THE MUSLIM BONAPARTE

THE MUSLIM BONAPARTE

DIPLOMACY AND ORIENTALISM
IN ALI PASHA'S GREECE

K. E. Fleming

PRINCETON UNIVERSITY PRESS

PRINCETON, NEW JERSEY

LIBRARY OF CONGRESS CATALOGING-IN-PUBLICATION DATA

FLEMING, K. E. (KATHERINE ELIZABETH), 1965–
THE MUSLIM BONAPARTE : DIPLOMACY AND ORIENTALISM IN ALI PASHA'S
GREECE / K.E. FLEMING.
P. CM.
INCLUDES BIBLIOGRAPHICAL REFERENCES AND INDEX.
ISBN 0-691-00194-4 (CLOTH : ALK. PAPER). — ISBN 0-691-00195-2
(PBK. : ALK. PAPER)
1. ALI PAŞA, TEPEDELENLI, 1744?–1822.   2. STATESMEN—ALBANIA—
BIOGRAPHY.   3. ALBANIA—HISTORY—1501–1912.   4. IŌANNINA REGION
(GREECE)—HISTORY.   I. TITLE.
DR965.F58   1999
949.5'05'092—DC21   98-36435 CIP
[B]

THIS BOOK HAS BEEN COMPOSED IN SABON TYPEFACE

THE PAPER USED IN THIS PUBLICATION MEETS THE MINIMUM
REQUIREMENTS OF ANSI/NISO Z39.48-1992 (R 1997)
(PERMANENCE OF PAPER)

HTTP://PUP.PRINCETON.EDU

PRINTED IN THE UNITED STATES OF AMERICA

1   3   5   7   9   10   8   6   4   2

1   3   5   7   9   10   8   6   4   2
(PBK.)

For My Parents

CONTENTS

ILLUSTRATIONS

ACKNOWLEDGMENTS

IT IS MY GREAT good fortune to have many people to thank for their role, witting or unwitting, in the successful completion of this book. I would first like to thank Dimitri Gondicas and Steve Ferguson at Princeton University for helping arrange for the reproduction of the illustrations that appear in this book. I am grateful to Firestone Library at Princeton University for permission to reproduce these rare engravings.

I have benefited greatly from the expertise and the time generously lent to my work by an array of scholars. Among them are Maria Kotzamanidou, who single-handedly has kept Hellenic Studies alive at Berkeley for more than a decade; Traian Stoianovich, who gave me careful comments and gracious encouragement on an earlier version of the manuscript; Robert Bellah, who taught me a good deal about civil religion and religious nationalism, read the manuscript, and made valuable observations; Eugene Irschick, who taught me new ways of thinking about history; Cornell Fleischer, who bore with me when my Ottoman Turkish was execrable; Ayla Algar, who taught me how to speak Turkish; Dimitri Gondicas and Alexander Nehamas, who showed an interest in my book and urged Princeton University Press to do the same; Ira Lapidus, my adviser at Berkeley; Lawrence Tritle, one of the few classical scholars who find modern Greece, too, to be worthy of study; and Liana Theodoratou, who read the manuscript, helped me think about its broader theoretical implications, and became a friend in the process.

In the course of researching for this book, I was the lucky recipient of hospitality on three continents. I would like particularly to thank Nick and Roula Ieromonachos; Nikolaos Patroudakis; Sevgi and Gürbüz Yıldız; Hamid and Nazura Sattar; Arshia Sattar and Sanjay Iyer; John and Margaret Newman; Diana and Arthur Newman; Elizabeth Newman; Carol Cohen-Romano and Israel Romano. I would also like to thank the Regents of the University of California, Berkeley's Center for Middle Eastern Studies, and the Mellon Foundation for the generous grants that made much of my travel possible. In addition, I would like to thank my superb editors at Princeton University Press, Brigitta van Rheinberg, Molan Chun Goldstein, and Dalia Geffen.

The completion of this project was aided by the support of a uniquely close-knit and intertwined group of friends, all of whom I have known since grade school. Even though most of them could not say just what it is I have been at work on all these years, they have given me more assistance than they know. They are Leslie Bienen, David Lafleur, Vinca Showalter Lafleur, Carol Tate, Michael Timoney, David Schrayer, and

Johanna Wilson. Friends of a slightly more recent but no less fine vintage have also given valuable encouragement: Eleanor Bergstein, Tom Carlson, Carol Cohen, Adnan Husain, Jacob Kinnard, and Sean Wilentz. Chris Stansell, oldest and best of friends, is in a category of her own.

Finally, I would like to thank the members of my immediate family, whom I do not quite know how to categorize, as they are both scholars and friends. First, my brothers: Richard, a polymath and autodidact who manages to make my interests seem commonplace and mainstream, and Luke, who survived the worst of my doctoral meltdowns in Vermont and Santa Fe and who shared some of my happiest times in Greece. My husband, Brian K. Smith, has supported me in ways too great and small to mention adequately. Both he and our daughter, Sophia, have been invaluable reminders that some successes are more important than others. Finally, my greatest thanks are to my parents, who have my great devotion, gratitude, and admiration and to whom I humbly dedicate this book.

THE MUSLIM BONAPARTE

ONE

INTRODUCTION

I FIRST LEARNED of Ali Pasha when I was a teenager, while on a now-distant family holiday to Greece. In the course of our mapless meanderings, I went to Ioannina, in Epiros, and saw the remnants of the city as it was in Ali's day, with its defensive walls and semipreserved old quarter. Many sites seemed to be under reconstruction, but they were being worked on at such a desultory pace that it was difficult to determine whether buildings were in the process of being demolished or revivified. At a local mosque we found a lone workman sitting amid great heaps of rubble in the unlit gloom, tapping aimlessly with his hammer at what appeared to be a wall. A shovel stood propped against a pile of rubbish. When we expressed our surprise that he had all alone taken on so vast a task—one that clearly called for teams of workmen, engineers, architects, and specialist consultants—he shrugged his shoulders and said by way of explanation, "Tzami einai" (It's a mosque). Nationalist concerns, as often happens in Greece, were an obstacle to the preservation of what, even in its dilapidated state, was clearly an important artefact of the country's history. The fact that this building was associated with Islam and Turkishness condemned it to the status of a trash heap.

I have come to learn that one of the arenas in which this contemporary nationalist antipathy for the Turkish past is most pronounced is that of Ali Pasha of Ioannina. To this day he is viewed in Greece as a paradigm of Turkish cruelty and rapacity, the quintessence of barbarism, an Antichrist. Over the years that I have been at work on this book I have experienced many obstacles, most of which have their roots in such attitudes. Materials written in Ottoman are at best heaped together unread, unclassified, and unmanageable; at worst they are left to rot away. In many quarters my expressed interest in Ali was met with amazement, curiosity, and disgust.

Such attitudes are widespread indeed. In the autumn of 1996, at an academic conference, I presented what I thought was a thoroughly benign, if not boring, paper on the economy of the Aegean islands in the late eighteenth century. It was the paper's unspectacular contention that the economy of the Aegean in this period saw some improvements, which I linked to an array of causes, ranging from the 1774 Treaty of Kutchuk Kainardji to the policies of various mainland Ottoman governors, among them Ali Pasha. After the conference I was accosted by an apoplectic man who said to me sarcastically: "Po, po, ton agapas poli! Ti, na ton agiaseis theleis?" (My, my, you love him a lot! What do you want, to canonize him?). As a historian, one scarcely knows where to begin by way of an answer to such a question. It is in the nature of the nationalist mind-set to be binary; if I was not defending Ali, then surely I was on the Greek side. Otherwise, I was clearly a Turkish apologist. If Ali was not to be made into a saint, then he should be demonized instead. It is not such a stretch of the imagination to see in such attitudes shadows of the tragic circumstances of so-called religious nationalism just beyond Greece's northern borders.[1]

This Manichaean vision finds its academic replication in a similar bifurcation, witnessed in the body of scholarship pertaining to the Balkans under Ottoman rule. In one camp stand those who argue that the nationalist tensions of the Balkans were created by the so-called millet system of the Ottoman state, under which subject populations were bureaucratically subdivided according to religious affiliation. In the other are those who argue in the Ottomans' favor, claiming that such tensions were preexisting and were kept effectively suppressed by the mechanisms of empire. According to the second viewpoint, the appearance and recurrence of such tensions in contemporary times can be linked directly to the absence of any unifying, all-embracing power.

In his introduction to a recent collection about this debate, L. Carl Brown rightly recognizes its polemical dimensions; he uses a metaphor of litigation in his reference to the two camps: "the prosecution (Ottoman legacy lying somewhere between the negative and the noisome) and the defense (continuing importance of certain Ottoman ideas and institutions)."[2]

Even the most cursory consideration of the problem thus construed is enough to show that both perspectives are laden with several troubling implications in terms of historiography and nationalism alike. The first implies, among other things, that the Ottomans are somehow to blame for the current crises; in the absence of any modern-day Ottomans wandering around, the Bosnians (among others) have constituted the handiest target for retribution.

The second position, which in contemporary scholarship has tended to enjoy greater popularity than the first, is just as easily given to national-

[1] I say "so-called" because the contemporary trend to attribute current conflict in the Balkans solely to religious causes is a dangerous one. Although religion is certainly mobilized as a useful *symbol* in national conflicts, it is often simply a smoke screen for the totalitarian impulses of specific individuals and groups. The current preoccupation with religious nationalism, moreover, creates the illusion of religious differences as being inevitably, hopelessly long-standing, entrenched, and irrational and helps any would-be interloper more easily shrug off any sense of responsibility for the ensuing horrors (Danforth 1995; van der Veer 1994; Denitch 1992; Denitch 1994; Bringa 1995).

[2] Brown 1996, 6.

ist abuses. Cemal Kafadar writes: "Most current historiography . . . tends to operate on the basis of a 'lid model' whereby at least some empires (the oriental ones?) are conceived as lids closing upon a set of ingredients (peoples) that are kept under but intact until the lid is toppled and those peoples, unchanged (unspoilt, as nationalists would like to see it), simply reenter the grand flow of history as what they once were. They may have experienced changes in terms of numbers and material realities but not in essence."[3]

It seems that nationalist rhetoric usually favors some combination of these two views. On one hand, the Ottomans (and, by extension, Islam) are blameworthy for having subjugated Christian and Jewish populations and rigidly hierarchized society according to religion. On the other hand, nationalists favor a model that assumes a fairly high level of societal compartmentalization, as such models allow for the illusion that religious and cultural syncretism is a nonexistent feature of their national histories.

. . . . .

It is certainly not this book's aim to serve as an apology for Ali Pasha. It is its aim, however, to focus attention on an individual who played a significant role in Ottoman, Balkan, and modern Greek history and who was a critical point of contact between western Europe and the Ottoman East in the latter half of the eighteenth and the first decades of the nineteenth century.

Greece in particular and the Balkans in general served not just as a geographic bridge but also as an economic and cultural one between western Europe and the Ottoman Empire. When the West spoke of the Orient, in many instances it based its vision not on the Far or Middle East but on the Balkans—a territory that was technically European. Ali's prominent role in the cultivation of the European romanticist, philhellene, and Orientalist sensibilities of the eighteenth century has long been overlooked.

So too has the part Ali Pasha played in the early stages of the Greek War of Independence, which broke out in Ali's lands just months before his death. The fact that both this insurrection and the failed uprising of 1770 had their geographic origins in territories under his sway is no coincidence.[4] Greek nationalists may be made uncomfortable by the notion that the success of the Greek revolutionaries depended in no small part on Ali's presence, but to fail to recognize this is to miss a significant dimension of the historical and cultural climate that gave birth to the mod-

---

[3] Kafadar 1995, 21.

[4] For the international and cultural context of the 1770 insurrection, see Constantine (1984, 168–85).

ern Greek nation-state.[5] There can be no doubt that Ali's declaration of independence from the Porte (the Ottoman government) provided an opportune occasion for the Greeks, too, to try their hand at freedom.[6] The ensuing Ottoman battle against Ali created an opportunity for Greek revolutionary rhetoric to be put into action. Indeed, one contemporary observer asserted: "It cannot be doubted that the declaration of the Porte against Aly was the immediate cause of the Greek insurrection."[7]

Ali's own conflict with the Porte tied up huge numbers of Ottoman imperial troops even while his infamy in the West encouraged European philhellenes to enlist in the battle against the Ottomans, a battle that, Ali's own attempt at secession notwithstanding, was widely perceived as a battle of Greeks against Ali. Thus both diplomatic and cultural history are necessary routes of inquiry for the study of this period in general and Ali Pasha of Ioannina specifically.

I hope that this book will make some small headway into an often-neglected period of Greek history and an often-ignored geographic terrain. It is a hybrid—part diplomatic history, part cultural history, part theoretical excursus—and I hope that in the attempt to cover such an array of approaches I have not fallen between a number of stools. Ideally, I intend to demonstrate that cultural and diplomatic history are not mutually exclusive; neither are Middle Eastern and European studies. Geographically bound categories of study are particularly frustrating to the Balkanist, and I can think of no focus of inquiry more amply poised to prove the relevance of the Balkans to both the East and the West than Ali Pasha of Ioannina. In any event, the fact that such nationalist discourses find their parallels—unwitting or not—in the pages of scholarship is worth the historian's attention.

Diplomatic and Cultural History

The turn of the eighteenth century marked perhaps the pinnacle of western European fascination with the Islamic East, as well as the birth of a widespread western European philhellene sentiment,[8] a sentiment that persists to this day[9] and that had a powerful impact on Greece.[10] These

---

[5] For an analysis of the historical and cultural climate of the revolution's early stages in the contexts of Wallachia and Moldavia, see Otetea (1966, 379–94).

[6] Skiotis 1976.

[7] Leake 1826, 38.

[8] Malakis 1925; Eisner 1991; Augustinos 1994; Silvestro 1959; Spencer 1954; Woodhouse 1969; Tsigakou 1981.

[9] Gourgouris 1996; Woodhouse 1992; Marchand 1996.

[10] Stoneman 1984, 1–15; Campbell and Sherrard 1968, 385; Augustinos 1994, 288.

two features of the early nineteenth century's intellectual-cultural landscape conspired to make Ali Pasha a focus of particular and concentrated interest.

Ali Pasha was the Ottoman-appointed governor of Ioannina, in Greek Epiros, from 1787 until his dismissal by the Ottoman Porte in 1820. From Ioannina, Ali ruled over a territory that when combined with the neighboring *paşalıks* (gubernatorial districts) of his sons covered almost the entirety of what today is mainland Greece. Only Athens and the surrounding portions of Attica were not under his control. Ali was thus the most immediate eastern neighbor of western Europe. This proximity had tremendous implications, both political and cultural, for the relationship between western Europe and the Orient, of which Ali's Greece was, in the eyes of western Europe, decidedly a part.

From a diplomatic standpoint, this proximity brought Ali in direct communication with the governmental representatives of various western European countries. Britain and France in particular established close diplomatic relations with him, and he in turn was eager to forge alliances with them, even when (or perhaps precisely because) those alliances were in direct contravention of the official diplomatic stance of the Ottoman state. Both Britain and France had consuls resident in Ioannina, both were eager to have Ali's approbation, and both clearly understood the pasha to be a major factor in the geopolitics of the day.

France was Epiros's closest neighbor, for the 1779 Treaty of Campo Formio gave to the French control of the Ionian Islands, and Napoleon's 1805 victory over the Austrian forces at the Battle of Austerlitz resulted in the French possession of Dalmatia. Britain, Russia, Venice, and Austria also came into close contact with Ali's territories, and the nature and content of the diplomatic negotiations between these powers and Ali effectively demonstrate that at the turn of the century he was regarded, as he wished to be, as a de facto sovereign political entity.[11] These negotiations make clear, too, that western Europe was discomfited by Ali's economic and military strength, and recognized him as a potentially formidable foe.

Whereas much of the Ottoman historiography of the last several decades casts the regional Ottoman governors of the Balkans as representatives of Ottoman weakness, "decline," and supposed ignorance of Western statecraft, Western diplomatic materials from the turn of the

[11] A Greek revolutionary tract of 1809 cited Ali's virtual independence from the Porte as clear evidence of Ottoman decline: "The Ottoman state finds itself today in its death throes, and can be compared to a human body, gripped by apoplexy. . . . Such is the tyranny of the Ottomans today, that in regions other than the capital it is not recognised to exist. . . . Take as . . . example, the tyrant of Ioannina [Ali], who, although he does not manifest it, all know well enough that he is not afraid, and that he never obeys the command of his Sultan" (Clogg 1976, 115).

eighteenth century suggest a more nuanced perspective. Such regional governors as Ali in Ioannina and Mehmet Ali in Egypt certainly represented a threat to Ottoman absolutism, but they hardly gave Europe an impression of vulnerability or weakness. In the case of Ali, for instance, France and Britain felt, if anything, a sense of threat, and clearly they perceived that he had the upper hand in diplomatic dealings for the better part of a quarter century. The more general backdrop of Ottoman decline should not overshadow the not insubstantial strength of a number of the empire's regional governors. Such governors were not merely symptoms of Ottoman weakness; in and of themselves they represented a new and fearful power in the path of Western designs on Ottoman territory.

Culturally, the implications of Ali's proximity to the West were twofold. First, this proximity meant that Ali became the most accessible and popular figure for fashioning the Orientalist[12] genre of literature then wildly popular in western Europe.[13] Second, the fact that Ali was in control specifically of Greece, a place to which the West also laid some sort of claim, meant that he played host to a huge number of Western travelers interested not in him but in the supposed vestiges of Greek antiquity contained within his lands.

The French and particularly the British fascination with the ostensible founts of Western civilization had, of course, a long and revered history; so much so, in fact, that travel to Italy was a virtually institutionalized feature of the education of gentlemen of a certain class. This phenomenon has been well documented.[14] In the seventeenth and eighteenth centuries, scions of the upper classes were expected to travel to France, Switzerland, and, especially, Italy, then considered the apogee of proximate otherness and the site of the roots of European civilization. By the end of the seventeenth century, this circuit had become so standard that it was given its own name; "the Grand Tour" had become a requisite chapter in an Englishman's education.[15] The eighteenth century saw unprecedented numbers of travelers, most with tutors in tow, set off for Italy and the surrounding lands.

By the century's end, however, Greece came to supplant Italy as the most popular destination of the gentleman-traveler. The reasons for this are complex and numerous, but one is obvious: the French Revolutionary and Napoleonic Wars (1792–1815) brought a necessary and abrupt halt

[12] Throughout this book I use the term *Orientalism* in its Saidian sense (Said 1979).

[13] Hugo 1829; Morier 1951; Davenport 1823; Davenport 1837; Byron 1901; Jókai 1897; Christowe 1941; Farwell 1981; Behdad 1994; Eisner 1991; Sharafuddin 1994.

[14] Augustinos 1994; Constantine 1984; Eisner 1991; Malakis 1925; Tregaskis 1979; Tsigakou 1981.

[15] This expression is found for the first time in R. Lassels's *Voyage of Italy*, published in London in 1670. It was rapidly adopted into common parlance (Tregaskis 1979).

to all travel in France and Italy.[16] English travelers were forced to venture beyond these familiar routes,[17] and Greece presented itself as the most logical educational alternative. In addition, the increasing sense of Ottoman decline, fostered during the eighteenth century by such popular writers as Dimitrie Cantemir (whose "insider" account of the Ottoman administration was widely read in Europe), made curious travelers eager to visit.[18]

Other, more subtle factors, too, contributed to the rise in popularity of travel to Greece. In *Early Greek Travellers and the Hellenic Ideal*, David Constantine has effectively demonstrated that even before the Napoleonic Wars, Greece was gaining in popularity over Italy as an educational travel destination.[19] Piracy in the Mediterranean was on the decline, and the establishment of Ottoman supremacy throughout the Greek islands following the 1669 Siege of Candia contributed to the overall safety of the region. Moreover, the strengthening of French and British mercantile relations with the Ottoman Porte facilitated travel in the area.

Cultural concerns, too, contributed to this gradual shift in the Western traveler's itinerary. By the eighteenth century some were beginning to feel that Italy was a bit too much "done," not exotic enough or far enough off the beaten track to provide the traveler with the desired sense of adventure and apprehension of Otherness. Moreover, there was increased interest in the classical civilization of Greece and the developing sense that Italy was but a poor imitation of the real thing. As Flaubert wrote after his first visit to Greece, "The Parthenon spoiled Roman art for me: it seems lumpish and trivial in comparison. Greece is so beautiful."[20]

Such comments arguably constitute one version of Orientalism. Flaubert's stance is authoritative, his dismissal of Roman art striking in its completeness, and his embrace of the Hellenic aesthetic paternalistic in its simplicity. But whereas so-called Orientalist discourse has most frequently had as its backdrop colonialism and Western imperialism, such mechanisms of Western political control are absent in the preponderance of the lands of the Ottoman Empire. They are completely lacking in the instance of the southern Balkans. Rather, in the territories with which this book is concerned the backdrop for discourse is travel—specifically, travel to "classical" Greece.

---

[16] Eisner 1991. On the demise of the Grand Tour and the Napoleonic Wars, see chapter 4 of Eisner's work, which is particularly relevant. See also Tregaskis 1979.

[17] There were, of course, early British and French travelers to Greece, but they became numerous only after the start of the Napoleonic Wars made travel in Italy untenable. For an excellent overview of early French travelers to Greece (1550–1750), see Augustinos (1994).

[18] Dakin 1955, 6. Cantemir (1673–1723) was Peter the Great's publicist, and his account of Ottoman decline was widely translated and read in Europe (Cantemir 1734–35).

[19] Constantine 1984.

[20] Flaubert 1979, 1:137.

Travel to Greece was not merely a matter of geography but also of chronology.. The breathless students who viewed a visit to Greece as an essential part of their educational curricula were not primarily interested in "modern" Greece or even in its Byzantine predecessor. Rather, they regarded travel to Greece as a sort of anachronistic interactive exhibit in which they could find nothing less than the vestiges of Periklean speech, religion, and philosophy. Indeed, even those travelers most critical of the Greeks saw in their failings some continuity with the past. In the words of one seventeenth century traveler, "Of their ancestors [the Greeks] have retained the worst qualities: namely, deceit, perfidy, and vanity."[21] Further, they believed that Greek physical and cultural relics represented not just Greece's past but also Europe's past, and accordingly they helped themselves to whatever they liked. As Lord Broughton explained, "No one likes to pass through such a country without collecting a little."[22]

The myth of Hellenic continuity fused with the European belief in Greece as the fount of all Western civilization to produce a strong proprietary interest in the southern Balkans.[23] The fact that these lands were under the control of Ali Pasha—not just a non-Greek, but a figure who by virtue of association with the Ottoman regime and religion was, to the Western Orientalist cultural imagination, wholly other—led philhellenes to believe that conflict with Ali would constitute a salvific and liberating act on behalf of Europe's own cultural origins.[24] Attendant upon such a view, of course, were powerful impulses of cultural superiority—superiority both to the modern Greeks, who if descended from the classical Hellenes were also regarded as poor shadow images of them, and to Ali Pasha, their "despotic" Oriental captor.

These two experiences of Greece—the diplomatic and the cultural— were thus at odds with one another. On one hand, French and European diplomatic knowledge of Greece was bound up with qualms about Ali's political and economic strength and his geographically strategic position. On the other hand, the cultural impulses of philhellenism and Orientalism cast him as weak, depraved, pathetic, and inconsequential. The tension inherent in the simultaneous adoption of these two points of view is one of this book's central interests.

[21] Sieur du Loir 1654, 166. Cited in Augustinos 1994, 67.

[22] Broughton 1855, 1:156.

[23] This myth was not without its opponents. Jakob Fallmerayer and post-war "neo-Fallmayerism" notwithstanding, the myth of Hellenic continuity has dominated since at least the late eighteenth century.

[24] Moreover, participation in a battle against Ali was understood by some as analogous to participation in ancient Greek battles against other "Oriental inva[ders]," such as Darius and Xerxes (Leake 1826, 1–12). By participating in the Greek Revolution, philhellenes could vicariously take part in the battles of epic tradition.

The Impact of the Eastern Question

Even just within the context of contemporary geopolitics, Ali's status vis-à-vis the West was ambiguous. The period of Ali's domination of mainland Greece coincided with the first decisive phases of the so-called Eastern Question, as the Russo-Turkish Wars of 1768–1774 and 1792 and the French Revolutionary and Napoleonic Wars brought to the fore the possibility of a European joint partition of the Ottoman Empire. Central to any such partition would be Ali Pasha and his lands, a fact to which the governor was not oblivious; Ali clearly recognized that European intentions of partition could, if finessed, meld nicely with his own plans for secession.

At the turn of the century the dissolution of the Ottoman Empire was regarded as an impending, if unwelcome, inevitability. In 1802 the British consul in Baghdad expressed both the hope that the Ottoman regime could be prolonged and the belief that it could not. "My situation and the duties of my office," he wrote, "have caused me to reflect on the probable consequences of the dissolution of the Turkish Empire; and the information I have obtained from channels not accessible to many makes me think a great revolution in the Turkish Empire is near at hand, unless . . . the period of it shall be protracted by some fortunate and unforeseen event."[25]

In Russian quarters, too, there was a sense of the inevitability of Ottoman demise, but the response to it was less fatalistic than that of the British. In 1804 the Russian deputy minister for foreign affairs made an urgent call for his government to delay Ottoman "collapse" for as long as possible: "There is no doubt that the Ottoman Empire threatens to collapse and that its future fate touches on the most essential interests of Russia. It is therefore urgent that our court should draw up a plan on this important subject. . . . Our objective at the moment cannot be other than that of preserving the Ottoman Empire in its present state and hindering its partition."[26] This was a dramatic reversal of the advice given the czar just five years earlier by his chief adviser on foreign affairs, Count Rostopchin, who had called for Russian collusion with Austria and France in the proposed Ottoman partition. This latter view prevailed again in the 1807 negotiations of Tilsit, where Napoleon and Czar Alexander I made contingency plans of a joint assault on Ottoman possessions in Europe.[27]

As far as the western European powers were concerned, Ali could play

[25] Vane 1851, 173.

[26] Prince Czartoryski, Russian deputy minister for foreign affairs, cited in Anderson (1970, 23–24).

[27] For the complete text of the agreement of Tilsit, see Adair (1845, i).

a part in either scenario, if more conveniently in that of Ottoman partition. If the Ottoman Empire was to be dismantled, then Ali's secession could, they hoped, be bought with promises of greater sovereignty, of ongoing control over the Greek mainland, and even of royal status: at one point Ali hoped to be crowned king of Dalmatia by Napoleon.[28] Conversely, were the Ottoman Empire to be propped up, suppression of Ali would allow the West, in one fell swoop, to save a huge portion of the empire's European holdings.

It is well known that the latter policy, as articulated by Prince Klemens von Metternich and the 1814–15 Congress of Vienna, dominated throughout the nineteenth century. Its dominance in the eighteenth century, although less systematically articulated, is amply testified by the fact that throughout the course of that century the only Balkan European possession lost by the Ottomans was the Banat of Temesvár, which had been the only shred of territory left to them by the 1699 Peace of Sremski Karlovci (Karlovitz). The Ottoman loss of the Peloponnese, also effected by that same treaty, was in fact reversed in the course of the eighteenth century.[29] As Peter Sugar has observed, the remarkable Balkan territorial persistence of the Ottomans throughout the century can in large part "be explained by the jealousy among the great powers that worked against each other always giving the Ottomans a 'friend' in the foe of their enemies."[30]

Such cobbled-together alliances were the precursors of the solution to the Eastern Question as articulated by the Congress of Vienna. The rapidly shifting alliances of the eighteenth century were closely monitored by Ali, whose cachet among the Great Powers rose and fell according to each new configuration.

Subsequent historical events, too, conspired to influence western Europe's impression of Ali Pasha. Even long after his death, contemporary international affairs conditioned depictions of him. By way of example, consider the tenor and context of the 1878 edition of Richard Alfred Davenport's biography *The Life of Ali Pasha, Late Vizier of Jannina: Surnamed Aslan, or the Lion*. In his introduction to the work, the publisher writes that Davenport's aim is to be didactic, aphoristically stating that he hopes "to point a moral and adorn a tale."[31] He goes on to elaborate on just what it is that Davenport aims to teach: perseverance brings results; a lack of religion and morality, when combined with unlimited power, leads to no good end; "passion must not triumph over reason."

It must be noted, though, that the publisher writes at a time when Eu-

[28] Hadji Seret, National Library of Greece.
[29] For a partial account of the Ottoman reconquest of the Peloponnese, see Brue (1870).
[30] Sugar 1977, 203.
[31] Davenport 1878, 1.

rope was still in the thick of its policy of actively supporting Sultan Abdülhamid II's failing efforts to strengthen the Ottoman Empire, as in the latter part of the nineteenth century it was widely believed that the perpetuation of the empire would maintain the tenuous balance of power in Europe. Indeed, this belief was in the publisher's day far less contested than it had been in Ali's own.[32] The publisher, then, cannot help but see Ali as critical to the process of the empire's decline and hold him in large part culpable for it.

In the publisher's preface to Davenport's work this is made explicit. "Ali," the reader learns, was "one of the numerous dilapidators of Turkish resources. . . . The reader will here see with what vampyre effect subaltern tyrants can exhaust the vital principle of an extensive empire."[33] The tenuousness that characterized the European power balance in the years prior to the Balkan Wars retrospectively colors the writer's view of Ali, who by the publisher's construct is not just secessionist but also morally and religiously depraved. Again, diplomatic concerns are here melded with cultural ones, and Davenport's publisher expresses his allegiance to the diplomatic policy of his day through the vocabulary of cultural observation and superiority.

Orientalism, Philhellenism, and Travel

I recognize that it is a convention of historiography to include bibliographic commentary at the conclusion of a work, rather than use it in the introduction. The nature of the available materials on Ali, however, is somewhat peculiar, and this peculiarity has colored my account of him, as it has others', although perhaps in somewhat different ways.

As I mentioned, the backdrop for the Orientalism fed by Ali Pasha is not colonialism and Western imperialism but travel, specifically, travel to classical Greece. The philhellene impulse underlying such travel can be seen as representative of a different form of colonialism, in which the history and ideology, rather than territory, of another country have been claimed, invaded, and annexed. Many of the philhellene European travelers who visited Ali's lands believed that they saw nothing less than the source of their own civilization and that its Greek inhabitants were the fossilized "survivals" of an earlier, more pristine, place and time.[34] In this belief, they were articulating a cultural, if not political, imperialist claim.

[32] Richard Alfred Davenport's dates are 1777–1852.

[33] Davenport 1878, v.

[34] Leake, for example, declared: "The domestic manners of the Greeks of Ioannina . . . seem not to have undergone any great alteration since the time of Homer" (Leake 1835, 4:145–46). On "survivalism" and Greek folklore studies, see Stewart (1991, 5–8).

For the student of Ali's time and place, this backdrop of European travel has significant implications. First and foremost is its powerful impact on the sources available for writing history. The secret nature of much of the diplomatic negotiations between Ali and the European powers makes for a relative paucity of consular archival materials, both European and Ottoman. Ali himself kept only a partial systematic archival record of his negotiations with the West.[35] Moreover, there were no Ottoman cadastral surveys of Epiros undertaken during any portion of Ali's rule. There are, though, in abundance, copious and comprehensive travelogues, kept by the numerous European travelers who visited Epiros in the course of their itinerant education. At the height of Ali's powers, many such visitors went to Greece specifically to document Ali and his renowned eccentricities.

The use of such materials is undertaken with some trepidation by historians of my generation. Edward Said's *Orientalism* is the most famous attack on Western writing that aims to portray non-Western peoples. Both predecessors, such as Hayden White,[36] and a slew of successors (ranging from post-Foucaultian critiques of power to Johannes Fabian to the emergence of such historical approaches as the subaltern school)[37] have provided ample corroboration of the basic problematics identified most famously by Said. Needless to say, Western travel literature on the Orient has not, as a genre, fared well in such a climate. It is widely assumed that such literature represents nothing more than the consummate illustration of Said's point. It is viewed as voyeuristic, manipulative, distorted, and thoroughly bankrupt.

This is a point of view with which I take issue, for a number of reasons. First is the fact that, in the completion of this project, I have had to rely heavily on travelogues for much of my information, particularly that pertaining to Ali's impact on the economy of his *paşalık*. More important, however, is my belief that the travel literature of the seventeenth, eighteenth, and nineteenth centuries constitutes a sort of protoethnography. The aim of travel to distant lands was not solely voyeuristic; the desire to apprehend the Other was not based only on titillation and thrill. In 1693 John Locke observed that ideally the traveler to France and Italy—then the de rigueur destinations of the educated English gentleman—would have the capacity "to govern himself, and make Observations of what he finds in other Countries worthy his notice, and that might be of use to him after his return: And when too, being thoroughly acquainted with the Laws and Fashions, the natural and moral Advantages and Defects of

---

[35] The Greek documents in Ali Pasha's archive are currently being edited and cataloged for publication by the Fondation Nationale de la Recherche Scientifique in Athens.

[36] White 1973.

[37] Fabian 1983; Guha and Spivak 1988; Guha 1985; Spivak, Landry, and MacLean 1996.

his own Country, he has something to exchange, with those from abroad. . . ."[38] In short, exposure to the foreign lent a critical ability to the traveler, who by comparing what was familiar with what was alien, was to both come to a better understanding of his own culture and have the means of improving it. Knowledge of the Other was viewed as playing an important critical function.

Arguably, this has been the fundamental approach guiding the relationship between travel, historiography, and ethnography since the time of Herodotus. In a recent and excellent book, Olga Augustinos forcefully demonstrates that "the importance of the voyage as an educational experience and a means of securing tangible and intangible gains became an ever increasing force in Renaissance Europe."[39] Central to this educational experience was the recalibration of one's understanding of one's own culture and history through the lens of the novelty of foreign lands.

This understanding of travel as having a large educative component both fostered and was fostered by philhellenism. On one hand, the belief in the pedagogically beneficial aspects of travel propelled classical scholars eastward in the quest to see their subject matter with a greater degree of immediacy. On the other hand, travel itself was understood to be a central feature of the lives of the ancient Hellenes whom these scholars studied. Classical tradition glorified travel, and the Hellenes themselves had preserved in their literary record the stories of mythic travelers and the importance of travel to their maturation and education. Again, in the words of Augustinos, "Their greatest heroes, Theseus and Jason among others, as well as their most original thinkers, used the voyage to accomplish their tasks."[40]

In undertaking the Grand Tour, Western students were engaged in an imitative act. In many instances, this imitation was both self-conscious and quite literal. Travelers attempted to retrace the steps of Odysseus, locate the mooring place of Theseus's ship on Naxos, and find the labyrinth where he had slain the Minotaur. And, again in the Herodotean tradition, one of the central educative features of travel was understood to be its benefits as a self-critical as well as a mind-opening enterprise. Finally, it was expected that one would write about what one had seen, both as a means of fostering such reflection and in the hope of spreading the educative benefits of travel to those unable to undertake it themselves.

The West's understanding of the critical function served by travel and, latterly, by anthropological ethnography endures today. George Marcus and Michael Fischer, for example, recently restated the case for study of the other as a self-critical enterprise. Writing of the dual function of an-

[38] Locke 1989, 263.
[39] Ibid., 57.
[40] Augustinos 1994, 57.

thropology, Marcus and Fischer claim that its first function is to identify and "save" distinct, non-Western cultural forms from "apparent global Westernization," and its second is "to serve as a form of cultural critique for ourselves. In using portraits of other cultural patterns to reflect self-critically on our own ways, anthropology disrupts common sense and makes us reexamine our taken-for-granted assumptions."[41]

Marcus and Fischer's point of view, that of Locke three centuries earlier, and that of Herodotus are in basic agreement. The end of travel aiming to discover that which is "not like us" is not merely voyeuristic entertainment but also education about ourselves. Self-reflection and self-criticism are at the heart of Herodotus's history, Locke's travel, and Marcus and Fischer's ethnography. Travel, like ethnography, is a possible form of cultural critique. Similarly, the travel literature of the seventeenth, eighteenth, and nineteenth centuries is a form of history and a sort of protoethnography; it is not just a critical but also a self-critical literary form.

Travel literature is the genre most liberally represented in the list of materials pertaining to Ali. It also is, incontestably, as many have noted, a genre that is not without its problems *qua* historical source.[42] The special circumstances of philhellenism and the educative vision that undergirded it, however, make the use of travel literature for the writing of modern Greek history not just inevitable but appropriate and necessary. These materials not only provide a repository of quaint, amusing, and colorful Orientalism, but also constitute an entirely viable and extremely rich source for the writing of history—not just of Greece, but of the countries from whence its authors hail. This, then, is a second significant way in which cultural and political concerns are interwoven in this book. I make use of European travel literature both as a source for Ottoman history and as a source for western European cultural history.

An Overview of the Contents

This book is divided into two sections, one concerned with diplomatic history, the other with cultural history. The first section also serves as an introduction and overview and provides basic information on Ali's historical context, the history of historiography on Ali, available sources, and a brief biography of the pasha.

I also include a more comprehensive, if synchronic rather than strictly chronological, biography based largely on the travel literature of the period. This biography provides material on the economy of Epiros in the

---

[41] Marcus and Fischer 1986, 1.
[42] Lewis 1968; Dodd 1982.

late eighteenth and early nineteenth centuries, a discussion of the various bases for nationalism within Ali's territories, and a survey of the relationship between the pasha and the powers of western Europe.

The core of the first section is a detailed examination of the political relationship between Ali Pasha and the West and is based largely on British and French diplomatic materials. It is the intention of this core material to demonstrate Ali's attempt to reconstruct himself according to his understanding of Western statecraft, to document his increasing dissatisfaction with the imperial system of which he was a part, and to illustrate the diplomatic insecurity experienced by the West in dealing with Ali Pasha. It is subdivided according to chronology so as to make it more accessible to readers who may want to learn about a specific period but may not want to read the chapter in its entirety.

The book's second section turns away from diplomatic history, focusing instead on the literary, musical, and artistic output generated in western Europe in response to the figure of Ali Pasha. It also suggests that Ali himself understood in some way the workings of western European philhellenism and Orientalism and manipulated them to his favor and benefit. Finally, this section highlights the inherent tension between the West's diplomatic and cultural understandings of Ali Pasha.

The process of researching and writing this book has raised for me some fairly substantial theoretical concerns. I have tried to avoid being driven by questions of theory and have not wanted my findings to be overly colored by them. I take the opportunity in a brief final chapter, however, to raise such questions as a way of suggesting the theoretical utility both of the types of sources used in this book and of their historical and geographic specifics. Although by now there is a fairly extensive literature concerning the theoretical implications of travel and the literatures it generates, little of this has been based on the Balkans; of the latter, still less has attempted to make fruitful use of contemporary sociological and literary theory. In addition to the ample possibilities for cultural and diplomatic study, the figure of Ali Pasha of Ioannina in specific has presented itself to me as ideally suited to theoretical work as well.

TWO

HISTORIOGRAPHY, HISTORICAL CONTEXT, SOURCES, AND A BRIEF BIOGRAPHY

The Lack of Scholarship on Ali Pasha

I have never followed any road previously travelled by Ali
Pasha, without seeing some newly filled up grave, or some
wretches hanging on the trees. His footsteps are stained with
blood, and it is on these occasions that, to display the extent
of his power, he orders executions equally terrible and
unexpected. Like Tiberius, his motto is "let them hate, so
they fear."[1]

ALI PASHA of Ioannina (1750?–1822) was indeed both hated and
feared, not just by his subject populations but by the powers of
Europe as well. The copious European literatures generated by
the governor, however, focus far more attention on their hate and revulsion for Ali than they do on the fear which he inspired.

During the decades surrounding the turn of the eighteenth century,
Britain and France found themselves confused, insecure, and fearful in
their dealings with the eastern Adriatic. Such feelings were the result not
simply of concerns that the Ottoman Empire might collapse but also of
the realization that Ali Pasha, whose government was richer, stronger, and
better prepared for war than was the Ottoman state, could dramatically
impede European designs in the southern Balkans. Yet as Ali's political
and military strength reached its peak, Europe saw the publication of a
veritable flood of plays, operettas, poems, paintings, novels, and travelogues portraying the pasha in increasingly belittling, comical, and Orientalist terms. One of this book's central claims is that there was a direct
proportional relationship between these two developments.

One of the most marked legacies of the Orientalist works inspired by
Ali is the academic assumption that although clearly a rich source of anec-
dotes and exotica, Ali is, from the point of view of Greek, Ottoman, and
European history, a relatively inconsequential character. Ali Pasha of
Ioannina, a figure who in his day enjoyed much international infamy, has

---

[1] Davenport 1837, 307.

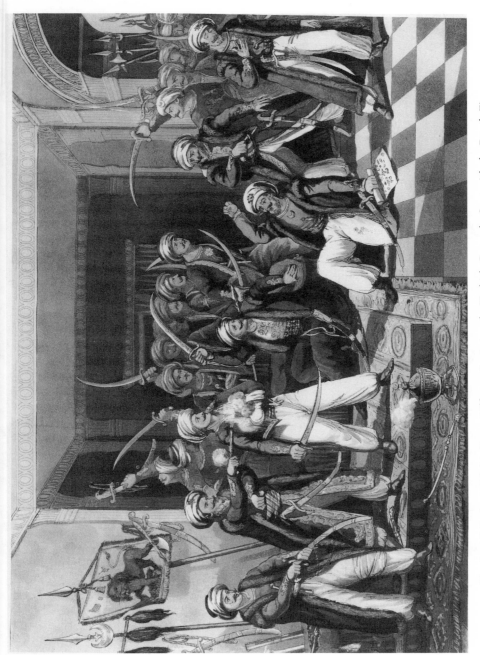

Fig. 1. Ali Pasha, with his Brave Officers, Resisting the Turkish Generals, Sent with the Death-Firman to Demand the Vizier's Head

been ignored almost entirely in contemporary scholarship on the later years of the Ottoman Empire and on the emergence of the modern Greek state.[2]

Indeed, Ali's time is, in general, neglected by historians of Greece and the Ottoman Empire. Because he lived in the years immediately preceding the Greek War of Independence (which broke out in the Peloponnese in 1821), the figure of Ali is somewhat overshadowed in Greek history by the events following him. On the Ottoman side, Ali's life competes for attention with the Napoleonic Wars, the aggressively expansionist governorship of Mehmet Ali in Egypt (1805–48), the struggles between the Porte and the Anatolian notability for administrative control of the eastern portions of the empire, and the myriad other symptoms of the empire's decline, well under way by the middle of the eighteenth century.[3] This lack of interest is exacerbated by the general dearth of scholarly interest in modern Greece, a problematic by-product of the classicistic and philhellene legacy from the time of the European Renaissance to the Enlightenment.

Insofar as Ali and his life have attracted outside attention, it has not been for his role in the historical intricacies of prerevolutionary Greece or for his contributions to the ultimate dismantling of the Ottoman regime. Instead, most works on Ali have had as the locus of their interest the hackneyed image of the cruel Oriental despot, and as a result they do not focus on Ali in the broader contexts of European and Ottoman history but limit themselves to lengthy tabloid accounts of his bedroom exploits, battlefield ferocity, and diplomatic treachery.[4]

Typical of this genre is Arthur Foss's *Epirus,* published in 1978. Foss's slim chapter on Ali opens with the observation that "cruelty is perhaps the characteristic most often associated with Ali Pasha." Foss then goes on to fill his few pages on Ali with accounts of Ali's various torture devices and double-dealings, even echoing the widespread but largely con-

---

[2] There is much debate over Ali's dates. Some diplomatic materials give the date of his birth as 1752 (PRO/FO 78/44, Morier to Hawkesbury, June 30, 1804; Psalidas 1962, 2:56). F. C. H. L. Pouqueville (1805) and Ibrahim Manzur Effendi (1827) date it much earlier, to 1740.

[3] Insofar as Ali is noted at all in this context, he is cursorily mentioned merely as representative of the increasing decentralization of the Ottoman regime. His struggle with the Porte is seen as only one of many such struggles between a central power and unruly regional rulers with pretensions to independence. Ali's role in broader historical events—the brewing Greek War of Independence; the power struggles between Russia, France, and Britain; the question of ethnic, linguistic, and religious identity in the empire—is overlooked as a result (Shaw 1988; Lewis 1968; Jelavich 1996; Sugar 1977; Campbell and Sherrard 1968).

[4] Vournas 1978; Davenport 1878; Plomer 1970; Aravantinos 1895; Lambrides 1887; Evangelides 1896; Beauchamp 1822.

jectural tales of Ali's sexual propensities: "His energies and appetites were enormous and to cater for these he maintained a harem of some five hundred women. In addition . . . there was a seraglio of youths, some of whom were in constant attendance, as his pleasures were rumoured to be mainly homosexual."[5]

In short, writings on Ali show a high titillation factor but are remarkably bereft of any attempt seriously to examine Ali as a participant in a broader and more important historical drama than the one being played out in the Orientalist imagination of the West. The most serious attempts to do so thus far have been in article form, and, with the exception of the work of such Greek scholars as Dennis Skiotis and George Siorokas, serious scholarship on Ali is by now well over forty years old.[6] There is virtually no contemporary academic work on Ali. In 1971 Skiotis observed that "the pressing need in Balkan historiography for a scholarly monograph on Ali Pasha based on documentary materials has been noted repeatedly."[7] Similarly, in 1961 Peter Topping wrote that "a modern account of the famous vizir [Ali] is a primary desideratum of Greek, Turkish, and Balkan historiography."[8] But Skiotis's 1971 article remains to this day one of the most complete and carefully written analyses of Ali's career. Recent biographies of Ali have reverted to the sensationalistic Orientalism evinced in F. C. H. L. Pouqueville's 1805 classic *Voyage en Morée,* long recognized as a colorful but highly exaggerated, biased, and unreliable account of Ali's temperament and exploits.[9]

---

[5] Foss 1978, 37–40.

[6] The most recent book-length biography of Ali, Tasos Vournas' *Ale Pasas Tepelenles: Turannos e idiofues politikos?* (Ali Pasha of Tepelenli: Tyrant or skillful politician?), although somewhat more rigorous in its analysis, is nevertheless highly dramatic and sensationalist. Its concluding sentence is not atypical of the mood throughout: "Who knows? Had his plans succeeded, perhaps the road of history might have been different in these lands" (Vournas 1978, 123). In addition, Vournas's work does not include a bibliography or an index, making even his more factual observations of qualified usefulness. Older biographies include Remerand 1928; Babaretos 1822; Beauchamp 1822; Richards 1823; Bessieres 1820; Malte-Brun (1822).

[7] Skiotis 1971, 224.

[8] Dimandouros et al. 1961, 165. See also Zotos 1938; Mihalopoulos 1930; Tomadakes 1960–61, 63 and n.

[9] Pouqueville 1805. F. C. H. L. Pouqueville, appointed French consul to Ali's court after the 1805 victory of Napoleon at Austerlitz, was the primary go-between in Ali's negotiations with the French. His assignation to Ioannina marks the establishment of Ali as a power in his own right, complete with his own set of independent diplomatic relations. When in 1807 under the Tilsit agreement control of the Ionian Islands reverted to the French, Ali was once again thwarted in his attempt to gain control of the Ionian mainland dependency of Parga. Furious with the French for what he perceived as a betrayal, Ali imprisoned the hapless Pouqueville. One cannot but suspect that Pouqueville's florid and unflattering portrayals of Ali are in some way the Frenchman's revenge. This floridity has to a large extent set the tone for all biographies of Ali, which linger in great detail on his physical appetites, atroc-

Without fail, the biographical accounts of Ali (both those contemporary with him and those written after his death) have as their central feature the repeated recitation of specific episodes in Ali's career: his drowning of a score of Greek beauties, whom he tied in sacks and dumped unceremoniously into Lake Ioannina; his raping of his own daughter-in-law; the revenge he wrought on the village of Gardiki, which had scorned him in his childhood; his fortuitous discovery of a pot of gold when as an impoverished youth he sought to gain power and wealth; and his endless battles with the independent Orthodox peoples of the villages of Souli.

The colorful repetition of such events—often with the addition of fictional dialogue, suspiciously apocryphal-sounding anecdotes, gory descriptions of physical suffering, and other novelistic embellishments—evinces the West's delighted belief that in Ali it had found the consummate Oriental despot, a cruel and wily ruler straight from the pages of such popular works as the widely read *Arabian Nights*.[10] By being cast in such terms, Ali was made instantly familiar, instantly known; as an individual he may have been obscure, but as an Oriental despot he became an Eastern everyman, a type.[11] As Edward Said famously writes: "The choice of [the term] 'Oriental' was canonical; it had been employed by Chaucer and Mandeville, by Shakespeare, Dryden, Pope and Byron. It designated Asia or the East, geographically, morally, culturally. One could speak in Europe of an Oriental personality, an Oriental atmosphere, an Oriental tale, Oriental despotism, or an Oriental mode of production, and be understood."[12]

Such episodes in Ali's life, then, functioned as tropes through which the West simultaneously verified and fed its imaginings of its eastern neighbor, the Ottoman Empire. Later I will turn my attention to the function such accounts of Ali have served in the ongoing construction of a Western image of the Orient, as well as to the ways in which Ali manipulated this Orientalist vision. Most immediately, though, it is necessary to note that for too many years these tales have stood as a feeble understudy for true scholarship. In the ever more dramatic and sensationalistic retellings of these episodes in Ali's life, attention has been deflected from the historically more significant, if also more staid, aspects of his rule. Irresistible and entertaining as these stories may be, they do not belong on the shelves of serious scholarship.

---

ities, and schemings while largely ignoring his broader aims and accomplishments. William Plomer's *Diamond of Jannina: Ali Pasha, 1741–1822*, the most reliable modern biography to date, nevertheless abounds in information of an anecdotal, rather than analytical, nature (1970). Vournas's work is of a decidedly softer sort (1978).

[10] Mardrus and Mathers 1989.

[11] Boulanger 1764; Springborg 1992; Morier 1951.

[12] Said 1979, 31–32.

Such unselfconscious storytelling not only overlooks Ali's influence on the eighteenth-century Greek economy, early Albanian and Greek nationalism, and relations between the European powers and the Ottoman state, but also distorts and falsifies what little historical information it may include. These biographers' insistence that their accounts of Ali epitomize the Islamic Ottoman Oriental despot completely mangles the truth of Ali. For Ali was none of those things. He was neither truly Muslim nor Ottoman, neither Oriental nor despotic.

An Albanian controlling mainland Greece, Ali was born to a family that recently converted to Islam. Ali himself seems to have had little or no interest in religion except insofar as it overlapped with his political concerns.[13] Acutely aware of his proximity to the West, Ali patterned much of his government on the ideals of Europe, soliciting counsel from both the French and the British and largely eschewing the diplomatic tactics of the Ottoman state. Deeply impressed by the Napoleonic Wars and the French Revolution, Ali in many ways sought to emulate the figure of Napoleon,[14] and at one point he even set about producing a constitution—based on the French one—for his own peoples.[15] In his aim to match Napoleon's fame, Ali met with no small success. Lord Byron, for one, dubbed him the "Muslim Bonaparte," a title more apt than perhaps even Byron himself realized. Most biographical accounts of Ali have a vested interest in seeing his exploits as somehow typical of Ottoman and Islamic statecraft; thus they are largely blind to or uninterested in these more unusual dimensions of his life and politics.

If Ali was in any way typical, this was so only because what in Europe was considered typically Ottoman was in fact quite far from it. Along with such other governors as Mehmet Ali of Egypt, Ali represented not traditional Ottoman despotism but rather a new breed of Ottoman governor

[13] The most recent estimate I have found for the conversion of Ali's family from Christianity dates it to 1716, when Ali's grandfather fought in the Siege of Corfu, where he is thought to have converted to Islam (Miller 1913, 19). The Turkish chronicler Moufit, however, claims that Ali's earliest known ancestor was Nazif, a Mevlevi dervish who settled in Tepelen in the early 1600s (Moufit A.H. 1324). This information seems to be based on Aravantinos's two-volume biography of Ali (1895). Finlay writes that Ali's family converted in the fifteenth century (1877, 6:57). In any event, most biographers of Ali agree that his religious sensibilities were guided more by political expediency than sincere spiritual belief.

[14] Spender 1924, 38; Tregaskis 1979, 73.

[15] Although it seems quite clear that Ali's proposal of a constitution marked a last-ditch effort to garner the support of the masses in his battle with the Porte and not a deeply felt or serious democratic sensibility on his part, it is significant nevertheless that Ali recognized the currency that the constitutional philosophy carried in his day. Ali requested Metternich (of all people!) to provide this promised constitution (Dakin 1972, 34–35). Although Dakin's primary interest is intellectual history, specifically the development of various phil-hellene movements, his works provide excellent, if brief, commentary on Ali and his role in the Greek War of Independence (1955, 1972, 1973).

who looked to the West rather than to the Ottoman bureaucracy for aggrandizement and political gain.

Ali found his political origins in the complex and ancient legacy of Albanian banditry. His noble title and rise to prominence, as was the case with his father and grandfather before him, owed more to successful brigandage than to the political and social structures of the Ottoman state.[16] His appointments—first to *derbendler başbuğu* (head of police of the mountain passes) and later to the *paşalıks* of Trikkala and Ioannina— were not so much conferred on him by the Porte as wrested by him from the sultan. Seeing that Ali planned to rule various territories of the empire regardless of what the central government might intend, the Porte's only recourse in several instances was to save face by retroactively "conferring" on Ali the lands already under his de facto (as far as his subjects were concerned) official control.

Ali's links to the Ottoman body politic were tenuous, and so were his cultural ones. Whether he knew any Turkish at all is a topic of no small debate; in any event, it is clear that his Turkish, even by the most generous estimate, was not very good. His idiom by birth was Albanian, and the tongue of his courtly business and correspondence was demotic Greek. So dominant, in fact, was demotic in his official business that the language's later champions in the great language debate of the early years of the independent Greek state found their position greatly helped by the existence of a courtly, rather than exclusively folk, demotic literary tradition. In being the first to use demotic as a formal language of state, Ali unwittingly aided the only recently regnant demoticist cause in a debate that was to see one of philhellenism's greatest victories: the decision of the new Greek state to use *katharevousa* (an artificial hybrid of modern and classical Greek, forced to fit classical grammatical forms) as its official tongue.[17]

Nor was religion a point of correlation with the sultanate in Istanbul. Although portrayed by Greek polemicists as a cruel Muslim who despised all things Christian, Ali seems to have had little or no abiding personal religious faith; aside from what a few advisers characterized as misguided dabblings in Sufism, there is nothing in the historical record to indicate that Islam was a major feature of his self-identification.[18] As for the reli-

---

[16] BA, Cevdet Tasnifi, Dahiliye, 11047.

[17] Demotic has been in wide official use only since the Karamanlis regime of 1975, and this more in reaction to the absurdity of this ossified and stilted language than to the junta of 1969–74. Since the time of that regime's use of *katharevousa,* the language has come to be seen as a symbol of reactionary leanings (Woodhouse 1992). For more specific information on the demoticist/classicist debate, see Kitromilides (1985).

[18] Such advisers felt that he was being taken advantage of by unscrupulous *shaykh*s hoping to capitalize on his wealth.

gion of others, he saw it entirely through the lens of politics, and he made religion his concern only insofar as the religious establishment of the day was to a large extent the same as the political establishment.[19]

How Ali has gone down in history as the typical Ottoman despot is no small curiosity.[20] Like so many features of the Western body of literature on the Ottoman Empire, perhaps it must be understood not by historical actuality but rather, as a Saidian critique would argue, by the discursive mechanisms of power through which the West "knew," and thereby mastered, the Orient.

Ali's Historical Context

It is unfortunate that Ali's time has often been neglected, viewed as an unimportant lacuna lying between the heyday of the Ottoman Empire and the rise of various modern nation-states in its stead. From the point of view of Greek history, his time is important, most obviously for marking the decades preceding the first outbreak of the War of Independence; as such, a study of Ali brings to light much new information on the spread of the Filiki Etairia,[21] the rise of literacy among the Greek population, the spread of philhellenism in the West, and the contacts—mercantile and otherwise—between Greece and the powers of Europe.

Balkan historiography, too, has much to learn from Ali: his life and rise to power demonstrate some of the social functions of the Balkan tradition of banditry; his familial and personal history represents an important view of the Albanian political scene of his day. Ottoman history, too, finds in Ali not just a fecund source for the mechanisms of decline,[22] but also a

[19] If Ali was despotic, he was at least an equal opportunity despot. As William Miller wrote in his classic work *The Ottoman Empire,* Ali was famous for "the impartial destruction of both a Christian and a Mohammedan community" (1913, 19). Although Miller is not entirely correct about Ali's "destruction" of the communities under his rule, his observation of Ali's impartiality regarding things religious seems very much on the mark.

[20] Indeed, it is remarkable that the notion of the typical Ottoman despot has existed for so long. It there is anything typical about Ali, it is that he, like the numerous governors of the far-flung territories of the Ottoman Empire, showed a remarkable diversity of religious, social, and ethnic background. The notion that the numerous provincial governors of the Ottoman Empire can be gathered to make a composite of the typical Ottoman ruler is a myth whose death is overdue.

[21] The Friendly Society, founded in Odessa in 1814, played a decisive role in preparations for an organized Greek insurrection against the Ottomans. In contrast to earlier societies, it had as its central objective not the cultural features of Greek life but the political ones. Its stated aim was "the liberation of the Motherland" (Frangos 1973, 87ff.).

[22] For a recent overview of contributing factors to the latter stages of Ottoman decline, see "Social and Psychological Factors in the Collapse of the Ottoman Empire, ca. 1780–1918" (Reid 1993).

key to the West's vision of the Ottoman Empire in the late eighteenth and early nineteenth centuries, and the issues at play in Europe's grapplings for a foothold in the region. A study of Ali and the Ioannina of his time also provides a useful microcosm of the religious, ethnic, social, and linguistic diversity of the Ottoman Empire, and the ways in which this diversity represented both a weakness and a strength for the Empire.

International Politics

Ali's rise to power corresponds with some of the most significant episodes in the early stages of the modern histories of Greece, France, Italy, Russia, and Britain. The year 1770, the beginning of a decade that was to pave the way for Ali's control over much of mainland Greece, marks the fateful so-called coalition of the Russians and Greeks in Greece's first bid for independence.[23] Following this embryonic independence movement, in 1774, the Porte suffered the further Russian insult of the famous—and subsequently much debated—Treaty of Kutchuk Kainardji, which granted to Russia a protectorate of sorts over the Orthodox subjects of the Ottoman Empire, furthered Greek trade activity, increased educational opportunities for Christians,[24] and marked a major feather in the cap for Russia in its ongoing power struggle with the Ottomans.[25] (The treaty is now best known as the supposed moment of kickoff for the Eastern Question.)

About two decades after Kutchuk Kainardji came the 1797 Treaty of Campio Formio, which handed Venice over to Austria, shifting the Mediterranean trade balance in the process, and gave control of the Ionian Islands to France. This was followed by the brief (and somewhat anomalous) Russo-Turkish campaign against the French, to gain back the Ionians, capped off in 1805 by Napoleon's victory over the Austrian

[23] For documents relating to this early insurrectionist attempt, see *The Movement for Greek Independence, 1770–1821: A Collection of Documents* (Clogg 1976). For an interesting account of the 1770 insurrection as seen through the eyes of contemporary Western travelers, see chapter 8 of *Early Greek Travellers and the Hellenic Ideal* (Constantine 1984, 168–87).

[24] For the effects of Kutchuk Kainardji on education, see Skendi's "The Millet System and Its Contribution to the Blurring of Orthodox National Identity in Albania" (Skendi 1982).

[25] For some of the complexities and ambiguities of the Treaty of Kutchuk Kainardji, see Roderic Davison's "'Russian Skill and Turkish Imbecility': The Treaty of Kuchuk Kainardji Reconsidered" (Davison 1990, 29–50). Although the extent of the privileges granted to the Russians by this treaty is the subject of much debate, it is universally regarded to have marked a major blow to Ottoman power, and a significant gain both for the Russians and, as a consequence of the treaty's stipulations, for the Greeks.

forces at Austerlitz and the subsequent French possession of the territory of Dalmatia.

The period 1800–1807 saw the short-lived independent Ionian Republic,[26] which although quickly smothered in the cradle by the power-playing of the European powers, nevertheless provided a critical moment in the Greek popular imagination and Greece's ongoing hopes for freedom from Ottoman rule.[27]

Both Ali's geography and his chronology squarely overlapped with each one of these major episodes in the history of the endless tug-of-war between Russia, Venice, Britain, the Greeks, and the Ottoman Empire for control of the region's territories and trade. Kutchuk Kainardji paved the way for a Greek mercantile life which flourished under Ali, and the Treaty of Campo Formio conveniently removed the hitherto powerful Venetians from Ali's borders.

Even more central to Ali's own history as a ruler was the repeated changing of hands of the Ionian Islands. The mainland Ionian dependencies of Butrinto, Parga, Preveza, and Vonitza had long been the target of Ali's expansionist policies, and as they passed from Ottoman to French to British control and back again, Ali forged alliances with these various powers in his repeated attempts to add these mainland dependencies to his own territory.

The French victory at Austerlitz was a critical moment not just in the history of France but also in that of the *paşalık* of Ioannina. The French takeover of Dalmatia placed a European power at Ali's doorstep, and with the arrival of French troops on his northern border Ali for the first time established independent diplomatic relations with a Western nation.

Following the events at Austerlitz, the French sent the now-famous Pouqueville to Ioannina, to act as resident consul representing France.[28] Ali both welcomed this opportunity for a new, official role as international statesman and demonstrated his savvy about the often quixotic and tenuous balance of power of his day. Even as he wooed a French alliance, he fortified his capital city lest the warm French overtures turn chilly and their troops move farther south, into his own territories.

Formal diplomatic relations between Ali and the British, established in 1810 through William Martin Leake, were strengthened five years later

---

[26] De Bosset 1819; Duval 1820.

[27] Vaudoncourt 1816.

[28] Pouqueville, who had served time in prison in Istanbul and in the Peloponnese, spoke fluent Greek (learned in jail) and seems to have been in Ali's good graces and close confidences until 1807, when, after the Ionian Islands reverted to the French under the stipulations of Tilsit, Ali's request to the French that they cede him the mainland dependency of Parga was rebuffed.

when Georgios Foresti, a Greek with strategic contacts in the Ionian Islands, was sent to Ioannina to serve as British consul. Ali had begun clandestine negotiations with the British three years earlier, when in 1807 the Tilsit agreement gave the Ionian Islands back to the French, but without benefiting Ali as he had hoped; Parga remained beyond his grasp.[29] By 1809, when the British took possession of the island of Zákinthos, Ali's relations with Britain were so cozy that the British were supplying him with Congreve rockets with which to blast the French.[30]

Philhellenism

Ali was also at the center of the budding romanticist movements and their philhellene offshoots that marked the Europe of his time. Lord Byron, together with the traveler John Cam Hobhouse,[31] arrived in Ioannina in 1809, where he set up house and penned some of his most famous works, most notably *Childe Harold's Pilgrimage,* in which the figure of Ali plays a prominent role. Hobhouse, too, went on to write a chronicle of his time in Ali's lands, which, like other travel accounts of the day, captured the imagination of his fellow Britons back home.[32] Numerous other European travelers were also entertained in Ali's court, and upon their return home several published wildly popular travel accounts, accounts that gave both sensational portrayals of the "cruel and sensuous" Ali and tragic, stirring depictions of the enslaved state of the modern offspring of ancient Hellas.[33]

The Western press too was fascinated by the events unfolding in Ali's territories; European newspapers tracked the struggle for possession of the Ionian Islands, Ali's relationship with the Greeks, and the many tales of his exploits and, ultimately, published dramatic accounts of his death. So renowned was Ali that his death was for many years prior to the actual event the subject of many communiqués. Thus when his true end fi-

[29] Ali Pasha's preoccupation with Parga was almost as great as that with the peoples of Souli, and it received much attention in both England and France (de Bosset 1819; Duval 1820; Andreades 1912, 445–48).

[30] Broughton gives the account of this British "gift" (Broughton 1855, 1:105). Ali's diplomacy showed more savvy than to actually do so; he continued making various overtures to the French for several years after. The rockets, however, were welcomed, albeit for other uses.

[31] John Cam Hobhouse's voluminous writings are among the most important travel documents of the period.

[32] Hobhouse 1815. See also the papers of Lord Broughton (Hobhouse) in the British Museum, London (36, 457–36, 464), for more on Hobhouse's time in Ioannina and its environs.

[33] Dodwell 1819; Eton 1798; Holland 1815; Hughes 1830; Leake 1835, 1 and 4.

nally came, the reports of it were treated with some reserve.[34] Ultimately, his death, as with most events in his life, was converted into an entertaining tale rather than considered for its political implications. Having barricaded himself within his island citadel, where all of his munitions were kept, Ali arranged a contingency plan with one of his most loyal followers to blow up all their stores and munitions rather than risk being captured by the Ottoman troops sent to defeat him. If Ali felt that such drastic measures were required, he would break his signet ring and send it to this follower as a sign that he must light the fuse. "Two thousand barrels of powder were piled in this gloomy vault, at the entrance of which, with a lighted match in his hand, stood a fanatical partisan of Ali, who was willing to sacrifice himself by exploding the mine, the moment that the signal was given by his master."[35] The vignette became the subject of a painting and a drama.[36]

The philhellene backdrop played a significant role in the production of such entertainments and in coloring the accounts of Ali that these Western travelers generated. Philhellenism gave such texts a guaranteed readership, made European observers feel that they had a personal stake in Ali's lands, and cast Ali in the role of oppressor of the Greeks and, by extension, the West. Mocking Ali became a form of support for the Hellenic cause.

Trade and Economics

The rule of Ali is similarly central to the eighteenth-century mercantile history of the European territories of the Ottoman Empire. On the mainland route linking the Adriatic on the west with the Saronic Gulf on the east, as well as on the path from Europe to Constantinople, Ioannina was a key point for domestic and international trade.

The Greek populations of Ioannina and the surrounding territories, long a major force in the trade of the region, flourished in the late eighteenth and early nineteenth centuries, when such treaties as Kutchuk Kainardji and Campo Formio opened still more trade opportunities to them. Wealthy Ioanninite Greeks endowed schools in Ioannina, established guilds, and brought Ioannina in direct contact with the trade centers of Russia and Europe. Indeed, Greeks of the western regions of the

[34] For this and more general information on Europe's interest in Ali and the politics of his time, see *La guerre de l'independence grecque vue par la presse française* (Dimakis 1968). Just as, for example, Fidel Castro (also cast as a villain in the West) has been erroneously reported dead on countless occasions, so too was Ali.

[35] Davenport 1837, 414.

[36] Payne 1823.

Fig. 2. The Delivery of the Broken Ring to Ali Pasha's Faithful Slave in the Magazine of the Citadel

Ottoman Empire were so far flung in their merchant contacts that we have an account of a Greek Orthodox church being established in 1781 in Calcutta, through contributions raised by a Corfiote.[37] The mercantile power of the Greeks of this era was seen as a major threat, not just to Ottoman control but also to European competitors.[38] Ioanninite Greeks played a major role in overland trade, and Ali's territories came to include some of the most important sea ports on the Adriatic coast.

The Greek War of Independence

Finally, the lands and time of Ali were also at the center of the brewing Greek movement for independence from Ottoman rule. Ioannina's schools, major centers of learning, acted as feeder institutions for many figures who went on to share membership in the Filiki Etairia, or Friendly Society, the most important (if short-lived) secret revolutionary cell behind the Greek War of Independence.[39]

Ali's Greek secretaries Alexis Noutsos and Christos Oikonomou, along with his personal physician John Kolettis, were members of the Etairia, a fact of which Ali was aware and which he attempted to use to his advantage when it became clear that the Greek insurrection represented perhaps his best hope for success in his effort to break with the Porte.[40] Other important members such as Konstantinos Pentedekas and Nikolaos Patzimadis were also from Ioannina,[41] where the society was well known. In a last-ditch attempt to gain some Greek support against the sultan's troops, Ali in 1819 claimed to be a member of the Etairia himself, and he convened his Etairist secretaries in the hope of forging an alliance with the Greek revolutionaries against the Ottomans.[42]

The trade ties between Ioannina and Europe proved to be invaluable, not just in the dissemination of revolutionary ideologies but also in the provision of presses by which to spread revolutionary propaganda. The Greek mercantile diaspora, particularly in Russia, provided some of the key members of the Etairia, most notably the Russo-Greek prince

[37] "Parga" 1827, 221ff. Cited in Clogg 1973, 38.

[38] See, for example, the letter of British members of the Levant Company to the British consul at Smyrna, written in 1804, complaining of the dangerously stiff competition to British trade in the region posed by the Greeks (Clogg 1973, 41ff.).

[39] Although both Perraivos and Tricoupis claim that the Filiki Etairia was virtually unknown in northern Greece and Epirus, there is significant evidence to the contrary. For more on this debate, see volume 5 of Finlay's *History of Greece* (1970, 5:75–76).

[40] Whether his private secretary Thanases Lidorikes was a member of the society is unclear.

[41] For further information on the society's membership, see *Apomnimonevmata peri tis Filikis Etairias* (Xanthos 1845).

[42] Dakin 1972, 34–35.

Alexandros Ypsilantis, who took over its leadership in 1820. Finally, the protracted battle between Ali and the sultan's troops, which marked the last years of the pasha's life, tied up Ottoman troops at a critical moment in Greek revolutionary history, providing a key diversion that allowed for the successful outbreak of the revolution in the Peloponnese, just to the southeast of Ali's lands. The territory of the *paşalık* constituted a geographical buffer between the Peloponnese and Istanbul.

A Brief Biography and Overview of Ali Pasha's Ancestry

The exact date of Ali's birth is unknown; by the most liberal estimate he was born in 1740; by the most conservative, in 1752.[43] Sources agree that he was born into an aristocratic Muslim Albanian family in the Albanian village of Tebelen. His paternal grandfather Muktar, who had distinguished himself at the Siege of Corfu in 1716, was the son of a brigand leader of reasonable renown in the region of Argyrocastro, twenty-five miles to the north of which lies Tebelen. This ancestor, Moutzo (or Mustafa) Housso, gained through his brigandry the title of bey, and may have been the *mütesellim* (deputy governor) of Tebelen, which, along with its surrounding lands, was one of the *nahiye*s (subdistricts) of the *sancak* (provincial district) of Avlona.[44]

Muktar, like most Albanian Muslim beys of noble rank, was a brigand chieftain, maintaining his own body of fighting men and gathering as large a following as possible from among the region's population. Upon his death he passed on some of his followers, along with a title of nobility, to Ali's father, Veli. Veli's rivalry with a first cousin, Islam Bey (briefly *mutasarrıf*, or chief administrator, of the sancak of Delvino), resulted in 1759 in Veli's murder of Islam.[45] Three years later the Porte, formally recognizing Veli's claim to control of the region, promoted him to the post formerly held by his cousin.[46]

The dynamic through which this upward mobility was achieved—formal Ottoman recognition of power *subsequent* to an individual's seizing it, rather than conferral of power—was to be the cornerstone of Ali's rise to prominence.

Ali's lineage, then, found its roots in the highest-ranking sectors of the Albanian Muslim aristocracy of his time, an aristocracy that owed more to force and coercion than to official appointment or sanction. A con-

---

[43] For more details on this debate, see Skiotis's "From Bandit to Pasha" (Skiotis 1971, 228–29).

[44] BA, Cevdet Tasnifi, Timar, 4971, 2710, 2699.

[45] BA, Cevdet Tasnifi, Zaptiye, 1102.

[46] BA, Cevdet Tasnifi, Dahiliye, 14418; BA, Mühimme Defterleri, 163, 65.

temporary report to the Hapsburg court described Ali as a scion of "the noblest family of the Tosks and one of the first families in the whole of Epirus."[47] By the time Ali was born, however, resentful neighbors had claimed much of the family's lands and wealth, and by the time of Veli's death (when Ali was about ten years old), Ali's immediate family was virtually impoverished.[48] Starting in his early teens, Ali set about replicating his father's successes as a bandit and made rapid gains both socially and financially. He established vital connections with the klephts of the region, which would later recommend him to the Porte to fill the post of *derbendler başbuğu*, a post he held from 1787 to 1820. It consolidated his 1786 appointment as *mutasarrıf* of Tirhala (Tríkkala) and served as a stepping-stone for his ultimate ascendancy to the *paşalık* of Ioannina.[49]

As Ali's territories and sphere of influence grew, so too did his pretensions to independent rule, and by the height of his powers (about 1812) his relations with the Porte, though still officially amicable, were strained. As he increasingly turned away from the Ottoman Porte, looking instead to the European powers for assistance in his hope of still greater territorial gains, Ali became more problematic to the Porte.

Particularly intolerable for the Porte were his negotiations with Britain and France, which were often at odds with official Ottoman diplomatic policy. Finally, in 1820, the Porte officially stripped the pasha of his title, declared him an enemy of the state, and dispatched troops to Ioannina. Ali retreated to his island stronghold on Lake Ioannina, and there he remained imprisoned for two years before the sultan's troops ultimately killed him.

Primary Sources

The paucity of secondary scholarship on Ali is made all the more puzzling by the fact that primary sources for such work abound. In addition to the numerous eyewitness accounts of the European travelers of the day, there is much archival and diplomatic material, providing invaluable information for the student of Ali.

The French Consular Archives in Paris have comprehensive and im-

[47] Laios 1783, "Perigrafe tes Bor. Albanias kai tes Bor. Epeirou apo to G. Demetriou ex Argurokastrou" (Description of northern Albania and of northern Epirus by G. Demitriou of Argyrocastro), trans. and ed. G. Laios, in *Epeirotike Estia* 5 (1956): 650 n. Cited in Skiotis 1971, 227 n. 4.

[48] BA, Cevdet Tasnifi, Dahiliye, 14418, shows Veli arriving to take control of Delvino in 1762. He apparently died shortly thereafter; Ali probably was between eight and twelve years of age.

[49] Skiotis pays close attention to the significance of this post in Ali's later career (Skiotis 1971, 231–43).

portant information on the political dealings of the pasha with the French; the Venetian and British diplomatic papers from the period are also voluminous and detailed, and support the contention that Ali was regarded as a key figure in European negotiations in the region. Of these, British and French materials are most useful for the last decades of Ali's life, Venetian and Ottoman for the first. Documents pertaining to Ali are also found in the Staatsarchiv of Vienna; these are fewer in number than those in the other European archives, and almost all have to do only with the end of his career. All of these European archives have especially useful collections regarding the Ionian Islands.

Greek and Turkish materials are, for an array of reasons, more difficult to access but no less sizable. The National Library in Athens contains portions of Ali's archive, as well as more general information both on the church's role in the Epirus of Ali's day and on the development of the Filiki Etairia, the most famous and effective secret revolutionary cell behind the Greek War of Independence. Greek documents in Ali's archive will soon be published by the National Foundation for Scientific Research in Athens. Finally, Istanbul's Başbakanlık Arşivi (Prime Minister's Archive) contains evidence of Ali's often complicated negotiations with the Porte and provides a useful foil against which to read the European sources; by far the most reliable biographical information is in this archive. The dates in most biographies of Ali are based on Pouqueville and are inconsistent at best. In this book I make use of only the tiniest tip of a very large iceberg of Ottoman material available for research on the eighteenth- and nineteenth-century Balkans.

In addition to the archival materials and travel literature, there is a wealth of primary material on the klephts and the *armatoloi* (policemen of the passes), two groups who were central both to Ali's social world and to that of the Greek independence movements of his day. This material includes memoirs and folk songs, which although of dubious reliability as precise historical sources, nevertheless shed much light on the ethos of banditry in late-eighteenth-century Greece, one in which Ali was fully steeped.

A number of comprehensive biographies have been written in the nearly two centuries since Ali's death. The most famous of these are Spiros Aravantinos's *Istoria Ale Pasa tou Tepelenle* (Athens, 1895); M. Gabriel Remerand's *Ali de Tebelen, Pacha de Janina (1744–1822)* (Paris, 1928); Ahmet Moufit's *Ale Pasas o Tepelenles (1744–1822)* (Ioannina, 1993); and, the big winner from a sales standpoint, William Plomer's *Diamond of Jannina: Ali Pasha, 1741–1822* (New York, 1970). With the sole exception of Moufit's, these works have as their central interest Ali's psychology and exploits. Plomer's work is, in this regard, most characteristic. None attempts systematically to situate Ali Pasha in the wider contexts of the economic, social, political, and intellectual history of his time.

．　．　．　．

As I have indicated, Ali's life straddles the two social worlds of tribal, bandit Albania and formal Ottoman politics; represents the convergence point of the lands of Christian Europe and the Muslim East; and overlaps chronologically with a critical juncture in the histories of Europe, Greece, and the Ottoman Empire.

A thematic approach to Ali Pasha's life will perhaps prove more historiographically constructive than the strictly sequential, narrative accounts written thus far. In examining him in light of broader historical concerns, Ali Pasha comes into clearer focus. Reciprocally, our understanding of some of the mechanisms of the westernmost terrains of the eighteenth-century Ottoman Empire is furthered by a careful look through the lens of one individual's historical impact.

THREE

ALI AND THE ECONOMY OF IOANNINA

ONE OF THE FEW AREAS regarding Ali in which there is a paucity of primary material is the economy of his lands. Ottoman cadastral surveys are unavailable for the region in this period, and as a result most of what can be known about Ali's role in the economy of his region must perforce come from less satisfactory sources, such as travelers' writings.[1]

What is by all accounts clear is that Albania and the surrounding territories enjoyed a reputation for economic strength throughout much of the Ottoman period. There were several trade centers in the region, most influential of which was Moschopolis, a large town whose Greek and Vlach merchants established chambers of commerce in Constantinople, Leipzig, Belgrade, Budapest, and Vienna.

The prosperity of the Moschopolis Greeks was such that in 1720 they established a printing press under George Constantinides. Until then there had been only one press in the entire empire.[2] In addition to being a center for the arts, Moschopolis was thus also established as a focal point of Greek intellectual and educational activity in the eighteenth century. Moschopolis, destroyed by resentful Muslim Albanians in 1788, served, along with other towns such as Korytsà, which was founded only in 1700 and had two Greek schools, as a center of both Greek trade and intellectual activity.

Most of these long-standing centers of wealth and education came ultimately under the sway of Ali and his policies. An avid territory builder, Ali married off his family members to surrounding chieftains so as to get a foothold in neighboring territories. His sister, Shainitza, was married to Suleiman of Argyrocastro, the pasha of Tríkkala. Earlier she had been married to Suleiman's brother Ali, who died under mysterious circumstances (it was widely rumored that Ali of Ioannina had him killed when

---

[1] Andreades' "Ali Pacha de Tebelen: Economiste et Financier," for instance, relies heavily on the accounts of Leake, Hobhouse, Hughes, Holland, Pouqueville, and Vaudoncourt (Andreades 1912, 427, 428, 430).

[2] Baerlein 1968, 22. For the importance of typography to the Greek national movements of the early nineteenth century, see "Nouvelles informations sur la création et l'activité de la typographie grecque de Jassy (1812–1821)" (Camariano 1966). For an overview of manuscript and print production under Ottoman rule, see "Post-Byzantine Hellenism and Europe: Manuscripts, Books, and Printing Presses" (Vranoussis, 1986).

he resisted Ioanninite expansion). Suleiman's son, also named Ali, was appointed governor of Libokhovo. Ali Pasha's own sons, too, were married off to the daughters of influential local rulers.

Ioannina itself was of tremendous economic and cultural importance. It had long-standing overseas contacts with Venice, Padua, and Livorno; by land it had important links with Belgrade, Sarajevo, Vienna, and other urban centers. Lord Broughton (Hobhouse) reckoned it was the most important city of European Turkey after Adrianople and Salonica, and its merchant community was among the most influential of the region. Travelers to Ioannina were uniformly impressed by its showy mercantile district—whose centerpiece was a *kapalı çarsı*, or covered bazaar—its large stone houses with gardens and courtyards, and its stables and warehouses. Broughton estimates its lowest possible population in 1809 to have been thirty-five thousand, of whom only 10 percent were Muslim.[3] A large portion of its population was engaged in mercantile activity.

There is much contradictory commentary on the effects of Ali's rule on his region's economy. Critics claim he wrought nothing but devastation upon a once-flourishing center for trade and agriculture, and his advocates (perhaps his apologists) argue that he single-handedly saved the region from political chaos and rampant brigandry and provided it with a much-needed infrastructure. Needless to say, what little modern-day scholarship there is on the topic is often informed by little more than nationalist sentiment.

Adding to the many difficulties inherent in assessing the economic health of a sparsely documented area of historical study is the fact that the few primary sources discussing the economy of Ali's lands are often impressionistic, unsystematic in their approach, and characterized by inherent bias. Ali's courtiers, for example, are, not surprisingly, full of praise for the pasha. Hadji Seret's long-winded, versicular *Life of Ali Pasha* is obsequious and servile and full of accounts of Ali's greatness; their very effusiveness makes them suspect.[4] European biographers, obsessed with Ali's vast personal wealth and reputedly great miserliness, have tended

[3] Hobhouse 1813, 1:60.

[4] The full text of Hadji Seret's verse biography of Ali is in the National Library of Greece, Athens. Portions of it also appear in *Tourkokratoumene Ellas, 1453–1821* (Greece held by Turkey, 1435–1821) (Sathas 1889). Sathas's work is in general a good source for primary material of the period, but the lack of notes and bibliography qualifies its usefulness. Leake makes use of Hadji Seret's 4500-line *stoihoi politikoi* (political verses) for his biographical note on Ali in his four-volume *Travels in Northern Greece* (Leake 1835). Leake refers to him as "Hadjiseret," and other accounts refer to him as "Hadji Sechrete." Of himself he writes "Sto Ntelvino en patridamou, sas grafo tonomamou / Hatji Siretes krazomai . . ." (My homeland is in Delvino I write you my name / I am called Hatji Siretes . . ."). Leake claims he was a Muslim Albanian unschooled in formal Greek. Hadji Seret's verse is known as the "Alipashade," but it has no title and is simply headed with a date: "1805, November 25."

to ignore the more general and beneficial dimensions of his policies and actions.[5]

Ali, most certainly aware of the critical position of his dominions vis-à-vis European and Ottoman trade, was far from myopically fixated only on his own coffers. Trade was used not just for economic gain but also as a political tool. At various points Ali cut off his ports to French ships, and fostered Greek shipping in the region at the expense of the European powers in order to bend them to his will.

As for accounts of his avarice, although Ali indeed seems to have been enamored of a burgeoning treasury, even policies designed strictly for his own personal gain often had broader implications for the region's economy. Many wealthy Ioanninite families, for example, hoping to evade Ali's claims on their holdings, attempted to emigrate to other territories of the empire as well as to various European lands. Recognizing that such emigration threatened his tax base, paved the way for depopulation, and could lead to the severing of Ioannina's important economic ties to the outside world, when petitioned for permission to travel Ali routinely took at least one immediate family member of the proposed traveler prisoner, thus guaranteeing the family's ultimate return. Although intended to safeguard Ali's own personal wealth, this policy had the long-term effect of establishing key links between Ioannina and the Ioanninite diaspora mercantile community, furthering international trade and bringing foreign wealth back to Ioannina. Many such families went on to endow schools and other organizations in their home city.

Just as some of the most felicitous aspects of the region's economy find their origin in policies designed for Ali's personal gain, so too do some of the bleakest ones. By virtually all accounts, Ali was highly parsimonious and would go to great lengths to avoid incurring personal expenses.[6] It is said that even in his last weeks of life, when he had barricaded himself within his island citadel in an attempt to escape Ottoman troops sent to assassinate him, his primary thought was for safeguarding his wealth.[7]

---

[5] Rumors of Ali's fabulous wealth and extreme parsimony comprise an important trope for the Orientalist literature about him. The lust for wealth is presented as evidence of Ali's insatiable appetites, and in the more moralistic accounts is also presented as his Achilles' heel. The British, in particular, whose advice to Ali to build fortifications against the onslaught of the Sultan's troops was not heeded, claim that only his avarice got in the way of a future as an independent ruler.

[6] Lord Broughton, for example, writes: "I have seen a computation which sets down his revenues at 6,000,000 of piastres. . . . Add to this, that all his work is done gratis, and his kitchens and stables furnished by the towns where he has any establishment. He pays his soldiers only twelve piastres a month, but insures that they are fed and boarded as he is, by local inhabitants" (Broughton 1855, 1:109). For an accounting of his overall expenditures, see "Ali Pacha de Tebelen" (Andreades 1912, 440–51).

[7] "Ali . . . with a singular infatuation which seems akin to insanity, was doing his best to

As a money-saving measure he would foist off expenditures that were rightfully the responsibility of his administration on his hapless subjects, instituting policies by which they were forced to take on his payments. Most burdensome of these seems to have been Ali's policy of forced quartering of his sizable Albanian troops; private homes would have the responsibility of housing and boarding several soldiers at a time, along with any horses they might have, over the span of many months. Virtually all travelers in the area document the local disaffection with this economically trying policy. Similarly, Ali's numerous public works projects—a category he expanded to include the construction of many private palaces, summer homes, and forts intended for his own use—were funded through raised revenues and built largely by unpaid laborers. Thus, even as Ali increased the productivity and trade of his regions, he depleted these increased revenues through extortion, high taxation, forced donations, corvée, and various other economically burdensome policies.

It is a clear measure of economic health that Ali, through his policies, was able to bring about a uniformity of economic law and freedom from piracy and brigandry hitherto unseen in northern Greece and Epiros. Oppressive as his financial demands were, his overall impact nevertheless saw its mark in increased trade, a more cosmopolitan and literate population, and a safer and more orderly society. Ali Pasha's rule from Ioannina corresponds to one of the most active periods in the history of the region's commercial activity. This historical context combined circumstantially with Ali's policies to make him economically influential.

Many of his policies actively encouraged trade and promoted agricultural activity. He established a comprehensive system of revenue collection and embarked on a widespread, if erratic, program of public works, building roads and khans, which fostered mobility and economic growth. Characterized by Greek polemicists as a rapacious and avaricious ruler whose policies wrought nothing but economic devastation on his subject populations, Ali actually enhanced the agricultural productivity of his territories and contributed to the growth of a robust Ioanninite mercantile class.

Indeed, the consolidation and centralization of Ali's power were effected most significantly not by military strength but by his economic policies,[8] which had the result not just of improving the economy of his day but also of transforming some of the most salient features of the social

---

disgust even his few remaining followers. Clinging to his gold, he evaded paying his scanty garrison, because he imagined that they were too deeply implicated in his treason to venture upon deserting him" (Davenport 1837, 413).

[8] As we have seen in the aforementioned example of keeping hostages to prevent family members' emigration from his lands, Ali's coerciveness often took the form not just of military, physical threat but also of economic threat and manipulation.

landscape. This dramatic influence of Ali on the economy of his territories and its surroundings is most clearly evidenced in six spheres: banditry, public works, trade and industry, taxation, agriculture, and landholding.

Banditry, Klephts, and Armatoloi

Ali's first foothold in the climb to power was the practice of banditry. Ibrahim Manzur Effendi, Vaudoncourt,[9] Broughton, and other biographers relate that as a child Ali had nothing and gained his first wealth through brigandry.[10] He also, at an early phase in his career, gathered together his own army of Albanians, whom he was able to pay only by plunder. "For he was then only a great robber," explains Broughton, "or one of those independent freebooters of whom there are so many in the vast extent of the Turkish empire."[11] Indeed, his family's noble title, with its right to hereditary transmission, had its origins in the successful brigandage of his father and grandfather.[12]

In eighteenth-century Albania and mainland Greece social rank and political power were regarded as the rightful reward for renegade activity. In fact, brigandry was recognized as the mechanism par excellence by which individuals could claim primacy in their region. The Greek revolutionary leader Kolokotrones, whose own career had started with banditry, wrote that in the eighteenth century "the name of a klepht was a boast. . . . The prayer of a father for his sons was that he might become a klepht. The klephtship afterwards lost its authority. In my father's time it was a sacred thing for a Greek to undertake."[13] Territories that were theoretically under the control of the Ottoman Empire were governed by leaders whom the Porte had no choice but to recognize, and the fame and success of a brigand leader held far more worth than a title bestowed by the far-away sultan. There was thus a long-standing meshing of the regional posts of the empire and the various bandit leaders of the region.

The relationship between a brigand chief and his gang of followers was parallel to that of a ruler and his supporting army. Indeed, the early relationship Ali had as a youthful brigand leader with his followers was later

[9] Vaudoncourt 1816.

[10] I must note, however, that the tale of Ali's impoverished youth also plays a significant role in the Western Orientalist construct of him. It was an essential element of the rags-to-riches account of his life that was so popular in Europe, and also provided a segue into the probably mythical account of his felicitous discovery of a pot of gold, a story whose veracity his European visitors hotly debated.

[11] Broughton 1855, 1:102.

[12] On Ali's background as a brigand, see Dennis Skiotis's excellent "From Bandit to Pasha" (Skiotis 1971), as well as the nineteenth-century biographical accounts of Ali.

[13] Kolokotrones 1892, 84.

replicated when as pasha he was supported by an exclusively Albanian military, many members of which had earlier in life been engaged in banditry.[14] As sociologists and social historians have noted, there appears to be a natural progression from brigandry to military activity when a society undergoes increased institutionalization. The Albanian territories under Ali provide a clear instance of brigands' taking on military roles as the increasing centralization of the government precludes traditional brigand activity.

Just as Ali's rise to power in the Albanian milieu of his childhood was paved by bandit activity, so too was his ascension to the highest ranks of the Ottoman Empire. Here the intimate link between banditry and policing is most salient. Much has been written on the close connection, in the Greek instance, of the so-called klephts and armatoloi, literally, "thieves" and "men at arms." The armatoloi, functionally a militia entrusted with the task of freeing mountain passes and other dangerous and isolated areas from klephtic brigandry, were established under the policies of the Byzantine Empire. As Byzantium gave way to the Ottoman Empire, armatoloi leadership remained largely in the hands of Orthodox Christians, and by tradition leadership was transmitted by heredity. In areas such as Albania, however, where conversions were numerous, many of these posts were taken over by Muslims, and gradually the empire came to have more and more say in their assignation. At the same time, the boundary between the two categories became, over the course of generations, increasingly fluid. The thieves and the militia that policed them often enjoyed joint membership, and the relationship between the two was not at always hostile. As J. W. Baggally notes, changing economic factors and the balance of power determined whether individuals would in any given period be found functioning as klephts or armatoloi.[15] Thus Ali was able to make a natural and smooth transition from banditry to his first official post within the Ottoman Empire—*derbendler başbuğu,* or chief of police of the mountain passes.[16]

The office of *derbendler başbuğu* represented the Ottoman ruling apparatus' assimilation and adaptation of the long-standing traditional office of chief of armatoloi. As Baggally writes, "One of the most important

---

[14] Eric Hobsbawm notes the similar function served by brigandry and military activity: both provided an outlet for surplus population. "Pastoral economies and areas of mountain and poor soil, which often go together, provide a permanent [rural surplus population of 'able-bodied men'], which tends to develop its own institutionalized outlets in traditional societies: . . . the supply of soldiers . . . raiding or banditry" (Hobsbawm 1969). Albania in particular, he notes, found its surplus population active in both brigandry and military activity. A quarter century later, Hobsbawm's work on the phenomenology of banditry remains unsurpassed. See also his *Social Bandits and Primitive Rebels* (1959).

[15] Baggally 1936.

[16] Asdrachas 1972, 104.

incidents in th[e] struggle [between the Ottoman state and isolated, quasi-independent regions] was the creation by the Porte of an office whose very existence was . . . inimical to the rights and functions of the armatoloi. This was the office of dervendgibashi (provost of the defiles). It appears that this office came later than that of the armatoloi, and was designed to hold in check the Greek armatoloi, who had already distinguished themselves by acts of resistance to the Turkish authority."[17]

In short, in the context of a largely autonomous, Orthodox-controlled society, the armatoloi functioned as a disciplinary force, controlling the chaotic and anarchic effects of klephtic activity. Once transposed, however, into a society dominated by Muslims and ruled by an alien, hostile power, these same armatoloi came to provide the very sort of resistance to order that they had previously contested. In an effort to curtail this evolutionary trend, the empire subsumed the entire system, created officially demarcated *armatoliks,* and to an extent broke the long-standing Orthodox monopoly over the position of captain. Ali's personal experience provides an illustration of the easy transition from brigand to policeman; indeed, it was precisely the contacts, knowledge, and training he had earned through his banditry that recommended him for the post of *derbendler başbuğu,* to which he was appointed in 1787 by Abdülhamid I.

The Ottoman usurpation of traditionally Orthodox armatoloi posts and the diminution of the traditional rights of the armatoloi reached their apex in Ali's day, when his tight control over the police apparatus did away with the hereditary transmission of captainships, and Ali himself made all appointments and assignations.[18] As a former brigand who had made the transition to de facto armatolos, Ali well knew the potential for resistance that not just the klephts but also the Orthodox armatoloi held. In fact, Ali himself switched not just from brigandry to policing but also back again. Just as the structural relationship between Ali the brigand chief and his armed followers was later replicated by the relationship between Ali the pasha and his armed forces, so too is there structural parallelism in the insurrectionist relationship of klephts and armatoloi vis-à-vis a hostile power and the relationship Ali himself came to have with the Ottoman state. When in the last decades of his career he attacked the neighboring Ottoman territories of other pashas, embezzled state funds, and otherwise undermined the central government, his behavior was once again functionally that of a bandit whose actions are not just criminal but also mark a low-level insurrectionist activity.[19]

[17] Baggally 1936, 6.

[18] In his monumental seven-volume *History of Greece,* Finlay comments on the tight controls Ali maintained over the armatoloi, who had enjoyed far-ranging freedoms in earlier times. Most Greek districts of Ali's time, Finlay reports, were forced to waive their hereditary privileges, and Ali handpicked their captains (Finlay 1970, 6:21–22).

[19] On the links between social banditry and revolutionary activity, see Hobsbawm's *So-*

Ali's claim that as a former brigand he could provide the Ottoman government with the best policing available seems to a large extent to have been true, although it is apparent that he did not so much extinguish brigandry as control it and manipulate it in such a way that it became one of his tools of governance. He was fond, for instance, of concocting outbreaks of banditry when such outbreaks suited him. There are numerous accounts of his arranging staged raids, which he promptly and dramatically squelched, making sure that word of his efficacy at taming thieves made its way back to Istanbul.[20] To facilitate this tactic, and to generally maintain close ties to the bandits of his lands, Ali interceded with the Porte on behalf of thieves and pirates from his territories. In 1809, when about six hundred Orthodox pirates were captured in the Aegean, Ali persuaded the Porte to repatriate them to his lands. The decision was announced with a *ferman* (imperial decree) that read in part: "Although the presumptuousness of these *raya* in undertaking these shameful things demands the . . . punishment of beheading . . . since my present High Admiral and Vezir Haji Ali Pasha, respected magnate, exceptional general, world governor, may his renown be forever . . . [requested] my Imperial Permission . . . that they be repatriated to their *kaza*s and villages, where they were born, my Imperial Decree has been published, that the leaders and followers with the women and children of one of the groups asking forgiveness who have been sent to you, be repatriated and established in their regions."[21] The individuals in question would, to say the least, have been indebted to Ali and willing to assist and collude with him in any way he required.

Accounts of Ali's life are unanimous in their observation that banditry dropped to an unheard-of low point during his rule. Lord Broughton, for example, observes that prior to Ali's time brigandry had been so pervasive in Epirus and southern Albania that travel was virtually impossible. He writes that Ali's curtailment of brigandry led to the opening of the countryside to merchants, increased revenues, and improved the overall living conditions of his subjects.[22]

Several European travelers give accounts of being accompanied on their travels in the pasha's territories by an Albanian guard of several horsemen, and of passing numerous mountain checkpoints and armed sentries in particularly dangerous spots such as mountain passes and ravines.[23]

---

cial Bandits and Primitive Rebels (1959) and *Bandits* (1969). Asdrachas's helpful article "Quelques aspects du banditisme social en Grèce au XVIIIe siècle" builds on Hobsbawm's model (Asdrachas 1972, 97).

[20] Davenport 1878, 50–56. For more general information on this modus operandi, see Hobhouse 1813; Leake 1835; and Pouqueville 1805.

[21] Vasdravelles 1970, 146.

[22] Broughton 1855, 1:105.

[23] Of course, the accompanying bodyguards would also have served the added function

Broughton himself reports that he and his party were accompanied through dangerous passes by four armed military guards; he observes that these security measures corroborated the widespread stories of the notorious safety of Ali's lands.[24] When Lord Byron and Broughton went from Ioannina to Tebelen to visit Ali in October 1809, they were accompanied by a complement of Ali's guards, and both registered approval of the extreme care with which Ali policed his roads. Such sentries also represented an important insurance to the goods and wares of regional traders.

Much of the land in Epirus and Thessaly was the crown land of the *valide sultan* (the sultan's mother) in Istanbul, and Ali is reported to have fostered particularly strong relations with her—sending sumptuous gifts and the like—with the result that she gave over to his control crucial mountain passes. These passes, he assured her, would be kept free of thieves by a handpicked Albanian guard.[25] Ali's reputation for controlling brigandry and his close ties with the thieves of the region in many cases persuaded the *valide sultan* to turn over these critical territories to him. Ali clearly understood that internal security was a key component of successful empire building.

Roads, Khans, and Other Public Works

Ali, aiming to be classed as a true world ruler worthy of the accolades of a Napoleon, set about leaving his physical mark on his lands. Upon assuming the title of pasha of Ioannina, he embarked on an ambitious program of public works, building roads and lodges, improving communications routes, and encouraging trade. Broughton was greatly impressed. "He has built bridges over the rivers, raised causeways across the marshes, laid out frequent roads, adorned the country and the towns with new buildings, and by many wholesome regulations has acted the part of the good and great prince, without perhaps a single other motive than that of his own aggrandisement."[26]

Ali, then, was clearly interested to some extent in portraying himself as a benevolent and protective ruler who improved the lot of his people by opening their lands and decorating them with architectural splendors. Moreover, through such works he was safeguarding himself against the possible revolt of his subjects. He well knew the catastrophic results of a decentralized regime, cut off from its territories and people. After all, his

---

of keeping an eye on these European travelers, monitoring their activities and ensuring that they saw only the more impressive aspects of Ali's dominions.

[24] Broughton 1855, 1:40ff.

[25] Leake 1835, 1:290ff.

[26] Broughton 1855, 1:106.

own rise to power had in no small part depended on inept Ottoman control of its more distant lands. Improved communications were to Ali's benefit as well as that of his subjects.

During his youth, Ali's career of banditry had given him an intimate familiarity with the lands he was to govern later. As with other dimensions of his career as a bandit, this knowledge was easily translated into his new role as pasha. Early-nineteenth-century travelers such as Leake and Broughton noted that Ali was frequently not in Ioannina but spent much of his time traveling about his territories. One European voyager claimed to have heard from reliable sources that Ali made a point of visiting each and every village in his dominions at least once a year.[27] A close familiarity with the countryside was one of the foundations of Ali's strength, and in addition to visiting outlying areas, he garnered information from native informants in various villages. Similarly, when in 1809 Broughton and Byron made plans to quit Ali's company and set out for the Peloponnese, the English visitors were much impressed by Ali's exhaustive knowledge of all the roads that such a journey would entail.[28] Ali, then, kept his government centralized by acting as a "hands-on," very much present ruler. Familiarized through his dealings with distant Istanbul with the inefficacy of absentee rulers, Ali made a concerted effort to maintain complete and direct control over and involvement in even the most remote of his territories.

The widespread construction of roads, khans, and storage houses had as its first underlying impulse the aim of making Ali's travels easier. Summer homes and secondary residences were built for him in all major towns for tactical reasons and in smaller villages for sentimental ones. For example, Ali built one of his most sumptuous secondary residences in his native village of Tebelen. In addition to facilitating his travels, such structures provided the local population with a physical reminder of its overlord's power over them. These works projects had the further effect of promoting facility of movement, not just for Ali but also for traders, itinerant artisans, and foreign travelers.

Other public works, too, were undertaken at Ali's command. The swamps and marshes north of Arta were drained under the supervision of European engineers so as to increase arable land in the area. Ali had teahouses and lodges established along the primary travel routes and paved the prime road from Ioannina to Preveza on the Adriatic coast. In 1804 Leake reported that the route between Ioannina and Tríkkala had khans

---

[27] Hobhouse 1813, 121. This is the first edition of Hobhouse's work. It was reissued after his knighthood as Lord Broughton's *Travels in Albania and Other Provinces of Turkey in 1809 and 1810*, 2 vols. (Broughton 1855). The 1855 edition has much added material.

[28] For a summary account of Byron and Hobhouse's (Broughton's) trip together, see Tregaskis (1979, 66ff.).

along its entirety, at intervals of about one hour's traveling time.[29] Ali increased the safety and reliability of other routes by strengthening extant bridges and building new ones. Government-operated ferries were established over the Drin and other rivers, and sentry booths and military lodgings were erected in the mountain passes.

These public works projects, along with the dramatic reduction in brigandry in the area, made Ali's territories accessible to foreign and domestic mercantilism. Piracy, rife in the Aegean and Adriatic Seas, had long led to the favoring of land routes for the transport of goods. Nevertheless, many of these routes, too, were made dangerous by thieves. Traders were thus delighted by the safe passes and clear roads offered in Ali's dominions. The control of banditry and the undertaking of public works, then, functioned as the joint foundations of a healthy and growing economy.

Trade and Industry

The lands of Ali's *paşalık* had a long history of international trade. Trade ties with Italy, in particular, had centuries-old roots, and many wealthy Ioanninite families maintained residences both in Ioannina and abroad. The primary Italian link was with Venice; Livorno, Ancona, and Padua were also well connected to Ioannina. This long-standing trade was augmented during Ali's time, not just by his own policies but also by changes in international politics. Leake notes that one result of the French Revolution was that the trade of the Black Sea and the Mediterranean was placed in Greek rather than southern French and Adriatic hands. This shift worked hand in hand with the treaty of Kutchuk Kainardji to guarantee the Greeks a virtual monopoly over seagoing trade. By the time of the Greek Revolution's inception in 1821, four to five hundred Greek vessels were engaged in commerce in the Black Sea alone.[30] The Greek shipping magnates favored their fellow countrymen in their business dealings, with the result that the merchant communities of such predominantly Greek trade hubs as Ioannina shared in their increased wealth.[31]

Ioannina's trade revolved around the export of both crude and value-added goods and the import of luxury items from the West. Textiles worked in Ioannina enjoyed particularly wide circulation. Silk braid (*yaitan* or *hrysoyaitan*) was exported to Italy and throughout the Balkans, as were scarves, blankets, gold and silver thread, and embroidered slippers

[29] Leake 1835, 1:420.

[30] Leake 1826, 24.

[31] For more information on how Europe fared against this surge in Greek competition, see *A History of the Levant Company* (Wood 1935).

and garments.[32] Spun cotton from the plains of Tríkkala, Thessaly, and Macedonia was routed through Ioannina, and imported textiles such as velvet were embroidered for re-exportation. Finely worked silver was also a major export of the area and was in great demand for swords and rifle and gun stocks throughout the Balkans.[33]

Crude goods from Ali's territories also enjoyed a wide exportation. For many years timber from northern Epiros and southern Albania was exported to Toulon for the construction of French ships. When in 1809 the British gained control of the Ionian Islands and became the major trading partner of the region, this timber trade was continued with the English.[34] The timber industry also provided the resin, widely sold domestically, used to flavor the retsinas (resinated wines) of the region. Henry Holland, another British traveler of that time, reports that cottons and yarns from Thessaly were routed through Ioannina for exportation to Italy and Germany, as were coarse woolens. Lemons, oranges, and hazelnuts from Arta were exported through the capital. Olive oil, corn, and Albanian tobacco were also thus routed for export, the latter being in particular demand for snuff. Albanian horses were sold throughout the Balkans.

In addition to serving as a regional center for this export activity, Ioannina functioned as the hub for the dissemination of numerous imports. Furs were brought from Russia; coffee, sugar, and caps were shipped from Trieste; French and German cloth was imported via Leipzig. Eastern Adriatic ports such as Preveza, Vallona, and Durazzo received these European goods, from whence they were brought on horseback to Ioannina.[35] Indeed, the large volume of trade in the Adriatic was a major reason why

[32] Salamanga 1959. Also helpful for a condensed summary, particularly of Jewish Ioanninite activity, is The Jews of Ioannina (Dalven 1990).

[33] Silver for guns and swords was worked throughout Albania and Epirus. Silver swords made up part of the unofficial national costume of eighteenth-century Albania and were in constant demand. Leake reports Delvino to have been a center for silversmiths (Leake 1835, 1:20).

[34] The Leake papers give detailed descriptions of the seven Albanian forests from which this timber was harvested, and show negotiations over the timber trade between Ali and the British lasting from February 1809 to February 1810. They are housed in the British Museum, London.

[35] Broughton's Travels in Albania, like many travelogues of the period, contains surprisingly detailed information on the exports and imports of the region (Broughton 1855). The most comprehensive contemporary account is probably Felix Beaujour's Tableau du commerce de la Grèce, formé d'après une année moyenne, depuis 1787 jusqu'en 1797 (1800). This work provides a very useful region-by-region breakdown of the economy, and under subheadings discusses various items in detail. For example, "rabbit pelts," "candles," "Turkish carpets," and "Greek shirts" are all given separate and careful attention. The value of this work is such that it was recently reissued in Greek as Pinakas tou Emporiou tes Ellados (Beaujour 1974). Long before, it was translated into English (Beaujour 1800).

Ali wanted desperately to take also the coastal towns of Parga, Vonitza, and Butrinto.

A central feature of Ioannina's primacy in the domestic and international trade of the region was its annual fair, held each spring on the plains one and a half miles southeast of the city. Lord Broughton, whose visit to the region corresponded with this event, recounts that for its duration all the local Ioanninite tradesmen and merchants shut down their shops and set up booths at the fair, which was attended by people from many distant and remote regions. By Broughton's account, the fairgrounds were so large as to resemble a small city, its trade booths set up in a grid, with pathways running between them. In addition to those who came to sell wares, there were also those who set up booths for the purchase of food and drink, and dancing and other entertainments were staged for the benefit of the attending populace. Ali himself made annual attendance at this event a personal policy, and he had his government regulators observe its goings-on.

Trade was fostered also, as previously noted, by Ali's policy of preventing the emigration of entire families from his dominions by taking "hostages" as collateral against émigrés' failing to return to Ioannina. As Holland observes, "This method of preventing emigration has the effect of retaining in Ioannina branches of all the ancient families of the place, and thereby of keeping up commercial connections, which otherwise might be transferred elsewhere." He provides the example of "a Greek family, with which I was intimate where, of four brothers, one was settled at Ioannina, another at Moscow, a third at Constantinople, and the fourth in some part of Germany; all connected together in their concerns." He observes this family to have been typical of wealthy Ioanninite Greeks, adding: "many other examples of the same kind incidentally came to my knowledge."[36]

Members of the Ioanninite mercantile diaspora contributed to the wealth and cosmopolitanism of their hometown, not just through trade activities but in other key ways as well. Such prominent local figures as the Zosimas brothers founded institutions for higher education, endowed schools, and underwrote the local priesthood. As a result, Ioannina came to gain such a reputation as a place of letters that it attracted students from throughout Greece. Virtually all contemporary accounts agree with Miller's assessment that "to Ioannina Greece owes the resurrection of education. . . . All Greek authors were either natives of Ioannina or pupils of the Ioannina school."[37]

This close link between economic prosperity and the rise in literacy

[36] Holland 1815, 149.
[37] Miller 1922, 10.

came to play a key role in the Greek War of Independence and made Ioannina a particularly desirable destination for a growing number of philhellenes interested in traveling to Greece. The Greek historian Georgios
Gatos points out the link between Ioannina's wealth and its erudition, citing the common saying of Ali's day: "Ioannina: first in weapons, in
groshen, and in learning."[38]

Agriculture and Animal Husbandry

Whereas trade was the primary economic activity of Ioannina, the outlying countryside depended on agriculture and pastoralism. Ali himself was
from a region heavily dependent on pastoralism, and a large portion of
his personal wealth (functionally indistinguishable from his government's
holdings) was based on shepherding. The statistics on Ali's personal flock
holdings can give an idea of the vast dimensions of pastoral activity.
Ibrahim Manzur Effendi, one of Ali's courtiers, reports that Ali personally owned about 500,000 sheep and 600,000 goats.[39] Further, Ali did
not incur any of the significant expenses attendant upon providing fod-
der, bells, and care for these animals. Corroborating Ibrahim Manzur Effendi, the traveler William Martin Leake writes of Ali that in addition to
his numerous other sources of revenues, "he is . . . the greatest proprietor
of sheep in Northern Greece, and owns flocks in every part of Epirus and
Thessaly. His shepherds are accountable for an increase of 120 per cent.
every year upon the number of animals, besides a certain quantity of
cheese. They pay all expences [sic], and reckon upon an average profit to
themselves of a piastre a year from each ewe, from which is to be deducted
a small loss upon the males."[40] Shepherds who tended their own flocks
still earned money for Ali. They paid an annual capitation tax (*kefali-
atikon*) for each animal, plus a pasturage fee (*nomistron*) for the right to
graze them. Under such terms as these, Ali's revenues from livestock could
not fail to increase. Sheep and goats were tended largely for cheese, wool,
and hides, and many were sold at the annual fair in Ioannina, both for regional domestic and for international export.

In addition to livestock, the region also enjoyed revenues from the fisheries of Lake Ioannina, over which Ali established a monopoly. The rights
to the fisheries of the lake were leased or "farmed" to the inhabitants of
the lake's larger island, who paid Ali about 15,000 piastres annually, plus
supply of firewood for Ali's island retreat, in return for exclusive rights to

[38] Gatos 1965, 18.
[39] Ibrahim Manzur Effendi 1827, 373.
[40] Leake 1835, 4:85–86.

the annual catch.[41] The fish were sold in Ioannina and to the numerous landlocked mountain villages nearby.

Agriculture was less central than pastoralism to the economics of Ali's (largely mountainous) *paşalık* but was nevertheless an important component of the region's economic health.[42] The plains of Larissa and Tríkkala had been devastated by banditry in the decades prior to Ali's accession to power. Bands of marauding thieves had become so powerful that they were no longer restricted to the mountainous regions of the Pindus range and the slopes of Olympus but had free rein in the agricultural flatlands as well. Fear and pillage had led to the widespread desertion of much of the arable land of these plains, and Ali's efforts were initially concentrated on repopulating the countryside and reestablishing its agriculture. Various public works, most notably the aforementioned draining of marshes, also had as their explicit aim the expansion of agricultural activity in the area.

The territories of Ali's *paşalık* provided for virtually all the agricultural food needs of the region. Arta provided Ioannina's fruits, vegetables, and nuts, and Leake reports that its peoples made use of highly developed grafting and planting techniques in their fields and orchards.[43] The Thessalian plain provided the *revithia,* or chickpeas, which were in great demand among the Greek population for use during their numerous fasts.[44] Large quantities of wheat and maize were grown on the plains outside Ioannina, and were brought through Ioannina en route to the port of Salaora, whence they were shipped for export.

Ali, in direct contravention of the policies of the Porte, established a near complete monopoly over all exportable grains of his territories. Holland, for example, reports that "of grain the vizier himself is the great monopolist for exportation."[45] The establishment of this grain monopoly

---

[41] Ibid., 154.

[42] Ali's greater interest in shepherding than in agriculture reflects his background. The mountainous terrain of Tebelen and its environs made it largely unsuitable for agricultural activity, and the region's primary economic sustainer was the tending of flocks. Moreover, the transhumant or quasi-transhumant lifestyle that goes hand in hand with shepherding is much more in keeping with the itinerant, roving attributes of a bandit's life. We have seen that even as pasha, Ali continued his peregrinations through the land. The highly sendentary, land-based life of the agriculturalist would have been inimical to Ali's personal experience and evident proclivities. His relative neglect of agriculture can in large part be traced to these influences.

[43] Leake 1835, 4:234.

[44] Most of the fasts of the Greek Orthodox Church involve not complete abstention from food but the omission of meat and, occasionally, oil. These substances are replaced by a wide variety of pulse, the most popular of which are lentils and chickpeas.

[45] Holland 1815, 150.

was one of the many ways in which Ali undermined the economy of the Ottoman Empire.[46] Of this monopoly Leake writes:

> The purchase of corn is a monopoly of the Porte and none can, according to its decrees, be embarked from Thessaly without an especial permission: the traffic however has always been carried on clandestinely, and Aly has even made it legitimate, by establishing, of his own authority, collectors at Armyro, Zituni, Salona, Talanda, and other principal places on the coast, who not only give permission to export but levy on his account 30 paras the kilo upon corn and 2 paras the oke upon other exported produce, such as tobacco, pulse, &c. He has lately attempted by means of an agent at Volo to follow the same practice there, but the Turkish collector, supported from Constantinople, has as yet been able to resist him.[47]

By establishing his own series of *gümrük,* or customhouses, Ali effectively co-opted a long-standing illegal grain trade, making it official, thereby guaranteeing his own monopoly in its place.[48]

Taxation and Ali's Personal Finances

In addition to fostering trade and agricultural growth in his territories, Ali made certain that he shared in its revenues by establishing a wide-ranging and complex series of taxation mechanisms. These taxes were so burdensome that they undermined many of the positive economic effects of his more progressive policies. Even as he encouraged growth in several sectors of the economy, he thwarted it in others with his increasingly unreasonable financial demands.

Rights to taxation were "farmed" to several regional beys and other individuals, who were responsible not just for raising the taxes Ali claimed as his right but also for generating the revenues demanded by the annual tribute to the sultan in Istanbul. In the event that these individuals failed to provide the stipulated amount, Ali imprisoned them until they or their families provided the missing sum as ransom for their release. He thereby

---

[46] The most famous renegade Ottoman governor who did severe damage to the empire through the establishment of personal economic monopolies was of course Mehmet Ali of Egypt, whose control over Egypt's cotton crop was devastating.

[47] Leake 1835, 4:335–36.

[48] This provides only one example of the many ways in which Ali institutionalized illegal activities. His treatment of the klephts, many of whom were integrated into his armies, marks another. The economy of Ali's region in many ways depended on such mainstreaming of long-standing institutions, which, while inimical to the power of the Porte in Istanbul, were, when properly guided, very useful to the consolidation of Ali's power.

rapidly established a reputation for being so fierce with inept tax collectors that the revenues raised by the collectors often were significantly higher than the amount originally demanded.

This taxation constituted an increasingly onerous burden to the common citizenry of the region. Leake provides an example of the rapid rise in taxation rated under Ali: "The inhabitants of Arta speak with great respect of Suleyman [a former pasha of the region], who was cut off by the Porte forty-five years ago, and in whose time those who now pay 700 piastres in khrei were not taxed more than 30, which, however, was equal to 150 at the present day."[49] Even allowing for inflation, this represents a fivefold increase in the tax burden of Arta's citizens. Ali had to meet the demands of the Porte, yet at the same time he wished to increase his own tax revenues. The net result was that the citizenry was exposed to a tax burden consisting of at least three tiers: the Porte sum had to be raised; Ali's additional demands had to be met; and the tax collector had to raise an additional amount so as to cover the costs of leasing the right to collect the revenues.

This increased tax burden depressed industry and agricultural output in several areas, as the perception among the public was that it was not worth striving for greater productivity, since whatever increased revenues were thereby obtained would simply be taken by Ali. This burden conspired with the oppressive effects of the quartering of soldiers to drain individuals of virtually all profits and in many cases to send them into debt. Of the citizenry of Arta, Leake writes:

> The expression "ekalasthike o kosmos" ("the world is ruined"), so common all over Greece, is repeated here loudly, not less by the Turks than the Greeks. They allude to the increasing poverty, and to the excessive rise in the price of provision, and every necessary of life within the last few years, which has been the ruin of many families. Its causes are the necessities of the Porte, the progressive debasement of the currency, the extortion of local governors, and particularly in this part of the country the destruction of industry consequent upon the oppressive government of Aly Pasha, his wars, his progresses, his arbitrary demands, and the forced maintenance of his Albanian soldiers.[50]

Leake provides a detailed account of the many different sources of tax revenues available to Ali. Arta, just one of the many *kazas* of his *paşalık*, provided enormous revenues. From Leake's account I was able to construct an approximate accounting, as shown in the chart.

These various revenues represented an enormous personal income for Ali, who was required to pay only one-seventh—300 purses—to Istanbul

[49] Leake 1835, 4:232.
[50] Ibid., 442.

Ali Pasha's Sources of Income

Agriculture		
1,400 purses	Ali's family lands. Provided revenues of 4/10 in kind of wheat, barley, corn, wine, oats, cotton, flax, rice, tobacco, and pulse. These are sold locally.	
1,000 purses	Exports of above, plus lemons, oranges, and hazelnuts of Ali's private gardens.	
Customs		
400 [est] purses	Underletting of customs, collected at Arta, Mytika, Luro, and Kastroskia.	
Tithes		
290 purses	Private lands.	
Duties		
16,000 piastres	Wine (collected at taverns and wine houses).	
16,000 piastres	Tobacco.	
16,000 piastres	*Kumerki* (excise on goods entering town) plus *statiri* (fee on public weighing).	
Tolls		
15,000 piastres	*Kumerki* on sheep and goats passing through town on the way from mountains of Spiros to winter pasturage in Acarnania.	
Fees		
14,000 piastres	*Subashlik* and *vostina* (fees paid to Ali as possessing the *ziamets* and *timars* of Arta, which comprised 25% of the district).	
Other contributions		
75,000 piastres	Special entitlements to Ali as governor.	
Total	2,000 purses*	

*Source: Leake (1835, 4:230ff.).

as the *mukataa* (rent on cultivated land) of the *voivodalik* (administrative region) of Arta. This required sum was met by the underletting of customs alone. Ali, then, would have had a profit of 1,700 purses—about 51,000 pounds sterling in the currency of the day—from Arta alone.

Regions not under Ali's direct control also paid him some form of tribute so as to remain in his good graces and stave off the possibility of an attack. Such was the case for the five hundred Vlach villages of Epirus, Thessaly, and Macedonia, whose revenues went to the valide sultan in Istanbul. Ali, whose desire to remain in good standing with the Porte, and particularly with the *valide sultan* (who he thought exerted significant influence over the sultan), dictated against his taking these regions by force. He nevertheless did not hesitate to use them as a source of corvée and free horses. By semiofficial agreement, he showed these towns leniency, and they in turn showed little resistance to his demands. Such crown lands, obliged as they were to pay both the central government and Ali, often found themselves with sizable public debts, serviced only by borrowing from Ioanninite moneylenders, often at rates starting at 15 percent.[51] This lending brought in still more wealth to Ali, who extracted in the form of tax much of the money gained by these Ioanninite financiers.

In addition to these "official" forms of taxation, Ali also gained a sizable amount of personal income from outright extortion. Not only did he take hostages to prevent emigration, he also, by numerous accounts, frequently imprisoned wealthy individuals so as to obtain a portion of their holdings. Demir Agha, the chieftain of Gardiki and a close friend of Ali's,[52] in 1804 informed Leake, for instance, that "Aly now has a Jew in prison at Joannina, from whom he has already extracted one hundred and forty purses, by threatening him with the loss of his head."[53] Similarly, Ali is widely reported to have made a point of keeping in close touch with the goings-on of his villages; in the event that a wealthy citizen committed an impropriety (real or imagined), Ali "fined" him for setting a bad example to the community at large. Such fines, random and unofficial as they were, went directly into Ali's personal coffers.[54]

Landholding

Another major component of Ali's personal finances was his practice of taking direct control of as much privately held land as possible. This practice was to effect the most dramatic change seen in centuries on the landholding patterns of the region. Leake reports that in the time of Suleiman, "*spahiliks* [fiefs given as payment to members of the Ottoman cavalry] of the district belonged to Turks, and the remaining lands almost entirely to Greeks, subject to the tithe of about an eighth, the kharadj, and a few other general or local taxes."[55] By the time of Leake's travels, however,

[51] Ibid., 1:278.

[52] Demir is known in most sources on Ali as Demir Dost (Iron Friend), owing to his close friendship with the pasha of Ioannina. He, like Ali, had great influence throughout the region, and the balance of power between him and Ali seems to have promoted tranquillity. In 1812, however, Demir lost his life in Ioannina after being imprisoned following Ali's massacre of the Gardikiotes.

[53] Leake 1835, 1:62.

[54] Ibid., 393ff.

[55] Ibid., 4:232.

Ali had successfully wrested control of these lands from the private land-holders of the area, thus undermining the long-established *timar* (fief) system of the Ottoman Empire.[56]

These private lands were usurped in various ways: in some areas the impositions made on the Turkish landholders were so great that many sold off their *çiftlik*s (plots of land that provided the basis for a share-cropping system) to Ali and fled to Larissa and other territories where they hoped to be beyond his reach. In other instances, Ali would buy the land of individuals who left no inheritors upon their death. In several territories, in fact, he instituted regulations whereby all land not claimed by inheritance would automatically revert to him. By all accounts, Ali, in the course of a few decades, seems to have brought about the complete dissolution of the Turkish landed gentry of his domains.[57]

Having thus gained territories through military conquest, usurpation of timar lands, and self-serving regulation, Ali naturally set about populating them as quickly as possible to ensure an increase in his own tax revenues. In many instances he not merely repopulated devastated areas but founded entirely new towns. This further changed not just the landholding patterns of the area but the demographics as well. On his first journey through Epirus, in the winter of 1804–5, Leake, for example, passed through a village that had been founded three years earlier by Ali, "peopled by the cultivators and pastors of the neighbouring plain, from the former of whom, Aly having lately made the land his own, receives a third of its produce."[58]

This radical shift in the landholding of the region represents precisely the type of wide-ranging "sociopolitical transformation" that Kemal Karpat argues is integral to the foundations of nationalism in the late Ottoman Empire.[59] Karpat's Western-style capitalist, "market economy" model has been contested by recent scholarship, which emphasizes instead the peripheralization of an Ottoman "command economy" during this period by European-Atlantic capitalism.[60] Such reevaluations are particularly useful in the case of Ali, whose economic strength was in large part based on his ability simultaneously to participate in the market economy of Europe and regionally to control traditional Ottoman economic structures in his own lands. This combination of economic approaches gave him the capital to, in effect, "buy out" the çiftlik system in his territories.[61]

[56] Beldiceanu 1980; Staab 1980; Hickock 1997; Mantran 1984; Eton 1798.

[57] Andreades 1912, 437–40.

[58] Leake 1835, 1:11.

[59] Karpat 1973, ii.

[60] Inalcık and Quataert 1994.

[61] I am hugely grateful to Traian Stoianovich for his observations on this combination of

This dramatic shift had strong implications for the events that followed, most significantly the emergence of a type of protonationalism within Ali's borders and the rise of a Hellenic nationalist consciousness. As Turkish beys were dispossessed of their lands, Ali's territories witnessed the supplanting of old social categories with new social organizing principles, and the rise to primacy of such long-standing markers of communalism as language, ethnicity, and religion.

---

economic models in the case of Ali. He points out that precisely this combination (domestic "command economy" coupled with mercantile participation in Europe's "market economy") made Ali Pasha and similar figures of such interest to the powers of Europe.

FOUR

ETHNICITY, LANGUAGE, AND RELIGION:

THE BASES FOR NATIONALISM

WITHIN ALI'S BORDERS

ANY WORK on the later centuries of the Ottoman Empire is, of necessity, concerned with the foundations of nationalism in the Ottoman state. The process that brought about the shift from a feudal system, marked by social estates, to one characterized by variegated economic classes in the modern sense of the term saw a parallel transition, similarly structural, from a system of religious states (millets) to modern nation-states. Both transitions, the result of gradual internal and external pressures spanning the course of several centuries, came to a climax in the late eighteenth and early nineteenth centuries, when widespread nationalistic uprisings, fueled by economic and religious internecine strife, cut across the communal categories of the empire in a new and destabilizing way.

The two primary ingredients in the societal brew of the late Ottoman Empire are thus best isolated as (1) a landed gentry and supporting bureaucratic class deeply invested in and closely tied to a feudal system and a permanent, imperial government; and (2) a religious establishment whose power derived from the central government and whose status was basically that of a state within a state. In the last century's scholarship on the dissolution of the empire, much has been made of the latter, and perhaps this is to the detriment of the former. Works on the late empire have tended to focus on the millet system, seeing in it a clear precursor of the modern nation-state.[1] Thus they have viewed the transition from empire to nation-state as springing from seeds sown by the Ottoman governmental system. In such constructs, the transition is seen as the natural outcome of the fusion of the Ottoman-imposed system of religious subnations with the popular nationalist movements of the day, particularly as exemplified by the French and American Revolutions.[2] The millet is por-

[1] Karpat 1982; Palmer 1992.

[2] This particular argument seems, in the Greek instance at least, doubly wrong. Just as religion did not provide the definitive nationalist building block for the Greek community, so the revolutions of America and France did not offer direct guidance for the Greek War of Independence. See, for instance, Spencer's observation in *Fair Greece, Sad Relic* that the abortive 1770 Greek uprising in the Peloponnese, doomed by the withdrawal of Russian

trayed as nationalism's fundamental building block, hardwired into the very imperial institutions it later came to destroy.[3]

Kemal Karpat's now somewhat dated but still invaluable *Inquiry into the Social Foundations of Nationalism in the Ottoman State* is in a different vein. Karpat's work attempts, in the author's words, "to break away from the parochialism which has been the mark of studies connected with the Ottomans; it . . . place[s] in one general framework the Muslim and non-Muslim subjects in the Balkans and the Middle East and analyze[s] their sociopolitical transformations as a whole."[4] Karpat and others who have followed his lead in the two and a half decades that have elapsed since his *Inquiry* was published demonstrate that the Greek War of Independence, like other nationalist uprisings that punctuated the empire's final centuries, was not a simple expression of religious and ethnic outcry.[5] The independence movements culminating in the formation of the nation-states that dot the map of today also find their roots in questions of class, social status, and economy.

Karpat argues that "the Ottoman economic system was open to a relatively free exchange of goods, to the holding of private property, and . . . could develop commercial relations within the framework of a market economy similar to the West. In fact, the social and economic order established by Sultan Mehmed II in the fifteenth century allowed not only for the production of surplus agricultural commodities and for home markets for such commodities within the framework of a controlled price system, but it also created the conditions leading to the rise of a new social

---

support, establishes an early Greek desire for freedom from the empire. Spencer writes: "Incidentally the whole history of the episode makes it very difficult for us to agree with the point of view of those who regard the Greek national movement of the early nineteenth century as merely a result of the backwash of the French Revolution. The rising of 1770 took place two decades before the Greeks had heard of the French Revolution" (Spencer 1954, 189). The events of 1821, although fueled in part by knowledge of French revolutionary ideology, mark the consummation of the secessionist tendencies of 1770. By 1821, this extant desire for independence was simply transposed into the revolutionary rhetoric of the day. One example of such transposition is Velestinlis' famous "Greek Marseillaise," a text that framed old notions of independence in the idiom of revolution. Similarly, David Constantine argues that philhellene sentiment leading to a sense of Greek nationalism, at least in an embryonic form, existed at the time of the 1770 insurrection (Constantine 1984, 168ff.).

[3] See, for example, *The Rise of Nationality in the Balkans* (Seton-Watson 1918), long a classic in the study of nationalism, and *The Arab Awakening* (Antonius 1938), similarly popular for several decades. Both works focus on ethnic and religious factors as central to the rise of nationalism and, to a great extent, demarcate the Ottoman Empire along Muslim and non-Muslim lines. In the same vein, many books on the Greek War of Independence view the Greek struggle as having its roots almost entirely in the religious categories propagated by the millet system.

[4] Karpat 1973, ii. I am much indebted to Karpat's work and have used his model as the basis for much of this section.

[5] McGrew 1976; Keyder 1987.

order not different from the one in the Western Mediterranean."[6] Karpat's claim is in direct opposition to the long-standing assumption that the Ottoman Empire represented a classless or preclass society, an assumption that has led to the favoring of religious factors over economic ones in the examination of nationalism.[7]

Although I disagree with a market economy model if applied to the entire Ottoman Empire, there is clear corroboration of Karpat's claim for a Western-style market economy in the mercantilism of Ali's territories. Also in keeping with Karpat's model is Ali's systematic destruction of old Turkish landed interests in the area and the consequent emergence of precisely the sort of "new social order" to which Karpat refers. These changes effected by economic policy worked hand in hand with long-standing communal tendencies to produce in Ali's day several protonationalist groups. These groups were defined by such factors as religion, language, vocation, class, and ethnicity, factors through which people found a sense of identity and communal meaning at least as significant as that lent by the Ottoman Empire.

These defining factors did not mark discrete categories; there was significant overlap between them, and the relative weight of each varied according to the circumstances of the moment. The history of the Orthodox Albanian peoples of the mountain stronghold of Souli provides an example of such an overlap. When Ali presented the most immediate threat to their independence, religion functioned as the most significant communal indicator, and they found allies in the Greek Orthodox peoples of the region, most notably those of the nearby coastal town of Parga. When, however, Ali in the last years of life found himself opposed by the sultan's troops, he managed to bring to life an anti-Ottoman coalition, gaining the Souliotes' support in part through an appeal to shared Albanian origins.[8]

Such ancient communal factors as language and ethnic origin, then, were at times at odds with one another and often confused by the exigencies of history, tradition, and politics. Albanians, for instance, who for several generations had been settled in Greece, used as their primary tongue Greek, but often practiced a form of Islam and identified themselves as Albanian. Similarly, Turkish beys, theoretically aligned with Ali and the ruling apparatus he represented, regarded him as an untrustworthy foreigner, whose Albanian, Bektashi background marked him as alien and suspect. Greeks, many of whom were integrated into Ali's govern-

[6] Karpat 1973, vi–vii.

[7] The claim of Ottoman classlessness is in part debunked by Maxime Rodinson's philological studies demonstrating that the Turkish term *sınıf* (commonly translated as "class") is in use in early Islamic writings on social position and rank (Karpat 1973, 17).

[8] For a detailed eyewitness account of Ali's battles with the Souliotes, see *Istoria tou Souliou kai Pargas* (History of Souli and Parga) (Perraivos 1857).

ment, although sharing a religious and linguistic heritage, were in many instances bitterly divided along class lines, the peasantry being divorced on one hand from a wealthy and corrupt ecclesiastical hierarchy and on the other hand from a Greek aristocracy or landed gentry.

Finally, in addition to the multivalent communal factors indigenous to the region, there were also external influences at work in the changing communal groupings of Ali's era. The European powers, most notably the Russians, sought to forge alliances with, at various times, the Souliotes, the Greeks, disenfranchised Turkish *ayan*s (who, like Ali himself, were notables with specific tax and revenue rights) and the imperium they represented, and Ali and his largely Albanian entourage. The Ottoman state variously opposed and sided with the French and the Russians in fighting for control of the Ionian Islands; the Greeks turned alternately to the Russians, the French, and the British for help in their fight for independence; the English manipulated klephts and armatoloi in the Morea to further their own interests; and Ali and his Albanian entourage were alternately seen as an obstacle and a stepping-stone in the fight for control of the region.

Ali was a master manipulator of these many internal and external crosscurrents, and he used the myriad communal groupings of his subject peoples in significant ways as he attempted to expand his power and establish his independence from the sultan. Just as his economic policies fostered the growth of various regional nationalisms, so too did this manipulation of the many socioeconomic divisions of his population.

Ethnicity: Nation as Territory

Despite the fact that he used Greek for all courtly dealings, Ali was regarded first and foremost as an Albanian. His use of Greek did not in any way make him Greek, any more than his status as Ottoman appointee made him in some way Ottoman. The Turkish beys of the region, often second-, third-, or fourth-generation residents, all of whom spoke Greek, were always referred to as "oi Tourkoi" (the Turks).[9] Similarly, the peoples of Souli, who both spoke Greek and practiced a form of Orthodox Christianity, were seen not as Greeks but as Albanians.

Clearly, there was no clear single marker of communal affiliation. How-

---

[9] Many of the Turks of Ali's day were the direct descendants of Turks settled in Ioannina following the surrender of the city to the Ottomans on October 9, 1430. About five hundred years later, when on February 21, 1913, possession of the city was given over to Greece, these same families still considered themselves Turkish, even though all spoke Greek, some had converted to Christianity, and virtually none had significant ties to the Ottoman bureaucracy.

ever, it seems that in the territories of Ali's *paşalık* historical geographic origin played the most pivotal role in one's identification by others as well as in one's self-identification. The various protonationalist groupings of Ali's territories coalesced, at least obliquely, around this question of geographic origin, and ethnicity was for the most part determined not by physiology, religion, or language but by geography.[10] If Bismarck's Germans were to "think with their blood," Ali's peoples were communally motivated by the physical land from which they came. This was the case not just of Albanians but of Greeks as well.[11]

In the instance of the Greeks and the Albanians, this geographic origin was often encapsulated in a reference to a sort of communal ancestor, a historical individual or individuals who functioned as national heroes and who served to remind people of their ethnic origins. Scanderbeg, the Albanian rebel famous for his opposition to the Ottoman advances into Albania, functioned as such a national hero for the Albanian community. Although not a bandit, Scanderbeg's rebellious activities served as an archetype for Ali and his insurrectionist Albanian forces. Indeed, the national consciousness of the Albanians of the region was shaped in large part by Albania's historical experience of resistance to Ottoman authority. First invaded by the Ottomans in 1385, the entire subsequent Albanian history down to the time of Ali was marked by insurrectionist movements. Scanderbeg's 1443 declaration of independence from the Ottoman Empire was simply the best known of many such instances. Even following the widespread conversion of the Albanian populations to Islam, noted by the famed traveler Evliya Celebi to be well under way in 1670, this legacy of resistance to the Ottomans remained central to Albanian national consciousness.[12] Nor did those Albanians who remained Christian feel any particular allegiance to the Greeks, with whom they shared their religion. Stavro Skendi has noted that only those Albanians who had long since emigrated to the Greek mainland or the islands participated in the Greek War of Independence.[13]

Just as Scanderbeg served as national hero for the Albanian community,

[10] There is a fairly ample theoretical literature on the connection between geography and nationalism (Carter, Squires, and Squires 1993; Jackson and Penrose 1994; Hechter and Levi 1979; Sugar and Lederer 1969).

[11] Petropulos 1976, 139–40.

[12] For particular attention to some of the nuances of communalism in the history of Albania, see "The Millet System and Its Contribution to the Blurring of Orthodox National Identity in Albania" (Skendi 1982, 243–57).

[13] Skendi 1982. Skendi notes that the Orthodox communities of Albania "possessed an Orthodox but not a Greek national consciousness" and thus did not participate in the Greek War of Independence. I contend that this was due to the lack of shared geographic origins; those Albanians who did participate did so not because they shared a religion with the Greeks but because they occupied the same lands.

so did the Greeks look to the figure of "Great Constantine, King of the Romans," for representation of a shared historical and geographical past.[14] In addition, more recent history provided Greeks with the heroic examples of klephtic leaders such as the rebel Vlahavas, who in 1808 led a Thessalian uprising against Ali's son Muktar.[15] As did Scanderbeg for the Albanians, Vlahavas and other klephts like him provided the Greeks with a model of resistance to the Turks. Indeed, Greek communal identity was so strongly shaped by this iconic image of klepht versus Turk that Greek children of the day played a popular game in which the boys divided themselves into two groups, the *tourkoi* and the *kleftes,* the would-be klephts hiding in the mountains and launching attacks upon the "Turks."[16] In their adherence to a national history that was powerfully informed by the experience of resistance, both the Greeks and the Albanians fueled their sense of place with the ressentiment that sociologists have argued is central to the formation of nationalist sentiment.[17]

In the Greek instance, the connection between ethnos and land became deeper still when philhellenes traveled the land, looking for the places written of by Homer, Virgil, Pausanias, Pindar, and Hesiod. The Greeks gradually came to see themselves not just as the descendants of the Byzantines but also as the children of Hellas, the land of the ancient Greeks. Their nationalist hopes were tied to geography. Observes Broughton: "It is easy . . . to see that the Greeks consider their country to belong to them as much as it ever did, and look upon their right to the soil as not at all affected by an ejection of three centuries and a half."[18] The Greeks may not have been in political control, but they certainly had not been "ejected," and their ties to the physical landscape remained potent.

The Souliotes, who are of Albanian origin but usually are grouped separately, also had ancestors who served as exemplars for the community of Souli. The rebel leaders Tzavellas and Botsaris, known through folk ballads telling of the 1792 Souliot war with Ali, provided a model of resistance and a unifying image for Souliot villages.[19] The Souliotes, whose rocky mountain strongholds were of virtually no economic importance, provide an excellent example of the way in which group identity in Ali's regions was linked to land. The Souliotes' sense of communal identity inhered in the land on which they lived. When offered clemency by Ali on condition that they evacuate to Parga and the Ionian Islands, many chose

[14] Broughton 1855, 2:3.

[15] For an account of Vlahavas and Ali's reaction to this uprising, see Hadji Seret's versicular biography in the National Library, Athens.

[16] Fauriel 1824–25, 1:lxxi.

[17] Greenfeld 1992, 7–17.

[18] Broughton 1855, 2:10.

[19] Baggally 1936.

to stay behind and die, claiming that leaving Souli would rob them of their identity. Souliot resistance to Ali provided some of the most sensational events of the period,[20] and the account of Souliot women throwing themselves and their children into the mountain gorge rather than surrender to Ali's forces stood as testimony not just to their pride but also to their allegiance to the land. The ersatz alliance between the Souliotes and Ali's Albanians against the sultan's troops was obtained only after Ali's promise that he would restore the Souliotes to their land.

Ali realized the centrality of geography in the communal groupings of his day. He insisted that Ioannina, in the Greek district of Epiros, was Albanian, and he viewed the Albanians who lived there not as immigrants but as indigenous inhabitants of the region.[21] He attempted to justify his designs on the coastal Ionian dependencies in part by claiming that they too were part of "Albania."

Language

Language was a central defining element in the identity of Ali, of his government, and of the district in general. Ali's natal tongue was Albanian, but he used Greek as the language of his court. The eighteenth-century phenomenon of Albanians and Greeks exchanging languages was fairly common.[22] All diplomatic business was conducted in Greek, and much formal correspondence was written in Greek. There are many reports that even when Ali employed Albanian or Turkish in his personal correspondence, he wrote in the Greek alphabet, transliterating whatever tongue he was using into the alphabet most familiar to him.[23] Ottoman, the formal bureaucratic language of the government in Istanbul, was entirely supplanted by Greek in Ali's lands.

Ali's use of Greek in his court dealings had a direct impact on language, education, and culture. The history of the Greek War of Independence is also in many ways a history of the Greek language. Central to the debate of what Hellenism consisted of was the question of language. Was Greek to be reformulated in such a way as to adhere more closely to its classical, Attic form, or was the popular, spoken form (demotic) to serve as the

[20] Even then the events of Souli captured the Western imagination (Dimakis 1968). All later biographies of Ali include lengthy chronicles of Ali's wars with Souli; Morier's novel *A Tale of Old Yanina*—published in 1857 as *Photo the Suliote: A Tale of Modern Greece*—centers entirely on the Souliote Wars (Morier 1951).

[21] This is not dissimilar to the current debate between Greece and the former Yugoslav republic of Macedonia over the rights to use the name Macedonia and its symbols.

[22] Baerlein 1968, 22.

[23] Marginal notes on some of the documents in Ali's Greek archive are in Turkish but written in Greek script; they seem to be written by Ali.

new nation's official tongue? Although such pivotal literary figures as Rigas and Solomos wrote in demotic—evolved from Byzantine Greek and the medium of folk traditions—their successors (Melas and Kalligas, for example) used the proclassicist *katharevousa*.[24]

In his overview of the history of the Greek language, Dakin observes that the prodemotic movement of the last quarter of the nineteenth century marked an attempt to restore the language, "[which] in its written form had been developed at the court of Ali Pasha, before the first Greek War of Independence."[25] Ali's adoption of Greek as the tongue of his court signaled a pivotal stage in the historical development of the language and played a central role in its academic consolidation, the furthering of its codification (first attempted in the sixteenth century by Sofianos, who had analyzed its grammatical forms), and its later popularity among the "New School" or "Demoticists," championed by Palamas.[26]

Ali's use of Greek for courtly business marks one of the many ways in which Ali represented a point of intersection between the several communal groupings of the day. As Dakin observes, "[Ali's] colourful career belongs to Greek as well as to Turkish history. His court was Greek and had been the centre of a Greek renaissance."[27] The population of Ali's territories was predominantly Greek speaking, and the use of its common tongue by the ruling class had the effect of linking them, albeit inchoately, with that ruling class. Greeks outnumbered Turks by ten to one in mainland Greece,[28] virtually all of which was under the control of Ali and his sons by the first decade of the nineteenth century. Whereas the sizable Greek-speaking populations of the Turkish provinces were cut off from the bureaucracy by their use of the Ottoman language—which used a foreign alphabet, borrowed widely from Persian and Arabic, and followed arcane and complex grammatical forms—those of Ali's lands spoke a form of Greek basically the same as the Greek used in court in Ioannina.

A second effect of Ali's use of Greek on the Greek populations was in education. Just as his economic policies furthered education within his borders, so too did his adoption of Greek for use in official business. Several wealthy members of the Greek mercantile diaspora[29] furthered educational opportunities in Ioannina by endowing schools there. In 1810

[24] Dakin 1972, 44ff.

[25] Ibid., 45.

[26] Ibid., 45–46.

[27] Ibid., 43.

[28] Dakin 1955, 9. Dakin estimates the population at the outbreak of the Greek War of Independence to have consisted of 1,500,000 Greeks and 150,000 Turks. Dakin's numbers are significantly higher than those of Colonel Leake, who estimated the 1822 population of the mainland to total not more than 1 million; the estimated ratio of Greeks to Turks is about the same, however (Leake 1826, 21).

[29] For a superb overview of Orthodox mercantile activity during the Ottoman period, see "The Conquering Balkan Orthodox Merchant" (Stoianovich 1960).

Broughton observed that there were two well-established secondary schools in Ioannina: "The principal was conducted by the celebrated Athanasius Psallida, and had 100 scholars; the other by the hereditary schoolmaster . . . Valleno [whose family had been in the teaching profession for three hundred years]. This school, founded 130 years ago, and having 300 scholars, was supported by the famous Zosimades, brothers, two resident in Italy, a third in Russia."[30] Broughton's fellow countryman Henry Holland noted two years later that the Zosimades brothers[31] alone contributed about twenty thousand piastres annually to Ioannina's educational establishment.[32]

The schools of Ioannina were staffed by a prestigious faculty, which included the philologist Psallida and the famed contemporary man of letters Georgios Sakellarius, who had penned several well-known works and who served as physician to Ali. These academicians, along with the core of Ali's court, comprised the academic elite of the day; many of these figures went on to play significant roles in the Greek movement for independence. John Kolettis, for example, who served as personal physician to Ali's son Muktar and who wrote and translated several scientific works, went on to become a central figure in the Greek Revolution of 1821.

The educational establishment and the courtly establishment, then, enjoyed significant overlap in their memberships. The schools of Ioannina, which grew to have a reputation for excellence throughout Greece,[33] served to some extent as feeder institutions both for Ali's court and for the growing Greek independence movement. Ali depended on the schools of Ioannina to provide future members of his court with a background in Greek. In so doing he also helped form a large Greek literary class, which became crucial in the first years of the Greek War of Independence.

Language, then, was a dominant organizational principle for the nascent nationalism in Ali's territories. His use of Greek as the official language of his government fostered literacy, and kept the predominantly Greek population of his territories connected to the governmental elite in a way alien to other provinces of the Ottoman Empire.[34] Albanians, Turks, and Greeks all spoke Greek, and the language was not, contrary

[30] Broughton 1855, 1:62.

[31] Lazarou 1965; Mihalopoulos 1930; Evangelides 1896.

[32] Cited in Broughton 1855, 62.

[33] This was particularly true of the gymnasium founded by the Zosimades brothers in 1769, which educated not just Greeks but Muslim and Orthodox Albanians as well. The school educated many who went on to have prominent roles in the Greek and Albanian independence movements. The Frasheri brothers, for example, who played a prominent role in Albanian nationalism at the end of the nineteenth century, were educated there (Skendi 1982).

[34] The reputed health of the Greek language in Ioannina also contributed to the city's popularity as a destination for traveling European philhellenes, who were interested in philological as well as anthropological study (Miller 1913, 25, 64).

to the claims of much of the historiography on this period, within the academic purview of only the Orthodox ecclesiastical establishment.[35] Rather, Ali's territories provide the interesting example of a non-Greek, non-Christian ruler who made significant contributions to the language of Hellenism and of Christianity. They also illustrate the fact that the Greek language was not the sine qua non of Greekness, but simply one of many factors in the construction of national identity.[36]

Religion

There were four basic religious groupings in the region. The Greeks were Orthodox Christians; the Turks considered themselves orthodox Sunni Muslims; the Albanians for the most part associated themselves with the Bektashi Sufi order; and there was a small Jewish minority, mostly refugees from the persecutions of Ferdinand and Isabella, many of whom still used Spanish as their primary language.[37]

The Greek Orthodox were the religious majority in the region. They defined themselves as Orthodox, in explicit opposition to the Catholic Christians of northern Albania and to the so-called Latins of the later Byzantine Empire. They had a religious affinity not with their western Venetian and French neighbors—whose form of Christianity was scarcely less offensive than Islam—but with the Orthodox Russians to the north.

The Orthodox sense of unity was fostered, on one hand, by a church hierarchy that was granted far-ranging privileges by the Ottoman regime and, on the other hand, by the simple fact of their constituting the vast majority of the population. Whereas in Albania large numbers of people had converted to Islam (largely to further their careers as mercenary sol-

[35] This was the case in Ioannina, at least. Whereas in many remote villages the priesthood encouraged the continuation of the Greek culture and language, in Ali's capital it was the government that did so.

[36] This point, however, can be overstated. Baerlein, for example, writes: "Now, since we find a Greek people largely talking Albanian and thorough Albanians writing in Greek, it is obvious that the languages which were used in the daily life of the two sandjaks [sic] gave little indication of the people's political sentiments. Yet there have not been wanting publicists who very rashly based their arguments on the habitual language. How far astray this leads one we shall see when contemplating the heroic Suliotes, who in Albanian shouted their defiance of the threatening Greek letters sent by Ali Pasha!" (Baerlein 1968, 22). The Albanian-speaking Orthodox Suliotes resisted domination of all sorts, Orthodox and Muslim, Albanian- and Greek-speaking, and their alliance shifted depending on who offered them the greatest chance of ongoing freedom.

[37] See, for example, Leake's observations on the Jews of Larissa (Leake 1835, 1:443–44). For more on the history of Jews in the area of Ioannina, see The Jews of Ioannina (Dalven 1990).

diers in the sultan's armies), the population of mainland Greece saw virtually no conversions.

The role of the church hierarchy was, however, double-edged: just as the privileges granted to them by the Porte allowed for the continuation of worship—an important aspect of the Orthodox sense of community—and to an extent fostered education (particularly the teaching of *koine* Greek, the language of the New Testament), so these same privileges made the Orthodox bureaucracy the target of accusations of corruption, abuse of power, and collusion with the Turks. Much Greek revolutionary propaganda of Ali's day viewed the Greek church hierarchy as being in collusion with the oppressive Turkish beys and with a wealthy, fatuous mercantile class. Lord Broughton, for example, reported in 1810 that "Lord Byron received as a present a long paper of verses to this import, which, in a dramatic colloquy between a Greek Patriot, an Englishman, Frenchman and Russian, a Metropolitan, a Waiwode of Wallachia, a merchant and a primate, and by the introduction of Greece, personified as a desolate female in tears, displays the apathy of the privileged classes, and concludes with the assertion of the Frank strangers:[38] 'We have found a Metropolitan and a Bey of Wallachia, and a merchant, and a primate, all friends to tyranny.'"[39]

Class concerns led to the grouping of Greek merchants, Turkish beys, and Orthodox religious leaders under one heading. Broughton commented that the Albanian Orthodox Christians, too, viewed the Orthodox hierarchy with disdain, writing that although fairly observant of fasts, they "pay no sort of reverence to the ministers of their Church, whom they abuse openly and despise because they are not soldiers, and are considered to be slaves, being usually Greeks by nation."[40]

The religion that mattered, then, was not the religion of the church hierarchy but rather that which existed at the level of the people, people who felt disenfranchised by the ruling classes of the empire, which included the so-called leaders of the Orthodox church. This faith observed not just the numerous fasts and holidays of the Orthodox Church, but also all manner of traditional practices, including magical rites, exorcisms, and the belief in numerous spirits and demons.[41]

Ali himself, although by most accounts interested in religion only when it was politically advantageous to him, appears to have been a follower

---

[38] This would have been a version of the so-called "Rossanglogallos" (The Russian-English Frenchman), a copy of which is translated in its entirety by Richard Clogg. See *The Movement for Greek Independence* (Clogg 1976, 96–106).

[39] Broughton 1855, 2:12.

[40] Ibid., 1:137.

[41] For an excellent overview of these numerous practices and their integration into Orthodoxy as practiced by the people, see *Demons and the Devil* (Stewart 1991).

of the Bektashis. Colonel Leake reports that Ali endowed a Bektashi *tekke* (religious school) in Tríkkala, but is quick to observe why Ali might favor that particular order:

> It is their doctrine to be liberal towards all professions and religions, and to consider all men as equal in the eyes of God. . . . The Vezir, although no practical encourager of liberty and equality, finds the religious doctrines of the Bektashli exactly suited to him. At the time that Christianity was out of favour in France, he was in the habit of ridiculing religion and the immortality of the soul with his French prisoners; and he lately remarked to me, speaking of Mahomet, *kai ego eimai prophites sta ioannina*, and I too am a prophet at Ioannina. It was an observation of the bishop of Trikkala, that Aly takes from everybody and gives only to the dervises [*sic*], whom he undoubtedly finds politically useful. In fact, there is no place in Greece where in consequence of this encouragement these wandering or mendicant Musulman monks are so numerous and insolent as at Ioannina.[42]

Leake's anecdote, if true, also provides a fair impression of Ali's low level of respect not just for Christianity but for Islam as well.

Ali did not, however, make a consistent practice of persecuting peoples on the basis of their religion. In fact, the Christians of Ioannina enjoyed the privilege of wearing green and yellow slippers (usually only Turks were allowed to wear colored slippers), velvet, and other sumptuous fabrics. Christians were so showy in their appearance that a traveling dervish complained to Ali that in Ioannina it was impossible to tell the difference between the Turks and the Greeks.[43] Ali's few persecutions of the Christian community had as their only objective the creation of a pretext for taking more of their money, as in an instance Leake heard of at the village of Kalarytes: "Not many years ago, the Kalaryiotes were moved with the desire of having bells to some of their churches, one of the attributes of the temples of the Oriental Christians, of which, because forbidden by the Turks, they are particularly proud; Aly, though generally very indulgent on the subject of building and repairing churches, did not omit so good an opportunity of making the Kalaryiotes pay for their vanity, and exacted 15,000 piastres from them for the permission to have bells."[44]

Ali's manipulations of religion, then, had as their primary aim the extortion of money from his subject populations. In the last years of his rule, he attempted to capitalize also on the communal implications of the religious subgroups in his territories. He announced his conversion to Christianity in a last-minute bid to gain Greek support and referred to the Greeks as his "fellow Christians." The insincerity of his conversion

[42] Leake 1835, 4:285.
[43] *"Tourkos Romios sta Ioannina den borokamo farki"* (Leake 1835, 1:495).
[44] Leake 1835, 4:283.

notwithstanding, this gambit was doomed to fail, as the Greeks sought not so much freedom from a Muslim ruler as the establishment of a quasi-democratic state. Class, not religion, was at the heart of the Greek movement. Although religion acted as an important symbolic point of coalescence, the evidence from Ali's lands, at least, indicates the presence of an overriding economic dimension to the Greek nationalist movements of the early nineteenth century.[45]

[45] This is anecdotally corroborated by such statements as Leake's: "In general, the condition of the peasant under the Greek proprietor was not much better than under the Turks themselves. . . . The most powerful were often in league with the pasha to plunder the Christians" (Leake 1826, 12–13). The role of economics in the rise of nationalism in the Ottoman Empire has been written about much more in the instances of Egypt and the lands of the Fertile Crescent.

FIVE

THE EUROPEAN CONTEXT: AN OVERVIEW

THE TRANSFORMATION of the domestic economy of the western Ottoman provinces and the gradual nationalization of Ali's subject peoples took place within the broader context of international affairs. Ali's rise to power in mainland Greece coincided with a period of heightened European interest in the region, complicated and shifting alliances between the European powers and the Ottoman government, and major political upheavals that definitively changed the face of Europe. Ioannina's territories, which encompassed almost the entire Greek mainland, included or bordered on some of the most politically and economically strategic regions of the day. Particularly central to the interests of both the European powers and the Ottoman government were the Ionian Islands, seven islands in the Adriatic Sea, directly off the western coast of the Peloponnese, Epiros, and Albania.[1]

The eighteenth century marked the definitive end of the Republic of Venice and the rise of Napoleon; in Greece itself it witnessed the rise of Albanian power and the collapse of the Turkish landed gentry. Ali's policies and life were very much at the heart of these latter events. The broader trends in European politics also came to have significant implications for—as well as to be shaped by—Ali Pasha.

The Venetians

Off and on over the course of several centuries, mainland Greece and the Peloponnese had as their western neighbor the Venetian Republic of Saint Mark. Venetian domination in the area was first undermined only in 1715, when the Turks finally reconquered the Peloponnese. This reconquest, however, left in Venetian hands the Ionian Islands and their four principal mainland dependencies, the coastal towns of Parga, Vonitza, Preveza, and Butrinto. In 1401 the peoples of Parga had established the precedent of colluding with Venice by placing themselves voluntarily under Venetian protection, thus staying the advance of the Ottomans.[2] Domestically, also, the dependencies had importance. These territories came to be known for their staunch support of the Greek revolutionary

[1] Corfu, Cephalonia, Zante, Santa Maura, Itháki, Cerigo, and Paxo.
[2] "Parga" 1820, 113.

cause, and Parga colluded with the independent Orthodox peoples of Souli in their chronic battles with Ali Pasha.

Once restored to the leadership of their Venetian suzerain and with the assistance of the free towns of Konispolis and Philates, these coastal towns provided ongoing resistance to the encroachments of the pasha of Delvino.[3] Thus was established a historical precedent for both hostility between the local governors of the region and Venice, and resistance to these local governors by the Greeks of the coastal Ionian dependencies. Venice was seen as a major obstacle to the expansionist goals of the various regional governors of the day, and the Venetian republic's long-standing control not just of the Ionians but also of the crucial coastal dependencies guaranteed them a dominant role in the region's trade. Venetian trade interests in the area favored the protection of the local Greek populations of the islands as well as of Parga, Vonitza, Preveza, and Butrinto, and the Venetians were widely regarded by these locals as their saviors in the face of encroachments from not just the Ottoman government but also various marauding bands common to the region.

Under the Venetians, then, the Ionian Islands grew to enjoy wealth and privileges uncommon in the other Greek territories of the region, and during this period of Venetian control the Greeks of the Ionians first nurtured the hope of forming an independent republic in the seven islands. The other European powers of the day well recognized the strategic and economic value of the islands and their possessions, and Venetian control over the region finally met its end in 1797 at the hands of Napoleon, who, calling the Ionians "the key to the Adriatic," took possession of them and garrisoned both the islands and their mainland dependencies.[4]

The Treaty of Campo Formio, signed on October 17, 1797, confirmed French possession of the Ionian Islands and effectively ended the Republic of Saint Mark, giving Venice over to Austria. Thus ended Venetian mercantile dominance in the region and with it the protection of the Ionians from encroachments from the east. Ali, long thwarted by the Venetians in his hope of gaining complete control over the islands and the western coast, immediately turned his attention to establishing good relations with the French, with the aim of persuading them to cede to him these critical territories.

The Ionian Islands and Their Dependencies

The first French possession of the islands was short-lived. Just one year later, in 1798, the French surrendered to an allied fleet of Ottoman and

---

[3] Baggally 1938, 3.

[4] For a detailed look at Napoleon's strategy regarding the Ionian Islands, see *Bonaparte et les Îles Ioniennes, 1797–1816* (Rodocanachi 1899).

Russian ships under the command of Admirals Oskaloff and Katu Bey.[5] The French position against the joint venture was further weakened by the threat of rebellion posed by the local Corfiote population.[6]

At this juncture Ali saw his first fleeting possession of the mainland dependencies of Vonitza, Preveza, and Butrinto; taking advantage of the struggle in the islands, Ali sent his own forces and seized the coastal towns. Sensing that French control over these territories would soon to fall to the onslaught of Ottoman forces, Ali, who had hoped to persuade the French to hand them over to him,[7] devised a new strategy. He turned his attention to proving his loyalty to the Porte.[8] With this as his aim, he unleashed the full extent of his might on the French troops garrisoned in the dependencies, slaughtering along with them any Greeks and Albanians who had sided with the French against the Porte.

Such tactics were typical of the first years of Ali's military and diplomatic engagement with France and England. Unsure as to whether his greatest hopes for success would be realized through collusion with Europe or through Ottoman patronage, Ali's treatment of France, in particular, was highly erratic, collusive at one moment and viciously hostile at the next.

With this military maneuver Ali came to the forefront of the Western media, and various accounts detailing his atrocities in the dependencies received wide circulation both in France and in England.[9] Of the four Io-

---

[5] "Parga" 1820, 114. The commanders' names vary from account to account, due to the poor system of transliteration; Jervis cites them as Ouschacow and Abd-el-Kadir Bey. See *History of the Island of Corfu and of the Republic of the Ionian Islands* (Jervis 1852, 164).

[6] Jervis writes: "The arrival of the French had been viewed with pleasure by none. The nobles, almost all of whom were of Venetian descent, regretted the loss of their trumpery titles; whilst the priests looked with dismay upon the innovations which their invaders were introducing, for their first acts had been to establish a primary school, to open a printing-press, and to form a public library with a collection of all the books which were found in the several monasteries" (Jervis 1852, 162). Bellaire's *Précis des Opérations Générales de la division française du Levant* provides the source for this information (Bellaire 1805). Jervis's observation is of further interest in that it alludes to the general hostility of the Greek Orthodox priestly class to Western "innovations," the government's usurpation of education and books, and the like. This hostility came into play later in the Greek independence movement.

[7] Up to this time Ali had been making friendly overtures to the French, but he had also sent them a somewhat threatening message demanding that Butrinto, Parga, Preveza, Vonitza, and the fort of Santa Maura be handed over to him. For the account of this letter, and the mixed French reaction, see chapter 14 of the informative eyewitness account of J. P. Bellaire 1805.

[8] Twelve thousand Albanian auxiliaries had participated in the Russo-Turkish expedition against the French, many of whom probably came from Ali's forces. Ali hoped that this, too, would raise his status vis-à-vis the Porte, thus increasing his chances of gaining control of the mainland dependencies (Jervis 1852, 185).

[9] "Parga" 1820, 114. The travelers Hobhouse, Holland, and Pouqueville also give varying accounts of Ali's military actions in Preveza, Butrinto, and Vonitza.

nian dependencies Parga alone resisted Ali's move, protected as it was by the French garrison within the town and its Souliote allies without. With the retreat of the French, Parga passed directly to the protection of a new, Russian garrison.

Ali, now with only Parga beyond his control, hoped to persuade the Ottoman government to allow him to maintain direct governance over Vonitza, Preveza, and Butrinto. Much to his fury, however, in 1800 the Porte concluded a treaty in Istanbul, under the terms of which the seven islands were to be established as an independent republic, at first placed under the sovereignty of Russia, then under the immediate protection of England. Parga, Vonitza, Preveza, and Butrinto were in return to be ceded to the sovereignty of the Porte for perpetuity.[10] In dividing the spoils of their joint expedition, the Russians and the Porte had left Ali entirely out in the cold. Adding insult to injury, the hated dependencies not only were once again out of his grasp but by this same treaty were granted wide-ranging privileges, to be guaranteed by Russia, in keeping with the stipulations of the earlier Russo-Turkish treaty of Kutchuk Kainardji (1774). The Greeks of the territories were now guaranteed free practice of religion, self-administration of law, subjugation to no governor except one resident Ottoman bey, and moderate taxation not to exceed that customarily paid to the ex-Venetian republic.[11] Abdullah Bey was sent from Istanbul to take control of the principalities, and Ali was forced to evacuate them immediately.

This marked a significant development not just for the Ionian Greeks— now the Septinsular Republic—and their mainland dependencies but also for Ali himself. Whereas earlier these territories had always been the possessions of enemies of the Porte, now they were governed by the stipulations of a treaty masterminded by the government of Istanbul. Any earlier show of aggression on Ali's part had always been construable as an act of fealty for the Ottoman government. Now, however, any action he might take to add these territories to his own lands would mark an obvious act of betrayal of the central power in Istanbul.

For the next six years, then, Ali was unable to make a move, fearful of the consequences of showing such flagrant disregard for the orders of the Ottoman government. Finally, in 1806, international discord once again provided him with the opportunity of attacking the Ionian dependencies. In that year, war again broke out between Russia and the Porte, whereupon Ali's son Veli, under the express orders of the Porte, seized Vonitza, Preveza, and Butrinto and confiscated the Russians' properties, ousting many Greek Orthodox inhabitants and planting several Ottoman fami-

[10] See *Della Repubblica Settinsulare* (Lunzi 1863) and *La Mediterranée de 1803 à 1805* (Douin 1917).
[11] "Parga" 1820, 114 n.

lies in their stead. (Once again, Parga resisted Ottoman aggression, calling a Russian force from Corfu to ensure its protection.)

Ali hoped again that through his son's show of loyalty to the Porte these territories would pass to his control. The following year, however, brought the Treaty of Tilsit, under which the Ionians once again reverted to France; the Ottomans were to maintain direct control over the mainland towns. Ali, fearing that the dependencies would slip from his grasp, began clandestine correspondence with Berthier, the French governor-general of Corfu, hoping to obtain his favor in the matter. Claiming to be acting on behalf of the government in Istanbul, Ali sent word to Berthier demanding that all French troops be withdrawn from Parga, the only town on the mainland's western coast to elude him. The Parganotes, however, informed of Ali's actions, sent their own delegation of primates to Berthier, and, as a flowery contemporary account would have it, "throwing themselves at the general's feet, implored his compassion for their unfortunate countrymen, and besought him not to surrender them to certain destruction."[12] Berthier, moved by this request, recalled his orders for a French evacuation of the town and, leaving his garrison in place, claimed Parga as a continuing appendage to the Ionian Islands. Parga once again had rebuffed Ali's advances.

The French maintained control of Parga and the seven islands for a few brief years, and the British soon wrested from them control of all the islands and their territories save for Corfu and Parga. In 1812 the Treaty of Bucharest, signed between Russia and the Porte, renewed and confirmed the stipulations of their 1800 treaty, and in 1815 the Septinsular Republic came once again under British protection as a result of negotiations at the Congress of Vienna.

Perhaps more than any other single factor, it was Ali's struggle to gain control of the Ionian dependencies that framed his gradual break with the Ottoman state. It was in the context of negotiations for the dependencies that he was first brought in direct contact with the western European powers, that he realized that his expansionist desires met with as much opposition from the Ottoman as from the European camp, and that he ultimately came to seek power through contact with Europe rather than with the Ottoman state.

Diplomacy with the British and the French

As the seven islands and their coastal dependencies passed back and forth between the Venetians, Russians, Ottomans, French, and British, Ali Pasha established multiple diplomatic ties with these powers in his ever

---

[12] Ibid., 115.

more frantic bid to gain control of the territories. His powers of diplomacy were sorely tried as he attempted to deduce with whom at any given moment it was most advantageous to form an alliance. The result of so much second-guessing was that Ali many times was simultaneously declaring loyalty to the French, the Ottomans, and the British, secretly colluding with powers that were often at odds with one another.

And just as he needed the friendship and alliance of these various powers, so too did they need him. Ali, in possession of the virtual entirety of the Greek mainland, wielded considerable influence in the region, and posed no small threat to the consummation of the territorial aims of the Europeans and the Ottomans.

The first European power with whom Ali began negotiations was the French, whose position in the Ionian Islands in 1798 was extremely tenuous. The local populations, consisting of a displaced Venetian gentry and a clergy stripped of its privileges, were hostile and threatened to revolt. Corfu's Latin archbishop was banished to Dalmatia so as to prevent his stirring the peasantry to revolt. The French force in the islands was small, and the promised support of Italian troops, ammunition, and provisions was not forthcoming.[13] The only remaining hope for supplies was Ali and his mainland territories to the east.

Ali, then, had considerable leverage in his demands that the French give him the islands' mainland dependencies. In 1798, however, he was still at a relatively early phase of his career and had neither the might nor the self-confidence to break with the Porte. His dealings with the French, the official enemy of the government in Istanbul, were concealed from the Porte, and as soon as war broke out between the Russo-Turkish alliance and the French, Ali abandoned his earlier protestations of friendship and attacked the French soldiers on the mainland. Not until several years had passed, when Napoleon defeated the Austrian forces at Austerlitz and occupied Dalmatia in 1805, did Ali establish formal, independent diplomatic ties with the French. Pouqueville was then sent to serve as French resident in Ioannina, beginning a complicated series of shifting diplomatic entanglements between Ali, the French, and the British.

As were the French, the British, too, were quick to realize the strategic importance of Ali's lands and the environs. About a year before Pouqueville's arrival in Ioannina, the British had sent to Greece as British resident and consul-general the Huguenot J. P. Morier, who was to drum up opposition to the French among the governors of Albania, Epiros, and the Peloponnese.[14] Most important of these, of course, was the figure of Ali Pasha, by then in control of a territory stretching from Livadia in the

[13] Jervis 1852, 163.

[14] For detailed information on Morier's mission, see British Foreign Office Papers, series 78/44, London.

south, to Pella, in Macedonia, to the north. The bordering *paşalıks* of Scutari and Berat were entirely dwarfed in significance by their Ioanninite neighbor.

Morier's meetings with the pasha made it clear that Ali was in no way committed to the French. Although eager to have good relations with them (they were, after all, threateningly close on both his northern and western borders), Ali was by no means about to abandon all other diplomatic routes. In the summer of 1804 Morier had the first of several audiences with Ali, laying the foundations for a diplomatic friendship that came to eclipse the one between Ali and the French and that endured until Ali's death, in 1822. Concealing his past overtures to the French, Ali told Morier of his suspicions of the French, the Russians, and the Ottoman government alike, inviting Great Britain (then politically aligned with Russia) to secure his position vis-à-vis these various threatening neighbors.[15] Morier, bound by the British alliance with Russia, was unable to offer any concrete support, but he promised future help and friendship in the hope of derailing a possible opposing alliance between Ali and the French.

Even as Ali was making these entreaties to Morier, he was in open communication with the French. Similarly, at later points in his career Ali would simultaneously profess friendship with the Ottoman government and the rebel Greeks, the klephts and the army that fought to suppress them, and both the Russians and their Ottoman opponents.

.   .   .   .   .

Ali's complex and contradictory diplomatic dealings have typically been cited as further evidence of his illogical, foreign, and untrustworthy nature, and these comprise an important element of the large body of Orientalist literature on Ali.[16] In reality, however, Ali's diplomatic tactics, though at times erratic and unorthodox, demonstrate a remarkable level of awareness of the intricacies of the political climate of his day. In these negotiations Ali proved to be a remarkable observer of world politics and a subtle manipulator of the complex and volatile international climate of the period.

Ali's gubernatorial tactics did not represent a reversion to the forms of ancient tribal politics. Instead they were a syncretism of Albanian, Byzantine, Ottoman, and modern European influences. Although Ali drew on his Albanian background of clannish warfare and brigandish activity, in his international diplomatic dealings he showed himself to be anything

---

[15] PRO/FO 78/44, no. 9.
[16] Leake 1826, 1835; Hobhouse 1813; Pouqueville 1805; Vaudoncourt 1816.

but provincial and naive. In fact, his diplomatic acumen in many instances outstripped that of the Ottoman central government, and through his brilliant international intrigues he came closer to achieving true sovereignty than any other ruler in his region. His paradigm for power was far broader than that provided by the categories of Ottoman politics, and in his career as a diplomat we see most clearly his pretensions not just to regional but to international importance as well.

In the world of international politics Ali found the cultural and symbolic idioms with which to express his vision of himself as an independent, non-Ottoman ruler. Archival and other primary sources depicting Ali's approach to international affairs demonstrate his self-conscious abandonment of the Ottoman imperial ideology and the adoption of a more modernist, European-influenced understanding of statecraft and of politics.

Paradoxically, though, Ali's fascination with the West and with being somehow Western was, to the Western eye at least, obscured by the West's own fascination with Ali as Oriental. Just as the pasha had a vested, self-conscious interest in seeing himself as Western, so too did Europe have much invested in an image of Ali as the quintessential Ottoman despot— irrational, cruel, old-fashioned, and wholly other. Thus countervailing representational forces are at work in the construct of Ali's identity: just as Ali attempted to push beyond the confines of the standard Orientalist models by which he was defined, so did those same models prove unable, from a Western viewpoint, to accommodate this attempt. How Ali has remained, to this day, a prime exemplum of the Oriental despot is a testament to the discursive power of such models.

SIX

INITIAL CONTACT WITH THE FRENCH

THE HALF CENTURY spanned by Ali's career saw him shift first beyond the confines of Albanian bandit culture to a solidly elite Ottoman milieu, then cast off Ottoman imperial ideology in favor of a form of pseudonationalist statism heavily influenced by the French Revolution and its leaders. Accounts by numerous European travelers who visited Ali in Ioannina, however, portray him in static terms. According to these texts, Ali's methods of governance remained basically unchanged from the time of his brigand activities in adolescence to the final decades of his life, when he controlled a vast territory, maintained independent diplomatic ties with Europe, and planned his break from the Ottoman Empire.

This complete lack of character development is adopted wholesale by Ali's biographers, most of whom based their accounts almost entirely on travel literature. Typical of this static portrayal is William Plomer's *Diamond of Jannina*, perhaps the most successful of the many biographies of Ali. In his concluding chapter, "The End of Ali," Plomer describes Ali's final moments, when, barricaded within his island fort on Lake Ioannina, Ali hears the voice of one of his former soldiers, now a deserter to the Ottoman troops. Already gravely wounded, Ali knows that his end is near but still can think of nothing but fury and revenge. "Anger, an emotion ready to the last to take precedence over all others in that turbulent heart, now got the better of pain, and Ali cried out."[1]

Ali's appetites, his rages, his quixotic moods: these are shown as the dominant features of his life and are the constants that guide his actions consistently throughout his long career.

Quite a different story emerges when we examine the available consular material pertaining to Ioannina's long and complicated diplomatic relationship with the powers of Europe. Diplomatic sources recording Ali's negotiations with the French and British evince a subtle yet distinct evolution in his political and ideological outlook.

· · · · ·

By the earliest years of the nineteenth century, Ali had managed to establish "a virtually independent State, with its own army, its own treasury,

[1] Plomer 1970, 275.

and an independent foreign policy."[2] As others have pointed out, it is a fair measure of his importance that during the Napoleonic Wars the British had sent Morier (in 1804–5) and the topographer Leake (in 1807–10) to Ioannina in order to persuade Ali that if the government in Istanbul were to lose control of its European territories, he was to assert his total independence and not succumb to the French.[3] Similarly, from the time of their first occupation of the Ionian islands in 1797, the French were secretly negotiating with Ali in the hope of gaining his support against the Ottoman government. He was significant enough in power and influence that the two leading European nations of the day felt the need in some way to address his presence and consider him, independently of the Ottoman Empire, in their plans for territorial and economic expansion.

Ali's stature was not merely the result of felicitous geography. Although anyone in control of the critical Adriatic coastal region would have elicited serious consideration and concern, Ali was regarded as a vital ally also because of his political acumen, his tremendous wealth, his large standing army, and his rich and cosmopolitan government. Ali, both in his own eyes and in those of such foreign powers as the British and the French, was functionally an independent ruler, with his own clearly demarcated territories, population, and economy. In negotiating with him, the British and the French knew full well that they were not dealing with a delegate or representative of the Ottoman state; they knew that Ali was not the mouthpiece for official Ottoman policy. He had fashioned himself a free agent and independent ruler, and in European political circles was treated as such.

Thus the nations of Europe provided the political recognition and affirmation long denied to Ali by the Ottoman Porte. Indeed, the position that Ali so desperately wished to hold—independent ruler of an independent nation—could never be recognized by the political system of which he was ostensibly a part, as the very role was inimical to the integrity of the ideology of empire. It is therefore no surprise to note that Ali reveled in the overtures of the Europeans, prolonging his negotiations with them for as long as possible, soliciting their counsel and giving them his, all with no concern whatsoever for the fact that his actions threatened to undermine the security of the Ottoman state. Gradually, as he became ever more convinced that his future lay not with the power to his east but with those to his west, he not only adopted aspects of their military and political policies but also began to see himself in ever more "European" terms, decorating his home with items redolent of French imperial imagery, framing

[2] Dakin 1955, 13.
[3] Ibid., 13–14.

his personal ideologies in the idioms of nationalism and atheism, and peopling his court with foreign, forward-looking secretaries and counselors.

Ali, however, did not simply mimic the actions and ideals of the European powers and eschew Ottoman ideology only when presented with this new, European alternative. Rather, the models of the West filled a vacuum that had long existed in his role as ruler. That is, since early in his imperial career Ali's aim had been the establishment of a quasi-independent nation or kingdom, free of the political and economic demands of the Istanbul government; but he did not, it seems, know how to give this venture shape. The European power crisis in the Adriatic merely provided him with a new paradigm for rule and a new political realm and sphere of influence in which to pursue his aim for independent rule. To a large extent the nation-states of Europe provided a model by which Ali could, tentatively, give shape to his long-held hope of being something more than an Ottoman governor.

In entering into negotiations with the British and the French, Ali's actions were significant not just for marking a break with the policies and wishes of the Ottoman state. For decades his behavior had been characterized by his contravention of the demands of his superiors in Istanbul. Rather, Ali's diplomatic relations with the French and the British are important for the implications they hold of self-conscious political evolution. They provide a picture that runs contrary both to the static, Orientalist, vision of him as unchanging and backward and to most contemporary historiographic depictions of Ottoman provincial rulers. One of Ali's chroniclers began his work with the declaration: "L'histoire n'est en Orient qu'un perpétuel recommencement."[4] The Orientalist myth of the eternal return, however, is seriously misplaced when applied to Ali of Tebelen.

Ali had long fostered the hope of independence from the central government but did not, in the first decades of his career, frame this hope in any terms but those of opposition to that government. His initial relationship with the central state was basically that of brigand leader, subverting and attacking the dominant power, but nevertheless defining himself in relation to it. When in the 1790s Ali entered international politics, however, he found the idiom with which to frame his hope for independence. As J. W. Baggally writes, despite Ali's power and skill, he "might have remained all his life an obscure local chieftain had it not been for the outbreak of the French Revolution and the rise of Napoleon."[5] Although Baggally did not intend the observation in quite the same way I do, there is truth to the statement.[6] The Napoleonic Wars brought western Europe

[4] Boppe 1914, vi.

[5] Baggally 1938, 7.

[6] Baggally evidently meant that the war advertised Ali and made him incidentally important. The war itself also made Ali see himself in a different way.

to Ali's doorstep and took him into a new political arena, one that had more to offer him than did the Ottoman government. The political system of which he had hitherto been a part did not provide a role which matched his aims and ideals. He found this role only through the French Revolution and the new ideological and political possibilities it brought in its wake.

. . . . .

Ali's career can be divided into two more or less discrete parts: the first three decades of his rise to power (from the 1760s to the 1790s)[7] and from 1797 until his death in 1822. The first period is characterized by Ali's ascension in the Ottoman provincial bureaucracy and his gaining power through mechanisms available in the contexts of the Ottoman government and the traditions of Albanian banditry. This period in Ali's life shows him working within the paradigms of power standard to his time, place, and personal background.

The second developmental period correlates directly with his interactions with the European powers. This period sees him looking beyond his familiar Ottoman and Albanian models and attempting to shift to a new role as independent ruler, international diplomat, and even constitutional monarch. These later years of Ali's career coincide with significant, irreversible changes in Europe—the final demise of Venetian primacy, the rise of independence movements, the emergence of British and French Mediterranean control—and reveal much about the process of Ottoman decline, as well as the European attitude toward the Ottomans in the early stages of the Eastern Question. Geographically, politically, chronologically, and ideologically, Ali was situated on the interstices of powerful imperial and counterimperial forces.

Ali's behavior during this later period demonstrates a tremendous awareness of the tidal changes taking place in world politics and signals his recognition that the old, Ottoman paradigms of governance, diplomacy and trade no longer provided the flexibility needed to adapt to a new world order and to a new approach to international relations. His proximity to the Ottoman regime, however, qualified his interest in and understanding of European colonialism, nationalism, and constitutionalism. His relationship to both east and west, then, was ambivalent and volatile, and his ultimate rejection of the Ottoman regime came only after many years of tentative overtures to the powers of Europe.

This second major period can in turn be broken down into several more or less discrete phases. The late 1790s are characterized by Ali's earliest

---

[7] For a detailed account of this early period in Ali's life, see the excellent "From Bandit to Pasha" (Skiotis 1971).

dealings with the French, who, as we have seen, first took possession of the Ionian Islands in 1797. During these years Ali was making his initial forays into the world of international diplomacy, but under the nominal sponsorship of the Ottoman Porte. The first decade of the nineteenth century saw Ali establish formal, independent diplomatic ties with both the British and the French. During this period the pasha became more confident, no longer seeking Ottoman sanction and legitimation, and his aspirations to independent rule broadened in scope. Finally, the last decade of his life (1810–22) saw the furthering of Ali's diplomatic relations with the Europeans, his increasing interest in European political ideologies and the nationalist movements of his own territories, and his ultimate declaration of independence from the Porte.

What follows is a detailed examination of Ali's diplomatic relations with the French and the British during the period 1797–1810, the years that most clearly document the significant ways in which Ali responded to and was shaped by the events on his western borders. This middle period of Ali's diplomatic career marks a subtle shift in his outlook from the ideologies of the Ottoman Empire to those of western Europe. Although this process is much more evident (most obviously with his declaration of independence from the Porte) in his later years, this central period of his career is most significant in that it shows the seeds of his discontent with the Imperial system by which he was bound. These years clearly chart Ali's development as a ruler and witness the gradual rejection of Ottoman political categories and the substitution of European ones.

The Ionian Islands

The struggle for control over the Ionian Islands brought Ali into the orbit of the western European powers. The seven islands in the Adriatic Sea (Corfu, Cephalonia, Zante, Santa Maura, Itháki, Cerigo, and Paxo) for centuries had been hotly pursued by, among others, the Genoese, the Florentines, the Maltese, and the Venetians. Long recognized as having geographic significance, with the rise of philhellenism in the late eighteenth century they came to be culturally desirable as well. "The position of the Ionian Islands will be found superior, in a variety of respects, to that of Malta; and of these its contiguity and relations with ancient Greece is not one of the least interesting. It is impossible to preclude feelings of regard for our masters in the arts and sciences."[8]

The islands were also regarded as central to the European effort to sustain the Ottoman Empire. Following the 1814–15 Congress of Vienna,

---

[8] Vaudoncourt 1816, iv.

General Guillaume de Vaudoncourt observed the centrality of the Ionians to Ottoman defense:

> The year 1811 was to the Ottoman empire the nearest and most probable term of its fall; the whole of the elements which might have accelerated it were then in one powerful hand. The decree of fate warded off the storm, and it cannot be again formed under so threatening an aspect, as long as the power, to whom the protection of the Ionian Islands is confided, equally wishes to shield the Ottoman empire, or at least, to promote the indivisibility of that part of the European continent over which the Crescent holds sway, should it be resolved that this shall no longer be under Mussulman dominion.[9]

The importance of the islands had long been recognized. From the fourteenth century on, Venice enjoyed primacy in the region, holding the island of Corfu, by far the largest and most productive of the seven islands. In the mid-sixteenth century Corfu was sacked by the Ottomans, but the Venetians managed to maintain possession of it.[10] Throughout the seventeenth century, the Venetian Republic hung on to its position of primacy but was constantly threatened both by the Ottoman Empire to the east and the European states to the west. Henry Jervis-White Jervis writes that the consequent cost of protecting the island was so great that there was little cultivation; thus the republic obtained only minimal revenues from the territory.[11] Nevertheless, Corfu's and the other islands' strategic position and mere potential for cultivation were thought to be worth the effort.

In the early eighteenth century the Ottoman government, under the leadership of Ahmet III, began a massive and ongoing effort to claim the territories of the Venetian republic. These hostilities culminated in the 1715–16 Siege of Corfu, in which Ali's paternal grandfather Muktar played a significant role and lost his life.[12] Fifteen thousand Ottoman troops were said to have been killed during this particularly bloody battle.[13] This defeat, however, only strengthened Turkish desire to lay claim to all territories held by the republic.

In July 1718, the Treaty of Passarowitz gave the Ottoman Empire the Morea, or the Peloponnese, legitimating its 1715 reconquest and decimating Venetian power by rendering all other Venetian territories virtually useless. Venice now maintained control only of the Ionian Islands and their mainland dependencies, Parga, Vonitza, Preveza, and Butrinto. By

[9] Ibid., 501–2.
[10] Jervis 1852, 121.
[11] Ibid., 125.
[12] Leake 1835, 1.
[13] Jervis 1852, 142.

the end of the century, however, these too would fall into enemy hands. In 1797 Napoleonic forces took control of the seven islands, and in October of that year the Treaty of Campo Formio formalized French possession of them, thus effecting the final demise of the Venetian republic. The fifth article of this treaty guaranteed that the French would soon come in close contact with Ali Pasha: "Art. 5e. L'Empereur consent a ce que la République Française possède en toute souveraineté les îles ci-devant Venitiennes du Lévant, savoir: Corfou, Zante, Céphalonie, Sainte-Maure, Cérigo, et les autres îles dépendantes, ainsi que Butrinto, L'Arta, Vonizza, et en général tous les établissements ci-devant Venitiens en Albanie, qui sont situés plus bas que le Golfe de Butrinto."[14]

Thus the French found themselves in control not just of the seven islands but also of several critical ports on the eastern Adriatic coast. Moreover, they found themselves having to deal with a new and cantankerous neighbor, one who for several years had been attempting to lay claim to the very same mainland territories granted to the French under the fifth article of the Treaty of Campo Formio.

The shift from Venetian to French control was not, from the point of view of the islands' citizenry, the incidental substitution of one foreign power by another. The Venetians, as a matter of policy, had relied heavily on an Italianized local aristocracy to enforce their rule and had systematically cultivated dissension between various aristocratic camps so as to ensure that no uniform, organized opposition would challenge them; the Venetian nobility was renowned for its corruption. In an effort to extinguish national sentiment among the Greek population, the Greek language was banned for official business, and the cultural elite—Greek and Venetian alike—scorned it as a symbol of backwardness and lack of sophistication.

The French invasion of the islands was cultural as well as military. "The fall of the Venetian republic carried the French troops into the Seven Islands. They brought with them all the principles of the revolution, which at that time were entirely democratical."[15] One year later, but before their expulsion from the islands, the French managed to heighten Greek national consciousness by reinstating Greek as the official language, allowing and even encouraging Greeks to study in France and Italy, and articulating their rule over the islands as democratic rather than imperial.

Ali had long had as his primary territorial aim the acquisition of all the ex-Venetian properties, and had hoped that the Venetian collapse would be to his benefit.[16] Snatching the islands from the French, however, would be no easy task. Bonaparte was quick to recognize the dimensions of his

[14] Ibid., 284, appendix C.
[15] Vaudoncourt 1816, 61.
[16] Leake 1835, 1:105.

victory, noting in his memoirs the significance of the Ionian Islands, which, along with the other French possessions, would guarantee virtually complete control of the Mediterranean. "It seems to me," he wrote, "that the grand maxim of the Republic henceforth should be never to abandon Corfu, Zante, etc. In this way we will find resources for our commerce, which would be of great significance to us, and to the future course of events in Europe."[17]

Possession of these islands guaranteed dominion in the Adriatic, and Bonaparte wrote to the Ministry of External Relations expressing his delight that they had fallen into French hands: "Corfou et Zante nous rendent maîtres de l'Adriatique; ces îles sont pour nous de la plus grande importance."[18] Moreover, Bonaparte's ambitious fantasy of gaining control over the route to India was predicated on a weakened Ottoman regime.[19] Control of the Ionians and Greece's Adriatic coast was viewed as central to the desired scenario, and the terms of Campo Formio meshed perfectly with the French ruler's plans. Before taking the islands, Bonaparte had written to the Executive Directory, explaining the great significance of the takeover to the process of Ottoman decline: "Les îles de Corfou, Zante, et Céphalonie sont plus intéressantes pour nous que toute l'Italie ensemble. L'empire des Turcs s'écroule tous les jours; la possession de ces îles nous mettra a même de le soutenir autant que ce sera possible ou d'en prendre notre part."[20]

Thus Ali and the French were thrown together by the exigencies of global politics. The terms of Campo Formio, giving the French control of several key towns on Albania's western coast, made Ali quick to befriend Napoleon. The French, for their part, were bequeathed a strong and aggressive neighbor, one whose shared resentment of the Ottoman regime was seen as highly advantageous.

Just as the Venetians had kept possession of the mainland territories by maintaining a policy of befriending the many Epirote Albanian tribes who remained quasi-independent of the Ottomans, so too the French saw that the key to maintaining control of the Epirote coast lay in establishing good relations with Ali and his Albanian supporters.[21] Pierre-Jerome Dupré, French consul at Hagia Saranda (Santi Quaranta), Parga (Pargue), and Sayades (La Saillade), and his correspondent in Ioannina worked to gain the trust of Ali and initially felt that they succeeded in the effort.[22]

---

[17] Napoléon, 1823–25.
[18] Rodocanachi 1899, 33.
[19] Schenk 1947, 163.
[20] Rodocanachi 1899, 33.
[21] Finlay 1970, 5:270ff.
[22] Henin au Comité de Salut Public. Lazaret de Venise, 12 messidor An III, in *Correspondance,* by Napoléon (1809).

The period following the signing of Campo Formio thus saw communications between Ali and the French commence immediately. As early as the late spring of the preceding year, Ali, recognizing France's imminent dominance in the region, had written to Bonaparte through a French courtier avowing his admiration and promising his friendship:

> L'estime et la vénération que je nourris pour vous, général, pour une grande et puissante nation, me fait désirer son amitié, que je cultive avec ses ministres et ses ambassadeurs; vos actions héroiques que j'admire avec tout l'univers me portent a désirer votre amitié particuliere, et la sympathie de vos goûts guerriers m'est un sûr garant de la gagner. Il me sera agréable d'en recevoir le témoignage et de resserrer, avec les héros de la France, les liens de l'amitié dont mon coeur a toujours été pénétré pour votre nation.[23]

Once the French were fully encamped in the Ionians, more formal diplomatic correspondence began. As relations between the Porte and France were verging on the hostile at the time, these first communiqués were, for obvious reasons, kept secret. Sources thus pose a bit of a problem, and most accounts are not contemporary to the events and thus vary. One of the best contemporary sources for this earliest phase of Ali's relations with the French is J. P. Bellaire's *Précis des opérations générales de la division française du Levant*. At the time of the French takeover of the Ionians, Bellaire was infantry captain and attaché to the state-major-general of the French army, and he draws not just from his own experiences but from consular accounts as well.

In his account, Bellaire reports that General Gentili, who along with General La Salcette headed the French Levant Division, had been instructed by the Maritime Ministry of the Colonies to maintain the best possible relations with Ali, as this could prove very useful in the event of a resumption of hostilities with the Porte. Bellaire writes that, to this end, Gentili sent the French adjutant-general Roze several times to see Ali, both to establish political relations with him and "de tenter de nous ménager cet homme ambitieux et rédoute de la Porte."[24] He reports that Ali, in turn,

> étoit a l'époque de notre arrivée dans la mer Ionienne, le sincère admirateur des armées françaises; la gloire de Bonaparte, et ses nombreuses victoires en Italie et en Allemagne, avoient produit sur l'esprit de ce pacha une impression si forte, qu'il sembloit etre notre partisan zélé, mais sans doute dans l'espoir d'obtenir du gouvernement français les secours qui lui etoient nécessaires. Ali prouva qu'il avoit de grandes vues sur nous, en fournissant a l'éscadre de Toulon pour plus de quatre-vingt milles francs de vivres.[25]

[23] Rodocanachi 1899, 73–74.
[24] Bellaire 1805, 17.
[25] Ibid., Bellaire 1805, 18.

Letters from Gentili to Bonaparte confirm the basic content of these first meetings with Ali, but record not just Ali's admiration for the French but also his attempts to influence them. Gentili writes that he met with Ali in secret, on the site of "les ruines de l'ancienne Buthrote," and that in the course of this meeting the pasha made "quelques demandes fort indiscrètes."[26] In a letter to Bonaparte, these demands were spelled out: armaments, military technical assistance, and the right to have warships in the waters off Corfu.[27]

The result of these meetings was Gentili's decision to allow Ali to have armed ships navigating the waters of the Ionian Sea, a liberty that the Venetians had never permitted him.[28] This imprudent move, Bellaire observes, enabled Ali successfully to wage war on the territories of Mustafa, pasha of Delvino, who hitherto had provided an important check to Ali's power in the region.[29] Ali, who was in effect battling territories belonging to a fellow Ottoman appointee, was able to justify his behavior to the Porte on the grounds that several of the villages he attacked, notably Nivitza-Bouba and Aghio-Vasili, were populated by Christians whose privileges of semiautonomy had long been protected by the Venetians and who now threatened to revolt against the empire.[30] The Stephanopolis, two French spies—nephew and uncle—sailing down the Albanian coast at the time, report hearing the loud and relentless explosion of Ali's cannons attacking the villages of Nivitza-Bouba and neighboring Aghio-Vasili.[31] Gentili's decision of necessity led to the abandonment of a French plan to support Mustafa with the aim of guaranteeing that he and Ali would, as it were, cancel each another out. Similarly foolish in Bellaire's view was Gentili's granting to Ali of two noncommissioned officers of the French artillery to instruct Ali's cannoneers in the maneuvres of cannons and mortars. He also received, by most accounts, two warships, the *Medusa* and the *Ceres;*[32] indeed, it appears that these very ships were used in the attack on Mustafa.

Bonaparte himself, however, saw Ali's aggression in a different light, arguing that it would be to his benefit if Ali became as powerful as possi-

---

[26] Gentili to Bonaparte, August 1797 (Napoléon 1809, 3:522, 535).

[27] Ali Pacha to Bonaparte, June 1, 1797 (Napoléon 1809, 3:350).

[28] Rodocanachi 1899, 72. See also *A History of Greece* (Finlay 1970, 5:274) and *Istoria tou Soulliou kai Tis Pargas* History of Souli and Parga (Perraivos 1857, 1).

[29] Leake 1835, 1:15ff. The Venetians, on the strength of treaties with the Porte, had always denied Ali access to these waters. Leake writes of the total ruin of these coastal villages and adds "Their lands, divided into portions, are numbered among the Pasha's tjiftliks; and it is for the use of those who cultivate them that the Pasha has built the new village of the Forty Saints, while many of the inhabitants of Nivitza have been sent to labour on his farms near Trikkala in *Thessaly*" (Leake 1835, 1:17).

[30] Finlay 1970, 5:274.

[31] Stephanopoli and Stephanopoli 1800.

[32] Rodocanachi 1899, 76.

ble: "Il est de l'intérêt de la République que ce Pacha acquière un grand accroissement, batte tous ses rivaux, afin qu'il puisse devenir un prince assez conséquent pour pouvoir rendre des services a la République. Les établissements que nous avons sont si près de lui, qu'il n'est jamais possible qu'il puisse cesser d'avoir intérêt d'être notre ami."[33]

The few material and tactical assistances, however, were nothing compared with Ali's true hopes and expectations of the French. It appears that Ali had hoped for a massive French military assault on the Morea—the largest Venetian ex-possession—and had linked his plans for territorial expansion to this event. Bellaire, however, records that no such mission was in the offing and that Ali's hopes had been fanned intentionally so as to prolong his friendship with the French. Any troops that in Ali's mind had been preparing for a Peloponnesian mission were, in fact, otherwise engaged: "Il est cependant bon de faire observer," writes Bellaire, "que ce Pacha avoit été bercé pendant plusieurs mois par des promesses brillantes que MM. Brueys, Gentili et Roze lui avoient faites sur la destination de l'éscadre et sur l'envoi dans les îles Ioniennes d'un grand nombre de troupes."[34] Ali, however, not one to play the fool for long, soon lost patience with this French inactivity, and Bellaire reports that his manner became less warm and personal, with pretenses of friendship soon abandoned.

A 4,500-line versicular biography of Ali, attributed to the court poet Hadji Seret, also makes a lengthy reference to these first, abortive meetings between Ali and the French.[35] Dated November 25, 1805, these *stoihoi politikoi* (political verses) tell of Ali's rise to power in the region.[36] Of Ali's meetings with the French, Seret writes that Ali initiated contact with them by writing from Butrinto to the French governor in Corfu, inviting the French to a feast and conference on the mainland. Adjutant-General Roze ("o Rozos") accepted the invitation, and after dinner told Ali, falsely, that the French had purchased from the sultan all of Rumeli "as far as Ederne [Adrianople]," and that in the spring Roze was to take over its rule. Roze, according to Seret's account, then promised to make Ali king of these lands or to give him Venice instead.[37]

Ali, as is typical of Seret's account, is portrayed as wily, clever, and aware from the start that the French are not to be trusted. Feigning belief

---

[33] Bonaparte to General Gentili, November 10, 1797 (Napoléon 1809, no. 2343).

[34] Bellaire 1805, 19.

[35] The poem provides the basis for Leake's biography of Ali, *Travels in Northern Greece;* Leake provides excerpts in an appendix to the work (Leake 1835).

[36] The *stoihoi politikoi* is a common demotic versicular form with fifteen beats per line (eight, seven) in rhymed couplets. It is easily memorized and thus favored by oral tradition, and is the basic form of Greek *mantinades.*

[37] The British traveler Henry Holland reports that in a conversation with Ali it did seem that Napoleon had at one point promised him the position of king of Albania, but he also notes that Ali was not taken in by the offer, being wary of the French (Holland 1815).

in Roze's words, Ali agreed to side with the French, promising to abandon the sultan and hand over his land to the French in return for "20,000 purses." In response to this clever lie of Ali's, writes Seret, Ali was sent by way of thanks the two warships later used against Delvino. After gratefully accepting this gift, Ali promptly turned around and sent word to the Sultan that the French were planning an expedition against Rumeli. (This part of the story is most believable, as Ali, on several occasions—most famously at the time of the outbreak of the Greek War of Independence—used both sides of a situation to his advantage, gaining intimacy with one party so as to reap the rewards of later exposing those intimacies to the Ottoman powers.)

By Seret's account, the Porte disregarded Ali's warning. According to the biographer, this Ottoman failure to heed Ali's advice led to Ali's decision to gather together his own forces to prepare for a possible French onslaught. Seret writes that Ali appointed his *hasnadar* (treasurer) Yusuf Arapi to the post of *vekil* (deputy),[38] placing twenty four thousand men under his command.[39] The supposed French threat, then, may have been a ploy Ali used to justify the mobilization of a large number of his own Albanian troops, without explicit Ottoman approval.

This story of Ottoman disregard of Ali's warnings, moreover, represents a device, also typical of Seret, whereby Ali's aggrandizement comes at the expense of his so-called superiors, with whom he is favorably compared. It is important to keep in mind Seret's deployment of this device when considering Ali's political evolution: Seret, as one of Ali's courtiers, was no doubt writing his biography at the behest of Ali. It is thus inevitable that he would portray Ali in a light most closely approximating Ali's view of himself. At the time that Seret's poem was written, in 1805, Ali clearly regarded his past contacts with the French as proof both of the naïveté of the Ottoman government's international dealings and of his own masterly approach to negotiations with the Europeans. Ali clearly regarded himself as superior to the Porte in international diplomacy, and Seret's account provides one testament to this fact.

Although for obvious reasons the details of Seret's and Bellaire's accounts do not agree precisely,[40] the overall picture is the same. Two fea-

---

[38] When in Ioannina, Leake was a guest at the home Yusuf's son Bekir Agha, who helped manage the *dervenia* (mountain passes) and thus was quite familiar with Ali's lands. He was the source of much of Leake's topographic information.

[39] Hadji Seret, National Library of Greece. The truth of this particular story is borne out by several accounts of Ali's failed military expedition against the island of Levkas. This expedition was led by Yusuf and occurred some months after the events Seret here describes. It also would have been typical of Ali to seize any available excuse to gather together his own armies, despite the fact that he was really meant to act militarily only when ordered to do so by the Porte.

[40] Bellaire is, after all, writing as a representative of Napoleon's armies, whereas Seret is

tures of the accounts are most salient: first, this initial set of negotiations between Ali and the French was characterized by opportunism and duplicity on both sides; and second, Ali brought the meetings to an early close by favoring Ottoman interests over French ones. It is clear that at this early juncture in his dealings with the French Ali's interest in forging an alliance with them was merely utilitarian. Ali welcomed the gifts of military provisions and instructions, but was loath to commit himself fully to a power whom he knew to be on hostile terms with the Porte. As we shall see, the events that immediately followed this first set of negotiations with the French underscore Ali's continued fealty to Istanbul at this still comparatively early phase in his career as a diplomat. Ali's admiration for Bonaparte (which by all accounts seems to have been genuine) was still tempered by his awareness that he was using the French just as they were using him. At this point Ali was still testing the waters of international diplomacy, and he chose to take refuge under the cloak of Ottoman politics.

The meetings of Brueys, Gentili and Roze with Ali Pasha were, however, only a more diplomatic and overt method through which Bonaparte sought to gain access to the Ottoman possessions in Greece. The second, and more clandestine, dimension to French infiltration of the region hinged on an attempt to stir the passions of the Greek populace, with the aim of creating a divisive and diversionary uprising in the very lands the French soon hoped to conquer. Thus in 1797 Napoleon sent the Greek Corsican botanist Dino Stephanopoli, along with his nephew Nicolo, to the Ionians and the Morea where they were to sound out the feelings of the people and propagate the notion that the Greek East would find its liberator in the French.[41]

Napoleon's hope for Greek liberation hinged on not just the role such an event would play in the dismantling of the Ottoman Empire, but also on the acclaim that he would gain were he to liberate ancient Hellas. "Quelle gloire pour celui qui delivrera la Grèce!" he rhapsodized. "Son nom sera gravé a coté de ceux d'Homère, de Platon et d'Epaminondas. Moi j'ai nourri cette espérance quand je luttais en Italie, et des bords de l'Adriatique j'écrivis au Directoire que j'avais devant moi le royaume d'Alexandre."[42] In this latter venture of stirring revolutionary sentiments the French were somewhat more successful,[43] and although the travelers Stephanopoli did not obtain for Napoleon the desired foothold in the

---

a courtier, highly biased in favor of Ali. The difference in their tone is worth noting, in particular the dismissiveness of French accounts in terms of Ali's real viability as a political player in the international milieu.

[41] Stephanopoli and Stephanopoli 1800, 1:71–72.

[42] Rodocanachi 1899, 68.

[43] The Greeks seem to have regarded the French as their potential liberators.

Greek mainland, they nevertheless seem to have cultivated Greek revolutionary consciousness. The written account of their adventures gained great popularity in Europe, and their work *Voyage de D. et N. Stephanopoli en Grèce*, published in London in 1800, started a spate of travelers' books on Greece and greatly contributed to European philhellene sentiment.[44] In any event, it is clear from their account of the trip that the two Greek Corsicans took seriously indeed their role as investigators of a vast Greek insurrection and propagators of European philhellene consciousness.

. . . . .

At this early stage in his dealings with the European powers, Ali's political aspirations remained muted. The events immediately following these overtures toward the French demonstrate that Ali, in the last years of the eighteenth century, was torn between loyalty to the Porte and collusion with his new "friend," Napoleon Bonaparte.

Coincidental with the cooling of his relations with Messieurs Brueys, Gentili, and Roze, Ali received orders from the *divan* in Istanbul to gather six thousand of his Albanian troops and proceed immediately to the Ottoman camp in Vidin, on the Danube, to assist the Porte in putting down a rebellion led by Pasvan Oğlu.[45] Hadji Seret, who recounts these events, writes that the *ferman* (imperial decree) issued against Pasvan listed among his offenses the hoarding of *miri* income (state treasury monies) for himself, the doubling of the *haraç* (land tax) on non-Muslim subjects, and his disregard of Ottoman orders.[46] Seret notes that these were Ali's practices as well, and he claims that Ali, who to some extent had colluded with Pasvan, wrote to the Porte on his behalf.[47]

In addition to this conflict of loyalty regarding Pasvan and the Porte, the command to go to Vidin put Ali in a bind regarding the French. On one hand, he did not want blatantly to disobey the Sultan, but on the other hand he did not want the French to see that he was not so independent a ruler as he had claimed. Bellaire writes that Ali, having hesitated for several days to respond, ultimately sent word that he would provide troops and used up what little credit he held with the Porte "pour obtenir de ne point aller devant Viddin."[48]

The following series of events perfectly encapsulate the confusion and double-dealing which inhered in nearly all relations between Ali and the

---

[44] Baggally 1936, 90ff.
[45] Olivier, 192–223.
[46] Hadji Seret, National Library of Greece.
[47] If such a letter exists, I am unaware of it.
[48] Bellaire 1805, 20.

British, the French, and the Turks. General Chabot, the French comman-
der in Corfu, learned from local sources of the dilemma in which Ali found
himself, and reveling, it seems, in Ali's discomfort, sent his aide-de-camp
Captain Scheffer to Ali, ostensibly to settle amicably the borders of the
district of Butrinto but really to further complicate Ali's situation. In his
meeting with Scheffer, Ali complained of the broken promises of Brueys
and Gentili, whose claims of forthcoming French monies had not materi-
alized. Scheffer rebutted Ali's complaint by telling Ali that the French government was very displeased with Ali's declaration of war against Pasvan
Oğlu, who, said Scheffer, due to his military talents and principles "de-
voit être plutôt son [Ali's] ami que son ennemi."[49] Scheffer went on to tell
him that he had heard reports from Istanbul that the Porte by calling him
to Vidin simply was trying to get him away from the safety of his *paşalık,*
and that once the Turks had him in the midst of the Ottoman camp, they
would murder him at the express command of the sultan.[50]

Ali, obviously troubled by this information, pressed Scheffer as to its
source, whereupon Scheffer informed him that it was included in reports
from the Porte to the French government.[51] Scheffer thus claimed that his
betrayal of Ottoman confidences should provide ample evidence of
French fealty to Ali. Ali, however, was not humbled by the French rebuke
for his participation at Vidin; instead he turned the situation to his advantage by letting Scheffer know in the clearest terms the price the French
would have to pay for his friendship: "A moins que l'on ne me donnes dix
milles Français et cent mille sequins [environs un million de francs], je ne
puis désobéir." According to consular reports, Scheffer, shaken by this
veiled threat, remained in Ioannina for two more days before returning to
Corfu.[52]

The French did not give Ali the money, and he did not give them his
friendship. However, Ali was prepared to take Scheffer seriously, and
when a few weeks later he finally went to Vidin, he took with him ten
thousand Albanian troops who had the clear command not just to fight
against Pasvan but also to protect him from the Ottoman troops should
any attempt be made his life.[53] Bellaire recounts the report of two French

[49] Ibid., 1805, 22.

[50] This is not improbable. Ali had long been known to the Porte as a potential source of
discord, and there are numerous reports, even as early as the late 1780s, of attempts, orig-
inating in Istanbul, to have him ousted in one way or another. In any case, Ali would have
taken this French account very seriously indeed, aware as he was of his limited popularity
with the Porte.

[51] I have found no such report.

[52] Bellaire 1805, 23.

[53] It is worth noting that Pasvan Oğlu was busy doing in the eastern part of European
Turkey precisely what Ali was doing in the western, only more overtly. Born in Bosnia in
1758, Pasvan Oğlu was similarly power hungry and expansionist but far more open than
Ali about his opposition to the Turks. He was a friend of the Greek Rhigas, who went on

artillery officers sent with Ali to Vidin that at no point during his stay there was Ali seen without a full guard of Albanian soldiers. (These two officers also convinced Napoleon of the Ottomans' degenerate state, reporting that the Ottoman armies were shockingly disorderly, fed on only dry bread and water, and were maladroit in weaponry and lacking in efficiency: "Une chose singulière et qui nuisoit beaucoup a l'attaque, c'est que chaque bouche-à-feu appartenoit a un maître particulier, et ne faisoit feu lorsque celui-ci le jugeoit à-propos. Le propriétaire d'une pièce de canon, ou d'un mortier, restoit a la batterie aussi long-temps qu'elle."[54]

Embellished as certain aspects of this story of Scheffer and Ali's negotiations no doubt are, the overall picture nevertheless agrees with the reports not just of Bellaire but also of the Porte and Ali's own chroniclers.[55] Ali and the French, both thinking to use the other for territorial and political gain, became mired in negotiations the duplicitous complexities of which are difficult fully to unravel. Perhaps most critical for our present purposes is the fact that Ali, despite his eagerness for French friendship, was unprepared to throw his fortunes completely into Bonaparte's hands. As Bellaire notes, Ali realized that he could not depend on the friendship of the French in the event that he broke ties with the Porte by refusing to assist at Vidin. In this early period of international negotiations (1797–1800), Ali recognized that his position would remain tenable only so long as he continued a formal policy of acknowledgment of the Porte's supremacy.

For their part, the French, too, were left with ambivalent feelings after these initial contacts with Ali Pasha. Talleyrand wrote: "On ne peut être trop en garde contre lui" He intimated that Ali's commitment to the Porte was perhaps greater than he claimed. "Les ouvertures qu'il ferait pourraient bien être concertées avec la Porte."[56]

. . . . .

---

to play a significant role in the earliest phases of the Greek movement for independence, and he appears to have adopted some of Rhigas's ideals. He appealed in revolutionary terms to downtrodden Muslims as well as to Greek Christians, and he promised to restore to them the privileges enjoyed under the rule of Suleiman. In his attempts at secession he also had the support of Grigorios, the Greek Orthodox metropolitan of Vidin (Dakin 1972, 25ff.). The similarities between Ali and Pasvan Oğlu are highlighted by the fact that, as Stanford Shaw points out, when the French abandoned their plan to put Ali on the Ottoman throne, deciding that he was too attached to British interests, they turned instead in the direction of Pasvan, who would be set up as a sultan under French protection (Shaw 1988, 267–71).

[54] Bellaire 1805, 31.

[55] See, for instance, the Istanbul Ayniyat Defterleri, no. 610, 3–4, 22 *Yanya Mutasarrıfı sabık Tepedelenli Ali Paşa maddesine dair* (Regarding the affair of the former governor of Yannina, Tepedelenli Ali Pasha) as well as Hadji Seret's *Life of Ali Pasha* (1805).

[56] Talleyrand to Comeyras, March 9, 1798. (cited in Boppe 1914, 12).

At this stage Ali was perhaps at the pinnacle of his career in the Ottoman service. Indeed, the very fact that the Ottomans, although not at all comfortable with Ali, nevertheless continued to keep him in their service corroborates Ali's basic loyalty to Istanbul. Ali had not yet developed to the point of breaking with the Porte, and his continued fealty, coupled with his expansionist desires, guaranteed the great gains he made for the government in Istanbul, his territorial victories ostensibly gained on behalf of the Ottoman government.

In short, troublesome as he was, Ali was more of a benefit than a detriment to the Ottoman government. As Leake, who spent several years in Ali's Ioannina, observed, despite Ali's hoarding of funds and clandestine negotiations, "it is probable that the Porte, during his reign, was more truly master of Greece than it had ever been before, and that it derived, upon the whole, as much revenue from the country and that the concentration of power in Aly's hands was the best protection which the Empire could possess on a frontier, where it was endangered by the increase of the power of France, not less that the North-Eastern side was menaced by the encroachments of Russia."[57] The benefits that Ali brought at this relatively early stage in his career still outweighed the problems created by his hesitation to follow the Porte's orders.[58]

[57] Leake 1826, 35.
[58] Indeed, this remained the case basically until 1820, when he declared his independence from Istanbul; there are, however, reported assassination attempts on Ali predating his official break with the Porte. Ali survived even the installation of Mahmud on the throne. Mahmud, recognizing the decline of the Ottoman Empire, took dramatic steps to concentrate his power. He ousted all the strong *ayan*s (notables) of the empire, and within ten years of taking power had purged all earlier governors except Ali Pasha and Mehmet Ali in Egypt. Leake's view is that this demolition of long-standing chieftains, designed to stop Ottoman decline, in fact had the reverse effect; although these individuals were an annoying thorn in the side of the central government, they were nevertheless the empire's best defense against the dangers of the French Revolution. Leake writes that the Porte committed the error of paying more attention to its own "wounded pride" than to European military superiority and imminent territorial threat from the Western powers (Leake 1826, 36ff.).

SEVEN

THE RUSSO-TURKISH ALLIANCE, THE SEPTINSULAR REPUBLIC, AND THE BRITISH

The Russo-Turkish Alliance and the French

THE EARLY DECISION over whether to participate at Vidin was only the first dilemma with which Ali had to contend. Just as the battle with Pasvan Oğlu was winding down, he faced a second situation that forced him to choose between his hopes for an alliance with the French and his continued loyalty to the Ottoman Porte. These subsequent events further illustrate his relative insecurity as an independent ruler in the 1790s and pave the way for his ultimate break with the Porte early in the following century.

In 1798 the French invasion of Egypt led to the Porte's declaration of war against the French.[1] In September of that year the Turks signed alliances with the British and the Russians, and the Russians, long the enemies of the Porte, were allowed to send their ships through the Bosphoorus Straits to join the Ottoman fleet in a campaign against the French in the Adriatic with the aim of ousting them from the Ionian Islands.[2]

This event provided an instant litmus test of the sincerity of Ali's touted friendship with the French. In response to the treaty, Ali immediately gathered his forces, assuring Bonaparte that he was preparing to launch an attack on the joint Russo-Turkish armies.[3] Sensing an opportunity of wresting the four mainland Ionian dependencies from Napoleon's grasp, Ali offered the French his support in return for the island of Levkás and the four former Venetian possessions. He also proceeded to demand instant payment of eighty thousand livres as reimbursement for provisions he claimed to have furnished the French under Admiral Bruix.[4] The governor in Corfu, however, instead sent a cannon by way of thanks, whereupon Ali, with the ostensible aim of discussing strategy but really to avenge this perceived insult, requested that Adjutant-General Roze return to the mainland to meet him in Tzamurià. It was Ali's plan to take Roze hostage.

---

[1] Finlay 1970, 5:274.
[2] Shaw 1988, 1:269.
[3] "Parga" 1819, 275.
[4] This seems vaguely to correspond with Ali's contributions to the French as documented by Bellaire.

Roze was the perfect target. Born in Patras, He spoke fluent Greek and was fascinated by the customs of the "Orientals."[5] Ali treated him with great favor, even going so far as to marry him off to Zoitza, a teenage girl of the palace, thought to be Ali's illegitimate daughter.[6] The wedding, in July 1797, was attended by all of Ali's family, and his son Muktar served as best man. As dowry, Roze is said to have received from Ali about 4,500 francs.[7]

In arranging this marriage, Ali was acting in perfect accordance with the diplomatic policies with which he had been raised. He was cementing his alliance with the French by marrying, as it were, the two families—his Albanian one and Roze's French one—in precisely the fashion by which conflicts between various Albanian tribes and families had traditionally been resolved. To name but a few examples, Ali's sister, Shainitza, had been married first to Ali of Argyrocastro, then to his brother Suleiman; his son Veli was married to his neighbor Ibrahim Pasha's daughter.

Ali had made important gains by these marriages, just as he did with the betrothal of Zoitza to Roze. In fact, it was partly in thanks for the generosities shown the French at the time of this wedding that Ali received the rights to the Adriatic, enabling him to attack the pasha of Delvino.[8] In response to this attack—ostensibly on the rebel Christian villages of the *paşalık* of Delvino, and thus in support of the Ottoman government— Ali received from the sultan the title *aslan*, or "lion." This marriage clearly had the effect Ali had hoped for, namely, of furthering his own opportunistic aims.

Thus Roze, who by then was Ali's pseudo-son-in-law, was fully convinced of the sincerity of his claims when in 1798 he was called back to Ali's lands. "Cet officier [Roze] se croyait sûr d'une amitié dont il avait reçu maintes preuves et a laquelle il avait dû jusqu'à sa femme."[9] Despite Ali's earlier actions regarding the situation at Vidin, Roze had managed to convince the French that in the coming war against the Porte they could count on his support.[10] The Frenchman thus went to meet Ali without guards or attendants when, upon his arrival, He was seized, tied to the back of a horse, taken to Ioannina, thrown into a dungeon, tortured to extract information on French military plans, and then sent on to Istan-

---

[5] Rodocanachi 1899, 75.

[6] Bellaire, however, claims that this girl was the daughter of one of Ali's principal officers (Bellaire 1805, 259). Pouqueville's account of the marriage is in his *Histoire de la regénération de la Grèce* (Pouqueville 1825, 1:134–36).

[7] Rodocanachi 1899, 76.

[8] This wedding was clearly a great event. Several of Ali's biographers mention it. One feature of the festivities was the release of a "ballon aerostatique" from the fairgrounds. The festivities lasted for several days.

[9] Boppe 1914, 17.

[10] Bonaparte to Adjutant General Roze, August 17, 1798 (Napoléon 1809, no. 3036).

bul as a token of Ali's loyalty to the Porte against the French. Roze is reported to have died soon after in the Istanbul prison.

Not only did Ali's action send a message of fealty to the Porte, it also dramatically informed the French of the demise of their short-lived alliance with Ali. Ali's attack on Roze, then, stood as his official declaration of war against the French.

This act of hostility, however, took some time to have an effect as the French, who knew that Roze's links to Ali were strong, assumed from his failure to return to Corfu that he had gone over to Ali's side and committed treason against the French.[11] Somewhat incredibly, then, when Ali, unable to extract from Roze the desired information, sent for the French commanding officer of the fort in Butrinto, his request was honored with the arrival at Ali's encampment in Kalispoli of M. Steil, the French sublieutenant at Butrinto, along with the fort's Greek chaplain, who was to serve as interpreter. Predictably, these two in turn were taken prisoner and tortured; they too revealed nothing and were subsequently returned to Corfu in exchange for the release of two of Ali's subjects who had been taken prisoner as an act of reprisal by Governor Chabot.[12] As late as December 1798, Bonaparte was still insisting that Ali's friendship was to be cultivated at all costs.[13]

The French were not wholly foolish, however, when before the Roze episode they continued to believe that Ali was on their side. Ali's hesitation to participate at Vidin had demonstrated just how close he was to breaking with the orders of the Porte, and although he did ultimately go against Pasvan, the French realized that his motivation was obligation rather than desire. What ultimately turned Ali against the French was events that occurred while he was away in Vidin and of which he was not meant to learn. As is standard, the details and underlying cause of these events are somewhat confused.

Once Ali had left for Vidin, the French decided to take advantage of his absence and sent Roze and other representatives to Ioannina with the aim of convincing the *arhontes* (the leaders of the Greek community) that the French would bring about Greek independence.[14] The Greeks, however, appear to have rejected this offer, so the French sent three thousand French troops to Preveza and another one thousand to Butrinto, and Roze attempted there, through various local agents, to incite the Greeks to insurrection. These Greeks, it seems, were more open to the suggestion, and not until Ali's son Muktar warned that Ali's return from Vidin was im-

---

[11] Bellaire 1805, 259.

[12] Ibid., 260ff.

[13] Bonaparte to Croizier, December 17, 1798 (Napoléon 1809, no. 5777).

[14] Hadji Seret, National Library of Greece. This attempt of the French to stir the Greeks to insurrection was effected by Bonaparte's "Manifesto to the Greeks."

minent did these regions close off their ports to the French (as they had been commanded to do earlier). Muktar and the metropolitan bishop then wrote to Ali, warning him of the brewing Greek insurrections in Parga, Preveza, and Arta, information that Ali quickly passed along to the sultan in Istanbul. By way of response Ali immediately received the order to leave Vidin and return to his paşalık in case he was needed to squelch any Greek uprising there. (Let us keep in mind, however, that the dimensions of any possible Greek revolt may well have been a good deal less than Muktar claimed, as it was likely that Ali manufactured the whole "threat" as a pretext to get himself out of the fight with Pasvan Oğlu and back to Ioannina.)

By Hadji Seret's account, when Ali returned to Ioannina and learned of Roze's actions, he approached Roze, subsequently taking him prisoner and having him sent, via his son Muktar, to the dungeon in Ioannina. Ali then led his troops against the French and Greeks first in Butrinto and next in Preveza, where on October 12, 1798, he decimated the rebellious local populations and took three hundred Frenchmen prisoner.[15] The heads of these prisoners, along with the barely alive Roze, were later sent to the Porte as a token of Ali's loyalty.[16]

Ali also took military measures against the French. In addition to providing a demonstration of his loyalty to the Porte, these actions had the aim of gaining Ali the mainland Ionian dependencies he had long desired. Ali now tried to seize by force the territories he had not been able to obtain through earlier negotiations with the French. His attack on these territories provides further insight into his relationship with the sultanate at that time.

The Mainland Dependencies

Under the command of Horatio Nelson, the British had by the time of Roze's abduction effected a stunning triumph over the French at Abukir Bay, on the coast of Alexandria, drawing French attention away from the Adriatic. In the midst of this battle, Ali, noticing that the French had no intention of giving him the four mainland dependencies, took advantage

---

[15] Seret's account is in basic agreement with Perrairos's *Istoria Suntomos Soulliou, kai Pargas* (Brief history of Souli and Parga) part 1 (1803; all parts 1815; English translation of the Italian 1823), written by a native Pargan, later a major in the corps protecting the Ionian Islands.

[16] For those who wonder at the impracticability of transporting three hundred severed heads over several hundred miles to Istanbul, the technique was this: The skin was peeled off the skull and packed down for transportation. Before presentation to the grand vizier, the skins were stuffed with straw, then moistened with water to revivify them (Leake 1835, 1:482 n).

of the confused situation. He moved to take them from the French by force, claiming to be doing so on behalf of the Ottoman government. Butrinto fell first and easily to his troops, who had long been poised just outside its borders. He then moved on to Preveza, with a body of men numbering in the thousands.[17] The Prevezans were better defended than the Butrintites, and the allied French and local forces tried desperately to fortify themselves against Ali's attack. They did not succeed, however, and their resistance to his advances was repaid with a brutal slaughter of the local population and the aforementioned imprisonment of several hundred French soldiers.

Ali now turned his attention to Parga, which of the four mainland Ionian dependencies had always been the most alluring to him.[18] Ali had long maintained a state of semiautonomy under the Venetians and, more recently, the French. He was therefore unsatisfied despite his recent successes in the other dependencies. He thus wrote to the Parganote leaders, telling them of his victory over Preveza and ordering them to turn against the French soldiers garrisoned in their town and to submit to his forces under penalty of death.

Ali, playing the role of the faithful subject, claimed to be acting on behalf of the Sultan: "I do not desire war with you, but only that three or four of you should come to me, that we may confer about making you fellow-subjects of my sovereign."[19] While implying subordination to the Porte, however, Ali also suggested that the fate of the Parganotes lay in his hands alone: "Whatever form of government you wish, I will grant to you. But if you refuse, I will deal with you as with enemies—and the blame be on your own heads."[20]

Some days later, a second threatening letter met with the following reply, later read aloud in the British House of Commons by Sir Charles Monck:

> To Ali Pacha: We have received your two letters, and we rejoice that you are well. The compliance which you require of us you will not easily obtain; because your conduct, exhibited to us in the fate of our neighbors [the Prevezans], determines us all to a glorious and free death, rather than to a base and tyrannical subjugation. You write to us to fall upon and slay the French.

[17] "Parga" 1819, 275. This number is not corroborated, but all accounts state that Ali's troops were numerous.

[18] The Parganotes had aided the Souliotes in their many wars against Ali, and for this Ali particularly hated them. The Souliotes, a Greek-speaking Orthodox tribe of Albanian origin, lived in a state of pseudo-independence in a mountain stronghold west of Ioannina. Ali had tried off and on over the course of nine years to take their villages and ultimately succeeded only through the treason of a Soulite. For more on Souli, see Perraivos (1857).

[19] The full text of this letter is included in "Parga" 1819, 275.

[20] Ibid., 276.

This is not in our power; but, if it were, we would decline to do it; for our country has boasted her good faith for four centuries past, and in that time often vindicated it with her blood. How then shall we now sully that glory? Never. To threaten us unjustly is in your power; but threats are no characteristic of great men; and, besides, we have never known what it was to fear, having accustomed ourselves to glorious battles for the right of our country. God is just; we are ready; the moment comes when he who conquers shall be glorified. So fare you well. Parga, Oct. 16, 1798.[21]

Before Ali could make good on his threats, however, the allied Turkish and Russian forces had secured the seven islands and the French garrison in Parga was replaced by a Russian one. By this series of events, it became clear to Ali that any aggression against Parga would be a de facto attack against the Porte. He therefore had to be satisfied with the possession of the remaining three dependencies: Vonitza, Butrinto, and Preveza.

In addition to sending troops into Vonitza, Preveza, and Butrinto, claiming them for the sultan, Ali ordered a military take over of the island of Levkás with about four thousand Albanian troops under the command of his "foster brother" Yusuf Arapi (known in the more florid accounts as "the blood drinker").[22] The Greeks, under the leadership of Count John Kapodistrias, famous for his later role as president of the first independent Greek state, repulsed the Albanian forces. At this time Ali also fortified Ioannina, ordering that a five-mile entrenchment be built around his stronghold. This venture was undertaken with great zeal, and "all the inhabitants, without exception, were forced to work with the shovel or basket. The Bishop and the Pasha's sons were required to set the example."[23]

Neither of Ali's military ventures, however, was to give him much success. The attack on Levkás was (with the help of French troops) completely thwarted, and Ali's possession of Butrinto, Preveza, and Vonitza was short-lived. He had assumed that the sultan would be so delighted with his military successes against the French that he would grant these three towns to him by way of thanks. Much to his dismay, they remained under the direct administrative control of Istanbul, and instead Ali was given the title of vizier.[24] He received a sword and a kaftan as symbols of honor, and upon his return to Ioannina was saluted with the honorifics *mübarek* (blessed one) and *gazi*.[25]

[21] Ibid.

[22] In the contemporary accounts Levkás was frequently referred to as Santa Maura. This island was protected against Ali by the French, then taken by the Russo-Turkish joint expedition.

[23] Leake 1835, 4:152.

[24] This was the title of "three horse tails" (Hadji Seret, National Library of Greece).

[25] Hadji Seret, National Library of Greece. This nevertheless would have been a great

Ali, who by then had lost virtually all interest in the hierarchy of the Ottoman government, was enraged by this turn of events, and redoubled his efforts to gain these territories from the Porte. By this point the enlargement of his territories was far more important to Ali than his rank. Nevertheless, for several more years he was to maintain at least nominal subjugation to his ostensible "superiors" in Istanbul, and he followed up his victory in Preveza by assisting the Turkish forces (with the help of the Russians, a fact that Seret pointedly omits from his account) in an attack on the French in Corfu.[26]

. . . . .

The years 1797–1799 thus saw the final fall of Venetian supremacy in the Adriatic, the brief French occupation of the Ionians, and Ali's first steps toward a new role as an independent, international diplomat. Ali, as we have seen, in these first years of negotiations with the French was very cautious. Although showing pretensions to independent rule, he still recognized that he had neither the strength nor the guarantee of European aid that he needed to act on his desires. This first period nevertheless marked a critical juncture, as he emerged from it at the very pinnacle of his career within the Ottoman ranks. This fact, combined with the confidence he had gained through successful negotiations with the French, paved the way for his next phase of political development, characterized by more aggressive international diplomacy and further steps toward secession.

The Septinsular Republic

Having reclaimed the Ionians from the French, the Russians and the Ottomans had to decide on the status of the islands. The history of ongoing

---

honor. Leake notes that it was extremely rare for an Albanian in the Ottoman service to attain so high a rank, and he writes that in order to offset the increased power that the rank of vizier gave Ali, his two neighbors, the pashas of Berat and Avlona, were also given the title (Leake 1835, 1:42).

[26] Baggally points out that it is possible that Ali may have ceased being allied with the French because the British had started intercepting his correspondence with the French and may have turned this information over to the Porte. Baggally's argument, presumably, is that Ali felt the need to demonstrate his fealty to the Porte (Baggally 1938, 8). However, this reasoning seems somewhat illogical, since had Ali truly intended to break with the Porte at this point and put in his lot instead with the British, he would not have had to demonstrate his loyalty to the Porte, as this would soon have been a moot point. The evidence that the British were intercepting Ali's communiqués with the French is found in a letter sent from Foresti to Grenville, November 21, 1798 (PRO/FO 42/3).

conflict between the Russians and the Turks made this a particularly delicate matter. There were three options: The islands could be placed under a second-order power, such as Naples; they could constitute an independent republic; or they could be determined a principality under the suzerainty of the Porte.[27] For several months in 1799 the Russians and the Ottomans argued for their respective points of view.[28] In March 1800 a convention between the Russians and the Porte was concluded, having effected a treaty under which the second option was chosen. Sultan Selim III ratified the treaty the following May and Czar Paul I of Russia followed suit in August.

This was a compromise position of sorts, for if the Russians did not want the Porte to have control of the islands, Istanbul, for its part, did not want the possibility of a strong Russian influence in the region. The Ionian Islands were declared a free republic, and the largely Greek Orthodox inhabitants of their four coastal dependencies were to govern themselves according to their own customs under the Ionian senate. They were to be granted freedom from direct Muslim presence, and had to pay by way of subjugation, only a small annual capitation tax to the Porte. The Septinsular Republic was to be independent, under Ottoman suzerainty, and protected by a joint garrison of Russian and Turkish troops.

A constitution for the new republic was drafted.[29] The islands were to comprise a federation, with each island having a local government consisting of the local nobility who would enjoy financial and political powers, appoint magistrates, and serve as commanders of the police.[30] The federation had at its head a senate, based in Corfu, to which the principal islands sent representatives.[31] The president of the senate had as his responsibility all foreign affairs, the command of the army, and the maintenance of the unity of the federation.[32]

The terms of the constitution were put into effect in the early months of 1801. Almost immediately, the many problems attendant upon holding such a federation together became manifest.[33] The islands, inherently

---

[27] Rodocanachi 1899, 176. See also Pauthier (1863).

[28] Rodocanachi provides excerpts of these correspondences, translated into French (Rodocanachi 1899, 175ff.).

[29] For the complete text of this constitution, see *Le tre costituzione, 1800, 1803, 1817, delle sette isole Ionie* (Paulini 1849).

[30] Jervis writes that Ali urged this support of the old nobility, finding it useful in maintaining a foothold in the islands (Jervis 1852, 187).

[31] Corfu and Zante, the largest islands, had three representatives each; Santa Maura and Cephalonia had two apiece; Cerigo, Paxo, and Ith-ki all had one (Rodocanachi 1899, 181).

[32] The result was, in effect, "a democracy for the nobles, and a despotism for the people." Minist-re des Affaires -trang-res, Paris, Correspondance relative aux -les ioniennes, vol. 22, 1814–23, Corfu, July 1, 1820, no. 200 insert (Corfu, May 1814).

[33] Letter from the deputation of the Onoranda to the government, cited in Paulini's *Le tre costituzione*, 27.

isolationist and self-contained, found it difficult to sacrifice specific interests for those of the greater republic, which was, after all, an oblique and new concept. By July of that year, Cephalonia and Itháki had effectively declared themselves independent, and Zante had turned to the British for protection. In Corfu, the peasantry was threatening to revolt.

Radical measures were taken to save the republic. The president resigned and the senate was dissolved. Sixty-four new deputies, elected by the people, drew up a new constitution, and the titles and privileges of the nobility were abolished on October 25, 1801.[34] This disenfranchised nobility, however, turned to their suzerain for support, and the Ottomans, only too happy to have a pretext for further military action in the region, prepared to intervene. The new government rushed to obtain approval of the revised constitution from Paris, Saint Petersburg, and Istanbul.

Once again, Ali planned to take advantage of a chaotic international situation and move into the troubled territories. Having learned from Ionian informants of the tenuous state of affairs in the islands, he sent word to the Porte that he would be happy to lend his military might to any mission undertaken to reclaim Ottoman possession of the Ionian Islands. The Porte, ostensibly acting on behalf of the nobles but really out of Ottoman interest in the region, took Ali up on his offer. Ali then gathered together a large force outside Butrinto and prepared to launch an attack. But whereas the nobility of the islands had turned to the Porte for protection, the people, threatened by Ali, now sought Russian intervention. Thus Ali's planned attack was halted only by the last-minute intervention of the Russian ambassador.

In the early autumn of 1802 Russian influence in the Ionians—which since Venetian times had been consistently strong—grew with the arrival of the Zantiot nobleman Count Mocenigo, a high-ranking member of the Russian service who was to serve as Russian plenipotentiary in the islands.[35] Under Mocenigo yet another new constitution was charted and ratified, on November 23, 1802.[36] This heightened Russian presence in the new republic in turn augmented the latent, long-standing tensions between Russia and the Ottoman Empire.

Because of the various schisms over the status of the Septinsular Republic, there was a gradual reversion from new global alliances (such as the one between the Russians and the Porte) to the more traditional, long-standing ones. This process soon hastened when in 1803 war resumed between France and Britain, and the alliance of Russia and Austria with Britain led the French to seek alliance with the Ottomans.[37]

[34] Vaudoncourt 1816, 67–72; Boppe 1914, 23–35.

[35] The posting of Mocenigo to the Ionians was a direct response to the mission of the Ionian senate envoy Naranzi, sent to the Russian government by the crisis-addled Ionian government. For an account of this mission, see *Quarterly Review* 23 (1820): 111–36.

[36] Vaudoncourt 1816, 68.

[37] Shaw 1988, 1:271. Of the period 1802 to 1807, Shaw writes: "The most salient char-

The treaty of 1800 had represented a major setback for Ali. Not only had the coastal dependencies slipped from his grasp once again, but their populations were granted even further-ranging privileges than before. In keeping with the earlier Russo-Turkish treaty of Kutchuk Kainardji, the Russian government was granted "guarantorship" of these privileges. Parga, after a desperate and unsuccessful bid to be incorporated into the new Septinsular Republic, had managed instead to have various stipulations included in the treaty by which the Parganotes were granted freedom from Ali's rule and placed under the direct sovereignty of the Porte (as were the other dependencies). Ali now had as an additional reason for hating the Parganotes the fact that their intervention had lost him control of Vonitza, Butrinto, and Preveza, which had, after all, been taken by his own Albanian troops. Adding insult to injury, the dependencies had then been granted numerous privileges by the Porte, including the free practice of religion and the self-administration of law. Moreover, the peoples of Parga were guaranteed subjection to no Muslim presence save one resident Ottoman bey and moderate taxation in accordance with the precedent set by the Venetians. Thus they were promised, as the treaty stated,

> that they should retain all the privileges they had enjoyed of old under the Venetians—that no mosque should be built within their territory, nor any Mussulman be allowed to settle or hold land within it—that they should pay no taxes but those which had been anciently paid to Venice, and should enjoy their laws both civil and criminal exactly as before—and, finally, that to secure the political rights of the new sovereign, a bey or officer of rank should be sent from Constantinople, whose functions, and the place of his residence, should be determined with the advice, and to the entire satisfaction of the republic of the Seven Islands.[38]

From the point of view of international relations the following few years marked a fallow stretch for Ali. Thwarted by the loss of the mainland dependencies and prevented by Russian intervention from military action against the new Septinsular Republic, Ali obeyed the wishes of the Porte and waited for a more opportune time to realize his expansionist dreams.

The shifting and somewhat anomalous global alliances that marked this period also necessitated that Ali temporarily shelve his international aspirations. Somewhat paradoxically, Ali thrived only with a hostile Western neighbor. With the French as his most immediate foreign neighbor, Ali had had ready opportunity to try the waters of international diplomacy.

---

acteristic of Ottoman diplomacy in this period was a reversal of the alliances molded by Bonaparte's invasion of Egypt and a return to the more traditional bonds forged by long-standing considerations of national self-interest."

[38] "Parga" 1819, 278.

Ali's negotiations with the French had been abetted by the low-level hostility that existed between the Porte and the French government. On the the one hand, this state of animosity had provided the French with proof of Ali's "sincerity." In dealing with the French he was, after all, contravening the policies of his own government. On the other hand, the hostilities between France and Istanbul made it possible for him to turn against France and claim to be doing so on behalf of his superiors. In short, during the French occupation of the seven islands, Ali had had two distinct political roads open to him. He could have sided with the French, playing the international diplomat for so long as the role was feasible; alternatively, he could have sought refuge under the umbrella of the Ottoman government if the situation with the French seemed untenable. Indeed, as we have seen, this is precisely what he did; when Ali realized that the French were unlikely to resist the Russian and Turkish forces, and that they refused to give him the territories he so badly wanted, he prudently chose not to break with the Porte.

Ironically, once the ostensibly hostile French at his borders were replaced by the ostensibly friendly Russian and Turkish protectorate, Ali found his hands tied. The Russians, Ali's long-standing enemies for having aided the rebellions of various Greek and Albanian Orthodox subjects of his *paşalık*,[39] were, as the newfound "allies" of the Porte, not a safe target for his aggressions. Similarly, the four mainland dependencies, which were under the direct administrative control of Istanbul, were also safe from his advances. Thus Ali now sought out a new foreign ally. Having met with little success in his dealings with the French, He turned to the enemy of the French in the hopes that they would prove more useful.

The British

In 1803 Ali sent word to the British embassy in Istanbul requesting that the British send to him an emissary, so that he might be given advice regarding the best course of action vis-à-vis the impending resumption of war between Britain and France. This petition resulted in a visit from William Hamilton, the secretary of the British embassy. Ali promised Hamilton support for Great Britain in the event of war with France, claiming that aid would be expedited by the assignation of a British resident to Ioannina.

---

[39] Indeed, during the period of their protectorate over the four mainland Ionian dependencies, they continued to do so. This period (1800–1802) marked the height of Ali's aggressions against the Souliotes, and the Russians were sending the Souliotes supplies via Parga (Baggally 1938, 9).

Thus in 1804 D. R. Morier took up residence in Ali's capital[40]—officially as a liaison between Ali and his government, covertly as a spy, observing Ali's economic and military situation. Ali made a great point of showing his fealty to the British, guaranteeing that his support and confidentiality could be depended on. Writing in Italian, Ali's dragoman Mahomet Effendi thanked Nelson for Hamilton's visit to Ioannina, stating that Ali's negotiations with the British were to be regarded as of the utmost seriousness and secrecy: "For the more secure conservation of this secret, I convey a copy of a mystic alphabet, which may be used for expressing the most necessary articles."[41]

Hamilton, for his part, implied great friendship on behalf of the British for Ali, but nevertheless went quickly about the business of clandestinely gathering as much information as possible on the pasha's populations, monies, and armaments. This way England would not only know how much help to count on from Ali, but would also be better prepared in the event of any future hostilities between him and the British. Hamilton, reporting back to Hawkesbury, the British foreign secretary, wrote that Ali was capable of raising thirty thousand troops in a matter of days and thus was truly a worthwhile ally.[42] In his letter to Hawkesbury we can see Hamilton's confidence in Ali's promises and, most important, note Ali's desire that his negotiations with the British be undertaken without the participation of the government in Istanbul:

> As this Pacha, whom Your Lordship knows to be one of the most powerful and energetic in European Turkey, is much attached to the English Nation, he invited me this morning to a secret conference, and repeated, in the most forcible of language, the fairest sentiments of a strict friendship towards our Government, which he expressed himself desirous of cementing by all the means in his power; and requested me to represent the same to His Majesty's Ministers; and *not*, he added, by way of Constantinople.[43]

Thus, at this intermediary stage in his career as an international diplomat, Ali was making few pretenses of acting on behalf of the Porte. Just as he had done with the French, Ali now entered into negotiations with the British without regard for the wishes of the sultan. The desire for se-

[40] Morier went on to write one of the many novelistic works inspired by the life of Ali. *Photo the Suliote: a Tale of Modern Greece* was published in three volumes in 1857. See chapters 8–10 for a discussion of this and other Orientalist works on Ali. David Richard Morier, son of Isaac Morier, Consul-General to the Turkey Company in Constantinople, was born in Smyrna in 1784 and went on to spend much of his life in the diplomatic service. He was just twenty when sent on his mission to Ali Pasha.

[41] Nelson Papers, Add. no. 34919 f. 20 (translation of a letter in Italian from Ali Pasha's foreign secretary to Lord Nelson).

[42] This is the same figure given by Bellaire (1805, 26).

[43] Nelson Papers, Add. no. 34919 f. 79 (May 6, 1803, Ioannina).

crecy not only marked an effort to go behind the Porte's back, but also inchoately bespeaks Ali's claims to independent leadership and unmediated international negotiation.

The immediate result of Ali's meeting with Hamilton was, as we have seen, the assignation of Morier to Ioannina. Morier's mission was not dissimilar to that of the Corsican Stephanopolis seven years earlier, who were sent, let us remember, with a particular eye to gathering information on the Greeks. Morier's first concern was to assess the frame of mind of the local populations: Could the French depend on Greek support in the event of a war with the British? The British feared a successful French invasion of the Greek coast, recognizing the hegemony such an event would grant them over the region.

Morier concluded that the Greeks of the Morea (the Peloponnese, directly to the southeast of Ali's territories), though not particularly fond of the French, would rise "to a man" in the event of a French landing on the western coast of Greece.[44] Denigrating both the French and the Greeks, Morier wrote that the Greeks "have heard of their [the French] gallantries, their atheism and their Sacrileges, and as the Greeks are jealous of their women, and bigoted in the extreme, they must possess a natural aversion and dread of French principles in those respects. In all other points the Greek character resembles the French. They are both equally false, vain and ambitious of power, which they ever abuse."[45]

The flames of British suspicion of the Greeks were later fanned by Ali, who had Mahomet Effendi advise the British that correspondence between Ali and his newfound allies must never fall into Greek hands, "whatsoever charge they may fill in these Islands."[46] Once in Albania, however, Morier's assessment of the situation was far more sanguine: "The inhospitable rockiness of the Adriatic coast, coupled with the immensity of the Pindus range," guaranteed the extreme difficulty, if not to say impossibility, of any hostile French landing there. Morier noted the great difficulty involved in transporting cannons across the terrain and "the invincibility of the native fighters, whose warfare tactics and intimacy with the geography of the region insured the defeat of any invader."[47]

Upon his arrival in Ioannina, Morier was received by Ali and reiterated the hope for friendship first stated by Hamilton.[48] In this meeting, the

---

[44] PRO/FO 78/44, no. 1. Lord Broughton later corroborated this point of view, writing that had Bonaparte been successful in his plan to march troops overland from Vallona, across Macedonia and into Constantinople, "there can be no doubt that every Greek would have joined his standard" (Broughton 1855, 2:8).

[45] PRO/FO 78/44, no. 5.

[46] Nelson Papers, Add. no. 34919 f. 20.

[47] PRO/FO 78/44, no. 10.

[48] Ibid., no. 9.

pasha expressed his fear and hatred not just of France but of Russia and the Ottoman government as well. Thus the British immediately found themselves in the peculiar and tenuous position of having to mediate between Ali and the Russians, who had been long at odds with one another. The British were eager to maintain friendship with the Russians, but they also feared that collusion between Ali and the French would ensure a French victory.

Morier, who seemed to recognize the greater significance of Ali versus the Russians, met with Count Mocenigo, a Greek from Zante and Russian plenipotentiary in the Ionians, with the aim of defusing the potentially explosive situation. Mocenigo urged the destruction of Ali (with the permission of the Porte), while Morier, familiar with Ali's formidable strength, reprimanded Russia for having given aid to Orthodox rebels, thus incensing Ali, and urged the Russians to pursue a policy of conciliation instead.[49] Morier, in a long report to the central office, naively wrote of the "great [Russian] error" of having assumed Ali to be in cahoots with France, "and even," he went on, "in actual correspondence with that country."[50] The fact that Ali *was* in communication with France seems entirely to have escaped Morier's suspicion, and Morier's report is testimony not just to his own naïveté but additionally to Ali's skills (not to mention duplicity) as negotiator and diplomat. Moreover, Morier defended Ali's loyalty in a letter to Lord Nelson, in which he wrote of Ali's preparations to resist the French when a false alarm of an impending French invasion of the Albanian coast had been sent out.[51]

For his pains, Morier received a rather terse missive from the British ambassador in Saint Petersburg, reiterating in no uncertain terms the relative rank of Ali and the Russians as far as British policy went: "To produce cordiality and confidence between the Russians and Ali Pasha is scarcely to be expected, but the influence of Russia may be usefully employed in restraining him from any projects which might again provoke the hostility of that power. He may be given to understand that considering the union between the Courts of London and St. Petersburg, he can only look for the support and protection of England by a reconciliation with the Russians."[52] Ali, then, was viewed as the source of tensions with Russia, and he was to be instructed to expect friendship from the British only within the parameters of the official friendship between Britain and Russia.

In part because of British hesitation to take his side over Russia's and in part because of his refusal to close off his options, Ali was far from es-

[49] PRO/FO 78/47. no. 4.
[50] Ibid., no. 9 and enclosures.
[51] Ibid.
[52] Ibid.

tranged from the French. Although relations established between Ali and the French in 1798 had lasted only a few months, they had been curtailed not because of mutual hostility but because the exigencies of global politics made any further friendship impracticable. The Vidin episode and subsequent Russo-Turkish alliance against the French had forced Ali's hand, and they did so at a time in his career when he felt that his fortunes still lay in a show of fealty to the Porte. Ali's immediate aggression against the French troops in his lands at the time of the outbreak of this war against the French had indicated his desire to please the Porte, rather than any specific animosity toward the French.

Seven years later, however, Ali was heartened by the interest the British took in him, and clearly he felt more confident about going about his business without the strictures of definite, formal alliances. Thus when in 1805 Napoleon's troops defeated the Austrian forces at Austerlitz and occupied Dalmatia, and Ali once again found himself with the French at his borders, Ali was eager to reestablish diplomatic ties with Napoleon.

Having avowed in various missives the steadfastness of Ali's support for the British, one can imagine Morier's surprise when early in 1806 he returned from a diplomatic visit to Thessaloníki and Istanbul only to find a French consul-general (the now infamous Pouqueville) resident in Ioannina. Pouqueville had visited Ioannina before, at the turn of the century, and had struck up something of a friendship with Ali. Pouqueville recalled Ali's earlier infatuation with the French and was certain that he could rekindle relations. After his earlier visits with Ali, Pouqueville had written of the pasha's fascination with the French: "La révolution française était, dans ces derniers temps, le sujet de toutes ses conversations, afin de s'entretenir de nos armées dont il admirait les succès. Il interrogeait les officiers français qui étaient ses prisonniers, et il leur demandait la cause de tant de triomphes, qu'il attribuait à une sorte de magie, à un prestige qui enchainait la victoire à nos drapeaux."[53]

Morier could only assume that there had been a secret collusion between Ali and the French. Morier was mollified, however, and his suspicions were allayed when Ali coolly told him that the French, not he, had initiated the move, obtaining a ferman from the Porte which made Ali's cooperation unavoidable. This explanation, of course, was vintage Ali, who often explained actions the Europeans found objectionable as resulting from the not-to-be-disobeyed command of his superiors.

Although Ali's subjugation to the Porte was awkward at times, he could use it for personal convenience. In a rhetorical move typical of Ali's negotiations with would-be allies, he went on to reiterate his friendship for the British, but concluded the meeting with a veiled reference to his dis-

---

[53] Pouqueville 1805, 3:25.

satisfaction with them, once again citing his grudge against the Russians for having aided Greek rebels in his lands.[54] This technique of concluding an ostensibly friendly meeting with an oblique threat was, as we have seen, one he used even as early as his 1798 meeting with Scheffer, in which he demanded payment from the French.

A few days later Ali met with Morier again, ultimately telling him that Napoleon had all but promised him control of Corfu (then in Russian hands) in return for allowing a French landing on his coast. This information must have been threatening to the British, and Ali must surely have intended it as such. The interview concluded, however, with Ali once again avowing his friendship for the British and stating his desire that his hostility toward Russia not upset the alliance between the Russians and the Porte. As a possible resolution of the tensions, he suggested that the four mainland dependencies of the Ionian islands—by way of which he claimed the Russians to have access to his Greek populations—could be handed over to him.[55] Ali clearly had not yet forgotten his earlier near possession of Vonitza, Butrinto, Preveza, and Parga.

Meanwhile, just as Ali was smoothing Morier's ruffled feathers, he was also listening with interest to Pouqueville's overtures of friendship on behalf of the French. Apparently stirred to some sort of territorial expansionism, however slight, Ali consequently dispatched several boats from the Gulf of Arta with orders that they sail up the Albanian coast and launch an attack on his local mainland enemies, the beys of Paramythia and Margariti. The result was increasing tensions between Ali and the Russians, who complained that the presence of these boats constituted a violation of the stipulations of the 1800 treaty by which the joint Russo-Turkish protectorate over the Ionians had been established. Morier attempted one last time to intercede on Ali's behalf in his ongoing battle with the Russians; once again he was unsuccessful. Morier thus withdrew from Ioannina, writing of his disappointment in his inability to reach a compromise between Russia and the pasha.[56]

William Martin Leake

In 1809 William Martin Leake was appointed British agent to Ioannina,[57] where he forged friendships of a sort with both Ali and Lord Byron.[58]

---

[54] PRO/FO 78/53, no. 5.

[55] Ibid., no. 6.

[56] Ibid., nos. 7, 13, 14, and enclosures.

[57] Letter of George Canning (October 21, 1808) appointing Leake special envoy to the court of Ali, Leake Papers.

[58] Byron's "friendship" with Leake appears, from the pertinent correspondence, to have been forced at best (Tregaskis 1979, 73).

Trained as a topographer, Leake in 1799 had been sent on a military mission to Istanbul, where he was to instruct Turkish troops in the use of modern artillery, as at that time the Porte anticipated an attack from the French.[59]

Relations between Ali and Captain Leake appear to have been ambivalent. By the end of his tenure in Ioannina, Leake was still addressed in all letters from Ali as "My most noble and beloved friend," but the reality, it seems, was not always thus. Indeed, during the early months of Leake's stay in Ioannina, when the French were still in possession of the Ionian Islands, Ali let it be known that he considered Leake not just a British envoy but also a potential hostage. He wrote to the British, informing them in the clearest of terms that were the British to desert him, leaving him unassisted against the looming threat of the French, he would not hesitate to detain Leake as a political prisoner.[60] For the most part, Ali and Leake appear to have gotten along adequately well. They could not rightly be termed friends, however, their own claims to the contrary notwithstanding.

Leake had had his first contact with Ali in 1807, when the British sent him to Ioannina to ask Ali what he would do if the Ottoman government lost control of its European territories. Leake was instructed to promise Ali that were he to declare himself independent under such circumstances, he could rely on British naval assistance against France and Russia. Leake was fully aware of the presence of French agents in Ali's court,[61] and so aimed to guarantee British confidentiality by proceeding to a designated port on the Albania coast where he knew Ali was receiving foreign letters for Ioannina.[62]

Ali used this meeting as a carefully staged drama intended to assure the French that he had no intentions of establishing relations with Britain. He rigged a fake meeting with the British, at which the French commissary Pouqueville was present, during the course of which the British were told of Ali's complete refusal to negotiate with the British so long as they were at war with the Porte. Prior to this meeting, however, Ali had managed to have secret word sent to Leake that he was to return some hours later for another, "real" meeting, which would be conducted without Pouqueville.

Thus Leake feigned departure, sailing a few miles out to sea, only to return that night to the designated secret meeting place on the beach north of Preveza. In this meeting Leake laid out for Ali the likelihood of a French attack on his dominions, and in particular the French interest in gaining control of Greece. Ali assured Leake that were "Albania" (which, by Ali's

[59] Spencer 1954, 207ff.

[60] See the memoirs of Robert Adair, then British ambassador to Istanbul (Adair 1845, 2:217).

[61] PRO/FO 78/57, no. 3, Leake to George Canning, November 18, 1807.

[62] This was the town of Hagia Saranda, or Forty Saints.

figuring, included sizable portions of Greek Epiros, Thrace, and Macedonia) attacked, he would not hesitate in taking military action against the French. Upon hearing this, Leake promised Ali that he could expect full British assistance in the repulsion of any possible French or Russian attack. Ali repeatedly requested that the British garrison Santa Maura, and that they help him expel the French from the Ionian Islands.

So began a somewhat lengthy correspondence between Ali and Lord Collingwood of Britain, with Ali repeatedly stating his request for assistance against the French in the Ionians and Collingwood promising assistance but stopping short of sending British soldiers to Santa Maura. From this correspondence it is evident that Ali felt that his fortunes no longer lay with Istanbul. Writing to Collingwood on August 2, 1808, he stated: "Whatever may be the event of affairs in the capital [Istanbul], it is evident I shall be the object of persecution; and as I have dedicated myself entirely to your nation, I hope that it will feel a pride in protecting me and assisting me in such a manner as may enable me to defend my person and property, and to accomplish those services which I feel the greatest inclination to render."[63]

Ali was employing a tactic with which we are by now familiar. Using his contravention of the Porte's desires as evidence of his fealty to the British, he attempted to make the British feel a reciprocal sense of loyalty toward him. Again, Ali paradoxically was more comfortable when dealing with his ostensible enemies than when confronting the Porte's allies. To further what Britain perceived to be a useful alliance, George Canning, on October 21, 1808, wrote appointing Leake special envoy to Ali Pasha's court.[64] Leake was to serve in this capacity for the next two years.

. . . . .

During the early portion of Leake's service in Ioannina, relations between the governments of Britain and the Ottoman Empire were hostile. A peace between the two was not signed until January 5, 1809. It is evident that by this point in his career Ali regarded himself as an independent ruler, and the powers of Europe recognized Ali as a distinct political entity. At the time, Britain was maintaining two separate sets of diplomatic negotiations in "Turkey," one with Ali, the other with the Porte in Istanbul.

Initially, British motivation for consorting with Ali had been Britain's weakened position in the face of Ottoman hostilities and French encroachments in the Adriatic. The British, however, even after signing the January 1809 peace, perceived the French as a grave threat and hoped in

[63] Collingwood 1829, 425.
[64] Leake papers.

particular that the Ottoman government would help the British push the French out of the Ionian Islands.[65] The Porte, however, maintaining a cautious policy, seemed unwilling to take any serious steps against the French. It therefore remained advantageous to maintain good relations with Ali, who, unlike the Porte, was obsessed with diminishing French power on the western Epirote coast.

Ali's friendship, however, would not come cheap. Adair was concerned about the pasha's extravagant and unrealistic pecuniary demands, and he was also troubled by his suspicions that Ali's Albanian troops might grow uncontrollable if allowed to take military action in the islands.[66] The British regarded only the remaining coastal dependency, Parga, as fair game for Ali. On the score of Parga, Ali remained inflexible, repeatedly insisting that the British make good on their promise to hand it over to him should the French be successfully ousted from the Ionian Islands.[67]

The circumstances of the struggle between Ali, the French, the Porte, and the British over the Ionian Islands changed dramatically in October 1809, when the British took control of Cerigo, Itháki, Cephalonia, and Zante. Ali immediately tried to turn this event to his advantage. In a letter dated November 27, 1809, he swore loyalty to the British and proposed that they hand over to him as hostages the two most powerful klephtic families of Zante, the Farmakis and Karaiskos clans. The klephts of the islands, who at this point were still working in the service of the French, were thus to be intimidated into submitting to their new British masters. Ali argued that such a move would be advantageous both to himself and to the British. Although the outcome of this particular proposal is not noted in the Leake papers (one would imagine the British to have been less than supportive of such a plan), as Baggally observes, "The

[65] See Robert Adair's *Negotiations for the Peace of the Dardanelles* for details of this period (1845, vol. 2). Adair, the British plenipotentiary and ambassador in Istanbul, was throughout this period in frequent correspondence with Captain Leake.

[66] Baggally 1938, 39–40.

[67] The British guarantee of Parga was first given to Ali in the letter from George Canning to Captain Leake appointing Leake envoy to Ali's court (October 21, 1808). In this letter Canning writes of Parga: "Should Ali Pacha determine upon commencing hostilities against the French, the Commander-in-Chief of His Majesty's Naval Forces in the Mediterranean has been instructed to employ his ships on that Station in effecting if practicable the Reduction of the French garrison in the town of Parga. Which instruction you will represent to have been given in consequence of Ali Pacha's request." (Leake Papers). This "promise" of Parga to Ali was ultimately fulfilled in 1819, when the British finally took the town from the French and gave it over to Ali's control. By 1819, British sympathy for the Greek was at a high point, as was anti-Ali sentiment, and this act was widely seen as of treason against the Parganotes on the part of the British. For details of this 1819 controversy, see Lieutenant Colonel C. P. de Bosset, "Proceedings in Parga, and the Ionian Islands, with a Series of Correspondence and other justificatory Documents." *The Quarterly Review*, Vol 23 (de Bosset 1820, 111–36).

rather daring proposal illustrates the efficiency of Ali's intelligence service and the tenacity of his resentments."[68]

At first the British had wanted Ali's friendship so as to recruit him against the French in the Ionian Islands. Now that the Islands were under British control, attention turned to the possible economic advantages attendant upon having Ali as an ally. The Leake papers report in very detailed terms on the seven Albanian forests that could supply timber for ship building, and they show ongoing negotiations with Ali over this timber from early 1809 to early 1810. Trade ties with Ali were all the more important for the British, as they suffered from the recent Peace of Schonbrunn, by the terms of which the Austrian Illyrian provinces were surrendered to Napoleon. This surrender had the effect of squelching British trade interests in that region, and they were now in search of new trading partners.

Throughout this period, the British followed a policy of appeasement in their dealings with Ali. British assistance for him came in the form of both supplies and technical know-how: ship builders were sent to consult and assist in the repair of Ali's vessels, and when in 1809 famine struck the largely Greek populations of Arta, Lepanto, and Missolonghi, the British supplied a warship to provide a protective convoy for Ali's ships transporting grain from his storehouses in Berat.[69]

It seems quite clear, however, that the British never came to trust Ali fully. British diplomatic records of this period indicate a hesitation to allow Ali's military power to go unrestrained. We have seen one example of this in Britain's refusal to allow Ali's Albanian troops into the islands. Similarly, the British later objected to his erection of fortifications on the Epirote coast facing the island of Santa Maura.[70]

The British nevertheless felt that these difficulties were well worth the risks. The alternative, after all, was the possibility of Ali's colluding with the French, forging an alliance against which the British would stand no chance. The French, moreover, were still in control of Parga, which Ali had long desired to possess. The French could (and did) attempt to use the promise of Parga as a carrot in an effort to lure him away from his alliance with the British.[71] So distressed were the British by this possibility that George Foresti, Leake's successor in Ioannina, wrote to his British superiors in March 1811 that the British should appease Ali by pushing the French out of Parga themselves.

> [Ali] does not hesitate to say to me that the Enemy [the French] had foretold him that the English would abandon him and that his Connection with them

[68] Baggally 1938, 42.

[69] Ibid., 43.

[70] British Museum, Add. MS. 20, 183, f. 13.

[71] Ibid., f. 67. Ali disingenuously led the British to believe that Parga was no longer of any interest to him.

would bring destruction upon him and upon his Family. You know enough of me to feel certain how embarrassed and overwhelmed I was going to add at hearing and seeing all this they had the effect on me [*sic*], not of inducing me to expect that the Vizir would give way to the Enemy, but only of making me feel the absolute necessity of giving him proofs that we are at least, equal to the Defence of His Coast [*sic*]. For this Reason I recommend strongly the immediate occupation of Parga by British Soldiers or Sailors or both.[72]

The incoherence of Foresti's missive notwithstanding, it is evident that the British felt that in dealing with Ali they had put themselves in circumstances not entirely to their liking or entirely within their control. This sense was heightened when Ali once again warmed toward Pouqueville while continuing correspondence with the British. As Baggally notes, "The Foreign Office drafts show strongly the embarrassment felt at the position into which Great Britain had drifted through official ignorance of the geography and politics of Albania and the Islands."[73]

European Insecurities

By the time of Leake's departure from Ioannina in February 1810, the British were solidly entrenched in a relationship with Ali in which they did not seem to have the upper hand. Ali's clever manipulation of the earlier diplomatic relations he had maintained with France, coupled with his vast and highly organized army, made the British loath indeed to incur his wrath.

By 1811, Ali had managed to establish a position of geographic, psychological, and strategic dominance over the British in the region of the Ionian Islands. He still enjoyed the possibility of Ottoman protection, in the event that he needed it, but he had managed to divorce himself from Ottoman affairs to such an extent that he now dealt with the French and the British on his own independent terms, with no reference by the European powers to his ostensible subjugation to the wishes of the Porte.

Moreover, Ali through his negotiations with the French and subsequently the British, had managed to make no small gains for himself and his people. Trade ties had been strengthened, resulting in increased revenues for Ioannina and its environs. Military assistance had been received, in the form of weapons and technology, and some monies (although not all he had hoped for) had been contributed to Ali's cause. In addition, by 1811 Ali found himself perhaps closer than he had ever been to possessing Parga. In the event that the British failed to help him obtain it, he could always turn his attentions back to the French.

---

[72] British Museum, Add. MS. 20, 182, f. 87.
[73] Baggally 1938, 56.

Psychologically, too, it is clear that Ali conceived of his territory in ever more independent terms. His correspondence and British correspondence refer frequently to "Albania" (namely, the territories under his control) and "Ali's Albanians." British concern over the tenuousness of their position had nothing to do with the Ottoman government but was based entirely on Ali's obvious strength and superior position. Indeed, as early as 1803 Hamilton had written to Lord Hawkesbury, the British foreign secretary, of Ali's power and influential position, observing that Ali was less needy of the Ottoman Empire than the empire was of him:

> Your Lordship is of course acquainted with the present situation and influence of Ali Pacha. Policy and Prudence alone dispose him to continue to profess, in form, his allegiance to the Porte; as in fact he is perfectly Independent of the Turkish Government; which is more in want of his assistance against the declared Rebels, than he is of its goodwill and favour. His influence extends over the whole of Roumelia, and he is immediate Governor of the most populous, richest and most Warlike Provinces in Albania. In the space of a few days he can raise 30,000 troops; and in case his first enterprises were successful, he would quickly be joined by as many more. He is prompt in his measures, full of energy, and professes a very quick and nice discernment of Individual Character; but his want of education, and a life spent in arms, have rendered him in his Government cruel and despotic, because he found it to his advantage. He has however established the most perfect tranquillity, and security of Persons and Property throughout his dominions, whose Inhabitants, Greeks and Turks, are richer, happier, more contented, and less oppressed, than in any other part of European Turkey.
>
> It is unnecessary for me to observe, that Ali Pacha is even able, by his influence throughout the whole of Greece, greatly to facilitate, or impede, the exportation of Grain from the Gulphs of Arta, of Corinth, of Volo, Saloniki, etc. etc.[74]

If in 1803 the British were worried by Ali, by 1811 they were positively fearful. According to Hamilton's account, Ali by then had military strength as well as significant influence over the economy of the region. He had brought virtually all inhabitants of Albania and Epiros under his direct control, subduing would-be rebels and co-opting the klephts. His methods had led to a "contented" and "secure" populace, whose loyalty was shown by the ease with which Hamilton assumed that Ali could raise huge numbers of troops in a short time.

·   ·   ·   ·   ·

In Hamilton's letter, the observation that Ali is "in his Government cruel and despotic" is entirely overshadowed by an otherwise glowing account

[74] Hamilton to Hawkesbury, Ioannina, May 6, 1803, Nelson Papers.

of the pasha, and it seems inserted more as a formality, a fixed form, than as a relevant part of the communication. Indeed, the observation is somewhat at odds with the rest of Hamilton's account, which details the contentment and security of Ali's peoples.

It is included, however, because descriptions of Ali's "cruelty" and "despotism" were ubiquitous, indeed de rigueur features of any account of him. As the British position in the Adriatic vis-à-vis Ali became increasingly tenuous, weak, and dependent, this denigrating, formulaic description was retained and heightened. It seems that it functioned almost as a compensatory device with which the British swept away their own insecurities in relation to Ali and heightened his otherness, portraying him in increasingly pejorative, Orientalist terms. Observations such as Hamilton's, which are rife in the accounts by later British travelers, as well as in Leake's, are a commentary as much on the relative weakness of the British in this period as they are on Ali himself.

Subsequent Western accounts, both diplomatic histories and biographies of Ali, have retained this heightened Othering while downplaying or eliding entirely the relative strategic weaknesses of the European powers in relation to Ali. Thus the bulk of biographical material on Ali focuses not on his diplomatic accomplishments but on personal anecdotes and tales of treachery. The results of this shift in emphasis are many. Most significantly, the product is a two-dimensional picture of Ali, a caricature that does not consider Ali as a changing, participatory entity. He is always described in the same terms, from a distance.

Texts such as Leake's four-volume *Travels in Northern Greece* are, according to a Saidian model, tours de force of Orientalist literature.[75] In them Ali is described in predictable and extravagant terms. He is "despotic," "cruel," "treacherous," "ignorant," "uneducated," "perverse," and other canonically Orientalist adjectives that spring to mind. Such works, however, are not mere Orientalist artefacts; they also constitute a form of self-criticism, an inchoate commentary on not just Western superiority but also Western weakness.

---

[75] Leake 1835.

EIGHT

ORIENTALIST STRATEGIES

IN HIS GRADUAL SHIFT away from the political framework of the Ottoman imperium, Ali deliberately and consciously styled himself on Western patterns of statecraft and politics. The development of his diplomatic contacts in the period 1797–1811 marks a pivotal point in the process whereby Ali dissociated himself from the Ottoman Empire and its mechanisms of power and turned instead to a more Western model based on the principles of statism and nationalism.

As pasha of Ioannina, Ali had risen to the highest possible position within the Ottoman provincial hierarchy. As his career progressed, he became ever more dissatisfied with the paradigms of rulership that the Ottoman imperial system offered, and increasingly he chose to align himself with the methods of his Western neighbors. Arguably the most important appointment of his official Ottoman political career took place as early as 1787, when he had been designated *derbendler başbuğu* (chief of police of mountain defiles), a position that gave him practical, if not formal, and direct control over Rumeli and Albania in their entirety.[1] Although the position of pasha was indeed prestigious within the Ottoman hierarchy, Ali's appointment to it also constituted an attempt on the part of Istanbul to coopt his power, influence, and prestige—gained largely through banditry and traditional Albanian social structures—by bringing him under formal state sanction. Although throughout most of the eighteenth century the Porte pursued a policy of controlling various provincial governors by playing them off one another, by the 1790s the general fear of runaway governors had coalesced into a fear of Ali in specific. In negotiating with the European powers, Ali was not just violating Ottoman policy but consciously seeking out a new framework for power.

The "West," however, was for Ali a place of vague and many signifiers. His own participation in that realm, he recognized, depended on an attempt to share in those signifiers, although in many instances, he did not fully understand their implications. For example, late in his career Ali promised his Greek subjects a constitution and wrote to Metternich requesting that he prepare one on his behalf.[2] Some Greeks evidently believed the promise.[3] It is not clear that Ali knew exactly what a constitu-

---

[1] Skiotis 1971, 232.
[2] Dakin 1972, 34–35; Miller 1913, 64.
[3] Makriyannes 1966, 14; Broughton 1855, 114.

tion was. The fact that he turned to Metternich, the least constitutionally minded European ruler, is a fairly clear indication that he did not, but it is obvious that he understood its symbolic implications. To him a constitution was something one offered to subject peoples as a gesture of appeasement when they made nationalist rumblings. Ali, master of the symbolic, cleverly used such signifiers of the West in his ongoing attempts to re-create himself in the image of what he imagined that West to be.

Ali thus turned away from the Ottoman imperial system and toward Europe both in his diplomatic policies and in his personal symbology. Even as Ali styled himself as Western, the West was busy representing Ali as the incarnation of all that the West was not. While Ali was insinuating himself into the heart of the European politics of the day, the European elite culture was positing Ali as the quintessence of the "mysterious Orient": sensual, cruel, whimsical, illogical, and, above all, unintelligible—unrecognizable as being in any way "like us." Ali inspired numerous European poets, painters, novelists, and musical composers, who invariably cast him as a villainous and dangerous figure, given to fits of whimsy and acts of great atrocity.

Works such as Victor Hugo's *Les Orientales* and Lord Byron's *Childe Harold's Pilgrimage*; dramatic musical compositions such as *Ali Pacha, or The Signet Ring, Die Entführung aus dem Serail*, and *Zémire et Azor*; the paintings of W. Davenport, which feature Ali lounging on couches, throwing Christian lasses into Lake Ioannina, and attacking the Souliotes: all are, in Saidian terms, prime exhibits of Orientalism, a category that now strikes most historians as hackneyed. In the case of Ali, however, it is worthwhile to look more closely at some of its most obvious features, for the Orientalist depiction of Ali was intertwined with Ali's own depiction of himself. Ali came to be intimately familiar with the Orientalist vision of him and he cleverly manipulated it to his advantage.

· · · · ·

The most famous literary works based on the life of Ali are Lord Byron's epic poem *Childe Harold's Pilgrimage* and Victor Hugo's *Les Orientales*. A host of other luminaries such as Goethe, Dumas, Balzac, and Lear also found him a literary inspiration, and as such he has had staying power. In 1973 James Merrill published his poem *Yannina*, first in the *Atlantic Monthly*, then on its own, as a limited edition monograph. Merrill's musings on Ali make up the work's core theme:

> Funny, that is how I think of Ali.
> On the one hand, the power and the gory
> Details, pigeon-blood rages and retali-

ations, gouts of fate that crust his story;
And on the other, charm, the whimsically
Meek brow, its motives ab ulteriori,
The flower-blue gaze twining to choke proportion,
Having made one more pretty face's fortune.[4]

Such fictional and artistic re-creations of Ali's life relied, almost without exception, on travel literature for their information. Merrill's work cites William Plomer's 1936 biography of Ali, which, although more academic than most of the biographies, is still clearly based largely on travelers' accounts.

Such accounts and the works they inspired illustrate the numerous ways in which the West represented Ali through its crude and fixed understanding of the East, just as Ali represented himself through his equally fixed and rudimentary understanding of the West. Even as Ali tried to adorn himself with the signifiers of modernity and nationalism, the West resolutely saw in him the signifiers of petty despotism and Oriental Otherness.

. . . . .

The mid-eighteenth century saw the rise to popularity of numerous musical and literary works that found their setting in the territories of the Ottoman Empire. The two most popular operas at Vienna's Burgtheater were set in an Oriental milieu: Gluck's *La rencontre imprévue* (Vienna, 1764)[5] and Gretry's immensely acclaimed *Zémire et Azor* (Paris 1771).[6]

In 1778 Emperor Joseph II established Vienna's national singspiel, founded as an adjunct to the Viennese National Theater. This move opened the Burgtheater to both a broader repertory and a wider audience, which now included not just the nobility of Vienna but its middle classes as well. Mozart immediately wrote of his interest in composing a German opera for the national singspiel, which resulted in his collaboration with the playwright-librettist Christoph Friedrich Bretzner for the creation of *Die Entführung aus dem Serail* (The abduction from the seraglio). After its Viennese premiere in July 1782, the work went on to be met with great acclaim in Prague and throughout Germany. Thus the European popular appetite for tales of the cruel and mysterious ways of Ottoman rulers was at its height during the life of Ali Pasha.

As the most immediate eastern neighbor to the nations of Europe, Ali was an appealing and a relatively accessible source of information on the

---

[4] Merrill 1973.
[5] Gluck 1923.
[6] Gretry 1771; Charlton 1986

fascinating Ottomans. His territories were entirely situated within the borders of the European continent, and his subjects were predominantly Greek Orthodox, two factors that contributed to the general impression of his lands as being somehow more familiar, less wholly Other, than those of other regions in the Ottoman Empire. Ali's lands were perceived as simultaneously European and Oriental, Christian and Muslim. Indeed, Said has identified this peculiar perception of simultaneous familiarity and foreignness as being one of the hallmarks of the orientalist viewpoint. Writing of the Islamist Duncan McDonald, Said observed that "all Arab Orientals must be accommodated to a vision of an Oriental type as constructed by the Western scholar, as well as to a specific encounter with the Orient in which the Westerner regrasps the Orient's essence as a consequence of his intimate estrangement from it."[7]

The observation is apt not just in the case of McDonald, but also for the numerous European travelers who visited Ali's Ioannina and the artists who based their creations in large part on these travelers' accounts. Such travelers for the most part considered themselves at the very least gentlemen scholars, and their writings on Ali were guided as much by what they, as scholars, already knew of the Oriental as a type as by their actual observations of—to use Said's terms, their "specific encounter" with—Ali. The "intimate estrangement" of the Western subject from the Oriental object was, in the case of these travelers and Ali, heightened, on one hand, by the geographic and cultural proximity of his lands and subject peoples and, on the other hand, by the Otherness of the Ottomans in general and Ali in specific.

Ali's territories were immensely popular with the numerous European diarist travelers of the day, many of whom not only passed through Ioannina but spent a good deal of time there, some even to the point of taking up part-time residence in Ali's capital. Lord Byron, for instance, maintained a house in the city. The last decades of the nineteenth century saw the passage of numerous eminent writers through Ioannina, all of whom published colorful accounts of Ali upon returning home. John Cam Hobhouse (Lord Broughton), F. C. H. L. Pouqueville, Henry Holland, Guillame de Vaudoncourt (who served in the Italian service), and William Martin Leake are the most prominent ones.

Many of the travel accounts penned by these Europeans had Ali as their central, if not sole, topic of interest. Virtually all included some sort of biography of Ali; indeed, some accounts (for instance, Vaudoncourt's 1816 *Memoirs on the Ionian Islands including the life and character of Ali Pacha*) included his name in their title. The famous British artist W. Davenport published his collection *Historical Portraiture of Leading Events*

---

[7] Said 1979, 248.

in the Life of Ali Pacha, Vizier of Epirus, Surnamed the Lion, in a Series of Designs.[8] The popular Roman artist Lusieri also created a series of paintings of Ioannina and its environs, which were purchased by the infamously acquisitive earl of Elgin (and unfortunately lost in 1828 when the ship on which they were being sent back to England, the HMS *Cambrian*, sank at Karabusa).

Clearly, by the later years of the pasha's life, his name was widely known among a certain class in Europe, and the West's generic interest in the East had coalesced into a specific interest in figures such as Ali of Ioannina.[9] Whereas Orientalist works such as Mozart's *Die Entführung* had had as their central characters fictional caricatures, now musical works, too, were based on the specific historical figure of Ali. Thus the Italian composer Giovanni Martino Cesare wrote the musical score *La Ioannina*,[10] his German counterpart Albert Lortzing composed *Ali Pascha von Janina*,[11] and John Howard Payne wrote *Ali Pacha; or, The Signet Ring*.[12]

Nor was the interest in Ali limited to the sphere of the artistic imagination. His varying fortunes vis-à-vis both the powers of Europe and the Ottoman Porte were a constant source of fascination, and the European press closely followed the political situation in his territories. In his *Précis des opérations Générales de la division française du Levant*, published in Paris in 1805, the infantry captain Bellaire writes that he is sure that his work will be of great contemporary interest to a European readership: "Tous ces observations et celles qui concernent Ali, Pacha de Jannina, ne peuvent qu'interesser dans le moment actuel, où l'accroissement des forces Russes dans la Republique des Sept-Iles et la situation politique de l'Albanie attirent l'attention de toute l'Europe."[13] In this assumption, it seems, Bellaire was not being overly optimistic. John Dimakis's *La guerre de l'independence grecque vue par la presse française*, for instance, effectively demonstrates contemporary Europe's attention to Ali and his actions.[14]

Moreover, Ali's impact on the Western artistic imagination was such that works inspired by his life continued to be created for more than a century after his death. The Hungarian novelist Mór Jókai, for instance, published his peculiarly titled *Janicsarok Vegnapjai* (the last days of the janissaries) in 1853 (the janissary corps plays virtually no role in the

[8] Davenport 1823.
[9] Mehmet Ali of Egypt was another such figure who attracted European attention of a more specific sort.
[10] Cesare 1979.
[11] Lortzing 1904.
[12] Payne 1823.
[13] Bellaire 1805, vii.
[14] Dimakis 1968.

work). The work was published in an English translation in 1898, under the more apt title *The Lion of Janina*.[15] It is clear from the translator's introduction to the 1898 edition that Ali was still, seventy-six years after his death, assumed to be well known by the novel's conjectured readership. No explanation is given as to Ali's political position, historical significance, or geographic location; indeed, no mention is made of the dates of his birth and death. All that is said by way of description of Ali is that he was "certainly one of the most brilliant, picturesque, and, it must be added, capable ruffians that even Turkish history can produce."[16]

Barely distinguishable from such self-avowedly novelistic works as Jókai's *Lion of Janina* and Morier's 1857 *Photo the Suliote* (issued in 1951 in a dramatically abridged version as *A Tale of Old Yanina*)[17] are a slew of "biographies" of Ali, some published as recently as three decades ago. Most such works pose as scholarly accounts of Ali's life but, in fact, are sensationalist pseudo-fiction, relying heavily on colorful (and quite possibly apocryphal) anecdotes of Ali's atrocities to fill their pages. Prominent among these is William Plomer's 1936 *The Diamond of Jannina: Ali Pasha, 1741–1822*.[18] Reissued in 1970, Plomer's book reads like a novel; although it is clear that Plomer made use of several primary sources, and for the most part is more accurate in his dating than other biographers, his biography is bereft of any attempt at historical analysis.

Another recent biography of Ali is Tasos Vournas's little-known *Ale Pasas Tepelenles: Turannos e idiofues politikos?* (Ali Pasha: Tyrant or skilled politician?), published in Athens in 1978.[19] Although Vournas's work, unlike Plomer's, attempts to address serious historiographical questions (What role did Ali play vis-à-vis his Greek subjects? What documents are available, and are they reliable?) this endeavor is undermined both by the fact that the sources for cited documents are never given and by Vournas's tiresome habit of inventing dialogue for his historical characters, thus giving his book, too, a distinctly novelistic feel. So up to the present, amazingly, the most "scholarly" comprehensive account of Ali's life remains the much outdated *Ali de Tebelen: Pacha de Janina (1744–1822)* written by M. Gabriel Remerand in 1928.[20]

The legacy of fiction and biography that Ali's life inspired presents us with two immediate questions. First, why was the literary, musical, and

[15] Jókai 1897.
[16] Ibid., iv.
[17] Morier 1951.
[18] Plomer 1970.
[19] Vournas 1978.

[20] I must repeat that some excellent scholarship has been done on specific portions of Ali's life. Most notable is Dennis N. Skiotis's superb article "From Bandit to Pasha: First Steps in the Rise to Power of Ali of Tepelen, 1750–1784" (Skiotis 1971). This, however, covers only the period up to 1784.

artistic interest in Ali so persistent that it continued for several decades, even more than a century beyond his death? Second, why has there concomitantly been such a striking paucity of scholarly biographical research on Ali? The answer to both questions is, I suggest, the same: Ali's ability, as it were, to attract attention remains to this day pinned to the fact of his being understood by the Western observer to somehow mark the quintessence of many of the most potent and long-held assumptions about the Orient, particularly the Turkish Orient. That is, despite the manifest importance, historically speaking, of Ali, he is fascinating to his biographers for almost nothing save his personal idiosyncrasies and anecdotally replete life. Ali's role in the decline of the Ottoman Empire, his contributions to the Greek War of Independence, and the economic transformations he effected in his territories have been eclipsed by the man himself.

What the numerous biographers, travelers, historians, and novelists have produced, then, is something other than historiography. Instead it is a vast body of representational literature, a literature that sheds much light not on Ali in his own time and place but on Ali as the West (for most of these writers were European) would have him.[21] Ali, then, has not been so much described as imagined and in these imaginings as much is revealed about the assumptions of those imaginers as about the figure of Ali himself.

The assumptions of Western superiority to and familiarity with the Ottoman Empire were in Ali's case challenged by the unavoidable fact of his strength and his potential military, strategic, and geographic superiority. These latter characteristics, however, did not serve to temper the former. Rather, feelings of geopolitical insecurity in the West amplifed the tone of belittlement and superiority that was the backbone of the West's cultural representations of Ali.

· · · · ·

I mentioned that a common feature of biographical accounts of Ali— whether novelistic or "factual"—is the repeated recitation of specific episodes in his career, which are largely anecdotal. By "anecdotal" I mean that these episodes do not, for the most part, convey information that casts light on anything other than Ali's personality; they do not refer to the broader political or economic scene, and they do not provide necessary background for future information, they do not contribute to the reader's understanding of Ali's time or place in any explicit way.

What matters to the teller of the anecdote is not accuracy but enter-

---

[21] Even a writer such as Vournas, a Greek, is heavily influenced by the Western point of view (Vournas 1978).

tainment value. Indeed, *Merriam Webster's Collegiate Dictionary* (tenth edition) defines *anecdote* as "a usu. short narrative of an interesting, amusing, or biographical incident." Its synonyms are usually given as "fable," "story," "tale," and "yarn," all of which carry the connotation of embellishment, if not outright fictionalization.

In accounts of Ali's life these anecdotal tales served as tropes through which European writers and their readership simultaneously verified and fed their imaginings of the Orient and by which they made Ali seem less threatening, altogether insignificant and ridiculous. Thus their relevance to the historian is redeemed, if reevaluated. Although these tales do not necessarily provide us with "the truth" and may not represent historical "fact," they are invaluable in demonstrating the process of historical representation at work. As products of their historical time, they reflect European concerns about Ali Pasha and should be seen not merely as exhibits in some great Orientalist museum.

Did Ali miraculously find a pot of gold beneath a tree just when his destitute state had grown intolerable? Did he really favor young boys over women? Did he truly have amorous designs on Lord Byron? Did Ali force his widowed sister to marry her dead husband's brother—and conduct the ceremony himself, in the presence of her former husband's corpse? Such literalistic questioning is in such a context both thankless and, ultimately, somewhat beside the point. What matters is not the historical authenticity or veracity of these accounts but the fact that so many people—even those who perhaps doubted them at the time of writing about them—included them, time and again, in their accounts of Ali and his life.

My purpose is not to go back, as it were, and make right the record. I have no particular interest in weeding out the "false" stories from the "true" ones, even if such an endeavor were possible. Rather, I am interested in focusing on such stories' testimony to the multifarious ways in which Ali was represented by—and represented himself to—the world around him, and to what end.

. . . . .

In the translator's introduction to the 1898 English edition of *The Last Days of the Janissaries*, R. Nisbet Bain writes of Jókai as "an absolutely impartial observer, who can detect the worth of the Osmanli in the midst of his apathy and brutality." It is, of course, temptingly easy for today's reader, a century later, to scoff at the naïveté of this claim. Jókai was no less impartial than we are today. What is interesting about Bain's observation is that it successfully debunks itself; it does not take the pretensions of a postmodern critic to observe the absurdity of Bain's statement. Bain does it for himself when he writes that Jókai's impartiality is signaled by his ability to say a few good things about the "Osmanli," despite his "apathy and brutality." That is, the Osmanli is outright assumed to be lazy and depraved; such an assumption is not considered to compromise the impartiality of the observer, because it is believed to constitute not partiality but fact.

As late as 1898, seventy-six years after his death, Ali was still a potent enough symbol to serve the important function of bolstering Europe's ongoing suspicion of and fascination with the Ottoman Orient. For the relevance and interest of Jókai's novel inhered not in the minutiae of history but in the ever elevant depiction it provided of a figure who corroborated and upheld the Western imagination of the Orient. In telling the story of Ali, the West was telling a tale that was at once exotic and familiar, foreign and hackneyed. For Ali represented the mysterious, alien East, even as those very qualities of alienness and mysteriousness were commonly known as the requisites of being Oriental. The story of Ali was thus a self-fulfilling prophecy, a story that both described and created the man behind it.

The representation of Ali met a demand that existed among the readership of Jókai's novel and similar works: the need to see that the fantasy and the reality were one. Through the representational process the West's "intimate estrangement" from the Orient was upheld. This need is still being met by contemporary works such as the movie *Byron*, starring Omar Sharif as Ali, and Plomer's *Diamond of Jannina* (not to mention such pop-cultural artefacts as the recent animated film *Aladdin*). The ongoing history of the biography of Ali is an ongoing history of the West's representation of the East.

There are some readily identifiable tactics and features of this representationalist viewpoint as it was applied to Ali. They play themselves out most markedly in the repetition of specific stories and characteristics of Ali throughout the corpus of Western travel literature on him and the novels and other artistic creations it inspired.

Birth as Destiny: The Genetic Features of the Oriental Despot

The most prominent theme running through the vast corpus of anecdotal material comprising the works based on Ali's life is treachery. Ali is presented as amoral and villainous. He is completely unforgiving and vengeful. The story of Ali's meteoric rise to power, from the impoverished scion of an obscure, pseudo-aristocratic Albanian village family to ruler of a vast and vastly wealthy *paşalık*, takes the form of an endless succession of atrocities, double-dealings, and criminal acts perpetrated by him. It is also characterized by his never forgetting any wrong (real or perceived), even those that occurred in the earliest years of his life.

As the starting point for this chronology, virtually all works on Ali provide one version or another of the death of his father (when Ali was about twelve), and his subsequent actions on behalf of his mother and sister. Ali, the story goes, was forced at an early age to fend for his female relations, protecting them against the aggressions of his cruel stepbrothers and stepsisters and the hostile community in which they lived. This story, however, is not presented merely as a sort of psychological exegesis for Ali's villainous character. Rather, Ali's ability, even as a young child, to act cruelly and aggressively is provided as proof of his amorality and ruthlessness. Ali's treacheries are uniformly viewed not as a psychological response to a difficult and brutal childhood but as a biological imperative, the inevitable outcome of his breeding.

In such a construct the very essence of the Oriental is marked by a depravity that is passed down by heredity, as if it were a physical, ethnic, or racial characteristic. (Needless to say, such a Darwinist or biological model is one of the uglier features of many forms of nationalist ideologies.) Ali's personal treacheries are an embellishment of the generically treacherous genetic type. Again, as Jókai's translator puts it, Ali was "one of the most brilliant, picturesque ruffians *that even Turkish history can produce.*"[22] In short, Ali's "Turkishness" alone (never mind that he was Albanian) was enough to guarantee his status as a ruffian; he was a particularly acute incarnation of an already well-established genre.

Similarly, the Greek historian Perraivos, who fought against Ali in the last Souliote war, refers to "To para tois Othomanois fusikon elattoma" (the natural defect of the Ottomans.)[23] By such a construct Ali is cruel by type, *by nature*, and as such is compared to other epic antiheroes of Middle Eastern, anti-Christian history: "Cent fois plus cruel que Neron, Ali."[24]

Typical of this type of "genetic" depiction of Oriental treachery is the account of John Cam Hobhouse (Lord Broughton).

> Ali's father, Veli, was a Bey of Tepeleni, but, being the youngest of three brothers, he was driven from the place by the other two, but returned at the head of a band of klephtes, took Tepeleni, and burnt his brothers alive. He was created a pasha of two tails, but was again driven from Tepeleni, and died soon afterwards, when Ali was only fourteen years old. The mother of Ali was named Kamko,[25] the daughter of a powerful bey of Konitza, the founder of all his fortunes, and with whose milk he seems to have imbibed his cruel and ferocious propensities. Kamko poisoned the other widow and the child of her deceased husband, and commenced a warfare upon the

[22] Jókai 1897, iv (my emphasis).
[23] Perraivos 1857.
[24] Bellaire 1805, 418.
[25] Esmihan Hamın; Kamko (also transliterated as Khamko or Chamko) is the Albanian.

neighbouring chiefs and clans, carrying her son Ali and her daughter Chainizza with her to the field.[26]

Ali's extreme cruelty is seen as inherited from his mother, Kamko; it is an organic part of both. The same image of Kamko's lethal powers of lactation was retained (or rather imitated) a some century later when William Plomer wrote of Kamko's relationship with Ali and with his sister, Shainitza:[27] "She had the most powerful influence over them, and with her very milk they drank in ambition, greed and hatred."[28]

The depiction of Kamko as cruel and overbearing and of Veli Bey as bellicose and vengeful is typical of Ali's biographies and has the obvious implication that Ali's character was determined by his lineage. His parents' atrocities are thus relevant to his biographers, as they explain Ali's later cruelty.

Thus stories of Ali's parents serve a critical function. They bolster and explain claims of Ali's extraordinarily sanguinary character and of his apparently inhuman behavior. Indeed, Kamko is often described as so bloodthirstily vengeful as to be inhuman. One of the most detailed such descriptions is found in Richard Alfred Davenport's biography, in which he describes the death of Ali's mother.

> After having poisoned the sole remaining half-brother of Ali, she spent her last moments in hearing her will read to her. This document, which rather resembled the composition of an incarnate fiend than of a human being, enjoined Ali and Shainitza [Ali's sister], under pain of her curse in case of their neglect, to exterminate as speedily as possible the hated inhabitants of Chormovo and Gardiki [villages whose inhabitants are reported to have raped Khamko shortly after her husband's death], pointed out various individuals who were to be murdered, and villages which were to be consumed, recommended to Ali to enrich the soldiery and to trample on the people, and directed that a pilgrim should be sent to Mecca, in her name, to present an offering on the tomb of the Prophet for the repose of her soul![29]

Kamko bears no resemblance to a human; she is a "fiend" incarnate. In the same vein, Tasos Vournas, in his recent biography of Ali, refers to Ali's

[26] Broughton 1855, 1:101.

[27] This is one of several instances in which Plomer's choice if diction is suspiciously similar to Richard Alfred Davenport's; it seems clear that he relied heavily on the account of the latter in writing of his biography. See, for example, Davenport's following observation: "The purport of the precepts delivered by Khamco to her son may almost be summed up in a few emphatic words, which Shakespeare puts into the mouth of the weird sisters in Macbeth—'Be bloody, bold, and resolute'" (Davenport 1823, 26); compare this with Plomer's comment, "her teaching was like that of the apparition conjured up by the witches in Macbeth: 'Be bloody, bold and resolute'" (Plomer 1970, 32).

[28] Plomer 1970, 32.

[29] Davenport 1837, 51.

Fig. 3. The Vow of Vengeance Made by Ali Pasha and his Sister Chainitza over the Dead Body of their Mother

mother as "e satanike Kamko" (the satanic Kamko).[30] In the context of Ali's biographies, the implications of such bizarre and horrifying characterizations of Kamko are clear: Ali, born of such a beast, could not fail, by dint of his genes, to share in her depraved and hateful character.

Similarly, Plomer, too, strikes up the theme of Kamko's inhumanity, in this instance attributing it to a speculative physiological abnormality. "There is no reason to suppose Khamko was mad," Plomer declares. "But she was certainly anything but normal, and the violence of her passions may perhaps be ascribed partly to some physical peculiarity."[31] Once again, we see the implication that her cruelty was inherent, biological, and therefore bound to inhere in her offspring like a physical trait.

The notion of brutality as a genetically transmitted feature of Ali's physiognomy is strengthened by the fact that Shainitza is also portrayed as demonic, inhuman, and bloodthirsty. Note, for instance, the following description of the death of Shainitza's last surviving son, Aden Bey:

> General alarm was felt in Jannina [upon Aden Bey's death] at the possible consequences of Shainitza's emotion, and all the shopkeepers hurriedly put up their shutters. It was the custom in that part of the world in those days for women to show the most excessive signs of grief for their dead menfolk; they did not mourn, they howled and bellowed, and it was not thought at all odd for them to howl daily at the tops of their voices for five and ten years. Shainitza, bereaved of her last male child, was not satisfied to be a blubbering and caterwauling Niobe. Foaming at the mouth, she demanded that the doctors who had failed to save her son's life should be delivered up to her so that she might drink their blood.[32]

Once over her initial shock, Shainitza retreated to her palace in the Albanian village of Liboovo, where she soothed herself by "ponder[ing] over ways and means of ruining or annihilating those whom she regarded as her enemies, an occupation to which her brother was always devoted."[33]

Shainitza, like her brother, Ali, and her mother Kamko, is described in inhuman terms. She "froths at the mouth" and howls like a rabid dog, and even in her time of despair her only thoughts are for those whom she hates. This description corroborates the genetic, familial quality of the cruelty that Shainitza and all her family members are said to share, and it supports the critique of Ali as brutal, cruel, and irrational.

This genealogy of brutality is also evinced by the European observers' comments on Ali's sons, who, like Ali and his sister, were thought to have been born with inhumanity in their veins.

[30] Vournas 1978, 16.
[31] Plomer 1970, 32.
[32] Ibid. 1970, 140.
[33] Ibid. 1970, 140.

The French general Bellaire recounts the story of Ali's devastatingly successful defeat of the Prevezans, a Greek Orthodox people living on the Adriatic coast to the west of Ali's capital. In this battle Ali's troops took, along with four hundred Prevezans, a handful of French prisoners, for the French army had collaborated with the Greeks in their defensive effort against Ali. These French prisoners were taken on a forced march to Ioannina, where Ali's son Veli was waiting to receive them. One of the prisoners foolishly sought clemency from Veli. Bellaire writes of the exchange: "Le sourire de l'antropophage devorant sa victime est plus doux que celui qui précéda la réponse de Veli: Maudit chien de Français, tu seras encore bien plus puni."[34]

Not only does Bellaire see fit, in the context of a précis of French military operations, to put conjectural dialogue in the mouths of his characters, but he is also prepared to describe their facial expressions, despite the fact that he did not witness the events. More remarkable still is his precise choice of diction in describing Veli: he is likened to an anthropophagus, a cannibal, an image at the heart of much orientalist literature of the Middle Ages.[35] Veli's cruelty, like the cannibal's partiality to human flesh, is both a cultural "habit" and so alien as to make him of a different race entirely. Just as Ali's mother is inhuman, so is his son completely, biologically, other.

In accounts of Ali and other Ottoman rulers, this depiction of the Oriental as genetically depraved, treacherous, and cruel corroborates Western assumptions of the essentially different, inferior Oriental vis-à-vis his European counterpart.

The Facade of Cultural Relativism

The assumption of genetic, essential depravity frequently serves as a device that allows for the gratuitous recitation of atrocities that have no relevance to the accounts in which they are included. In many travelogues and biographies, a list of brutal, amoral, or otherwise heinous Orientals is typically provided as an ostensible point of comparison for the subject in question. In reality, the list serves to titillate the presumably Western reader and to undergird his or her sense of horror and superiority regarding the Oriental.

An example of this device is in Richard Alfred Davenport's *Life of Ali Pasha,* published in London in 1878.

> The Europeans, having no connection except with two of the Ottoman pashas, have been struck by the ferocity of those monsters; I allude to Djez-

[34] Bellaire 1805, 425.
[35] White 1991.

zar and Ali. It is believed that those two pashas were the most remarkable for their tyrannical proceedings and their crimes; but if Europe had known the other Turkish governors, it would not have considered those two tyrants as exceptions. What would it have said of the vizier who was surnamed Kih Pasha, or the Stifler, from the pleasure which he took in strangling his victims? or of another, called Bekir who, when he condemned an unfortunate being, used to say to his sanguinary satellites, "Take away that dog, and give him a good lesson." The lesson was always death. A third pasha was called Cujudzy, because he ordered to be thrown into a well the victims who incurred his resentment. Haki Pasha, a governor of European Turkey, under the reign of Selim, always breakfasted in a turret of his palace, and this was the time that he chose for having brought before him, to be executed, the persons whom he had doomed to death. The Pasha of Widdin, Afiz Ali, having defeated some mahometan rebels, ordered their heads to be put into a sack, to be sent, with a letter, to the reigning sultan. By mistake the secretary stated in the letter a larger number of heads than the sack contained. He prepared to correct his error by recopying the letter; the pasha, however, simplified the operation. He ordered his officers to go through the streets, and kill men enough to make up the number which was mentioned in the letter. He was punctually obeyed; his officers murdered forty Christians, the first who came their way, and thus the sack was filled and sent off to the Porte. Such is the conduct of the provincial governors.[36]

We are told nothing of these other pashas (where did they rule? when did they live?), and their inclusion in Davenport's account—a work confined to Ali—is an irrelevant digression. By dressing them up, however, to appear to be a point of reference for Ali, Davenport justifies the inclusion of a long laundry list of horrifying and titillating tales of the random atrocities and perverse tastes of a host of Oriental tyrants.

The same device is at work when Leake describes a personal conversation he claims to have had with Ali during one of his numerous visits to Ioannina. The two men, by Leake's account, were discussing Demir Aga, the chieftain of Gardiki and a good friend of Ali. Ali, it seems, was particularly impressed with Demir's nearly total control over the inhabitants of his territories.

Leake's authorial commentary on this conversation is typical of this genre of "observation" of the East: "Aly [says of Demir that he] now has a Jew in prison at Joannina, from whom he has already extracted one hundred and forty purses, by threatening him with the loss of his head. *But this mode of refreshing a treasury is no novelty in any part of the east.*"[37] Leake's editorial comment serves three functions: It establishes his authority as a specialist of the East; it satisfies the Western reader's expecta-

---

[36] Davenport 1878, 36–37 n.
[37] Leake 1835, 1:62. The emphasis is mine.

tion of hearing gory anecdotes about cruel Eastern potentates; and it provides the illusion that Leake is a modern, relativistic observer who knows better than to judge the East by the mores of his own Western viewpoint. The last is a function served by much of the commentary of Ali's Western biographers.

Broughton was one of the more "enlightened" observers of Ali, and his account is full of references to cultural relativism. Having judged Ali's wartime behavior to be particularly brutal, for example, Broughton self-mockingly observes, "Voilà comme on juge de tout quand on n'est pas sorti de son pays."

His very stance as a cultural relativist, however, reveals his assumptions about the Oriental cultural milieu. Having somewhat priggishly observed that Ali's wartime atrocities are "too bloody and too brutal to pollute a Christian page," Broughton goes on to admonish his reader: "It is not fair to appreciate the merits of any man without a reference to the character and customs of the people amongst whom he is born and educated."[38] Life in Turkey, he explains, is so very cheap that brutality is to be attributed not to "singular depravity in an individual" but rather to "conformity with general practice and habits."[39] Even a practice as shocking as that of tying women in sacks and drowning them in a lake (something Ali is said to have done on numerous occasions) is explained as a cultural habit rather than a personal cruelty.[40] In short, depravity is not an individual peculiarity but a national trait.

Broughton is able simultaneously to expose Ali's moral depravity and to make a claim for his own cultural sensitivity.[41] The "open-minded" cultural relativism of the observer requires the otherwise irrelevant inclusion of anecdotes about Ali's cruelty and atrocity. Thus "open-mindedness" serves as an excuse for the inclusion of gratuitous, titillating stories of Ali's exploits. Note, for instance, Broughton's account of his initial entry into Ioannina.

> As we passed a large tree on our left, opposite a butcher's shop, I saw something hanging from the boughs, which at a little distance seemed to be meat exposed for sale; but on coming nearer I suddenly discovered it to be a man's arm, with part of the side torn from the body, and hanging by a bit of string tied round one of the fingers. We learnt that the arm was part of a robber who had been beheaded five days before, and whose remaining quarters were

---

[38] Broughton 1855, 1:109.

[39] Ibid. 1855, 1:110.

[40] Ibid. 1855, 1:110.

[41] Broughton, in particular, is full of forward-thinking, "enlightened" statements. See, for instance, his observation that the habits of the Turks have succeeded entirely in destroying "the natural equality of the sexes" (Broughton 1855, 1:137). This is one of many examples.

exposed in other parts of Ioannina. [But it must be said] that not fifty years [ago one] might have seen not dissimilar things passing through Temple Bar of England.[42]

Leake, another daringly forward-looking Englishman, provides another example of this culturally relativistic dynamic at work. "Scarcely any two persons agree," writes Leake, "as to the number of female children which Aly has had, but it is generally believed that several have been put to death." He immediately goes on, however, to excuse this behavior: "If the life of a man is worth little in the east, it is difficult to conceive how much more strongly this remark applies to the female sex."[43] In this case, the inclusion of what Leake himself acknowledges is hearsay provides an opportunity for him both to reiterate the moral depravity of the east and to present himself as worldly and contemporary.

Similarly, writing of the practices of the so-called *skipetars* (the Albanian warrior class of which Ali was a member), Plomer avers: "They were much given to homosexual practices, and were quite uninhibited about them." Lest the reader be shocked, however, Plomer didactically continues: "Parallels to this can easily be found amongst other races in various ages, living a formalized or stylized military life, keeping women in subjection or at least in the background, and having always before them as an image of perfection the young warrior."[44]

Thus the Orientalist appetite for titillation is often masked behind a facade of open-mindedness and sensitivity to cultural difference. It is critical to note that one of the most potent features of this type of culturally relativistic stance is that it enables its employer (for our purposes, the Western biographer) simultaneously to appear open-minded *and* to retain, indeed, corroborate, long-held assumptions about the Orient. The biographer may in the same breath provide the explanation for his protagonists' behavior (thereby in some way excusing it) and condemn the entire culture that has produced it. In short, this form of cultural relativism guarantees that the behavior of an individual can be excused only through indictment of his entire nation.

[42] Broughton 1855, 1:45.
[43] Leake 1835, 4:226–27.
[44] Plomer 1970, 28.

NINE

ORIENTALIST THEMES

JUST AS contemporary Western accounts of Ali are linked by a stance of authorial open-mindedness and a belief in a readily identifiable, quasi-genetic Ottoman "type," so too are they joined by the fact that they all share a number of themes or tropes repeated with near formulaic predictability. These themes are developed through the endless repetition of various key vignettes in Ali's life, episodes that may not be significant from a purely narrative, biographical point of view but that are essential in creating a general mood, in fleshing out the basic realities that are understood to undergird Ali's life and character.

The clearly identifiable themes that characterize the European accounts of Ali's life both inform the writing of his history and emerge from it. Even as Ali is portrayed as shockingly other, he is also paradoxically described much as we would expect him to be described. All of the central themes describing Ali's character and physical person are attributes that can be seen as the inverse of what, according to the Western point of view, is ideal. Where the authors of these texts value heterosexual manliness, rational thought, and Christian morality and charity, Ali is described as being given to homosexual behavior, illogical in the extreme, cruelly avaricious, religiously and morally bankrupt, and depraved.

The Feminization of Ali

At the same time as Ali is portrayed as bellicose, fearless, and cruel, the European biographical literature concerning him is full of references to his feminine characteristics, his dubious sexual orientation, and his overweening attachments to his mother and his sister. Just as Ali is painted with characteristics that are the inverse of the ideals for his gender, so is his mother, Kamko, characterized with traits regarded as traditionally male. We have seen Davenport's observation that Kamko was less human being than "incarnate fiend"; other biographers portray her in similarly overbearing, distinctly nonmaternal, and antifeminine terms.

The stage for the feminization of Ali is set with the occurrence of events that also are held to be responsible for his becoming a "true man" and "warrior," namely, the premature death of his father and subsequent need for the young Ali to strike out on his own and provide for his mother and his sister, Shainitza. The general points of the story are as follows: Ali's father, Veli, originally from Tebelen in Albania,[1] was at the head of a group of bandits based in the nearby town of Kormovo, from whence he and his followers waged an active campaign of brigandry throughout the surrounding countryside. Veli's father, Muktar, upon his death left a small patrimony with an annual income, which, while a fair sum of money, was nevertheless insufficient to maintain the rank of bey, a rank requiring the hire and maintenance of armed followers, horses, and the like.

Veli, the son of a slave, was ousted by his brothers Salek and Mehmet (born to Muktar's wife), despite the fact that under the law he too was a rightful heir. Jealous of his elder brothers' inheritance and good fortune back in Tebelen, Veli returned, at the head of his band, to his natal village, where he assassinated his brothers, thus gaining what he thought was his rightful share of the family's wealth.[2] Not satisfied with pecuniary reward alone, Veli went on, through elaborate and cunning intrigue, to lead the inhabitants of Kormovo to storm Tebelen and to kill his cousin Islam, then vice-governor of Tebelen.[3] As a result, Veli took the vacant vice-gubernatorial post and was awarded the title of pasha by the Ottoman Porte. There, however, it seems he reached his peak, for chroniclers indicate that he died poor, murdered by his enemies, in or about 1764.[4] Just how poor he really was is debatble; however, Ali's biographers were much invested in his being poor, as it constituted an important part of what is best termed his "mythic identity," allowing for the inclusion of the exciting tale of young Ali's discovery of a hidden cache of gold coins. This event, contested by Pouqueville but included by Vaudoncourt, is interpreted as providing the foundation for Ali's whole career, for it was with this unexpected windfall that he is said to have been able to hire his first band of soldiers.[5]

Regardless of the veracity of the reports of his later discovery of gold, upon his father's death Ali found himself poor and suddenly expected to provide for his widowed mother and his sister. He was then between the ages of nine and fifteen. (Again, accounts make much of his extreme youth at the time of Veli's death but are unclear as to the date of his birth.) The difficulties of Ali's task were magnified by the fact that Veli's brigandry and ruthlessness had earned his family many enemies, as well as by the claims to title and inheritance made by his step-brothers and sisters, the offspring of an earlier marriage of Veli's.

Finding the hostility of the residents of Tebelen, many of whom still

---

[1] Variously Tebelen, Tepelen, Tepeleni, Tebeleni, and other variants.

[2] In his usual deadpan style, Davenport referred to this episode as Veli's great "fratricidal triumph" (Davenport 1878, 23).

[3] BA, Cevdet Tasnifi, Zaptiye, 1102.

[4] BA, Cevdet Tasnifi, Dahiliye, 14418.

[5] Davenport 1837, 35.

Fig. 4. Ali Bey Discovers the Chest of Treasures Near the Ruins of an Old Monastery in the Mountain

sided with the survivors of Veli's cousin Islam, overly unpleasant, Kamko installed herself at the head of Veli's band of followers and led them in a new series of campaigns of banditry and theft. Following her husband's example, Kamko now incited the Kormovites to march once again on the town of Tebelen; Islam's widow and his survivors were killed in this raid.

. . . . .

Before continuing with this tale and examining its specifics as they pertain to Ali, I would like to analyze some of the more general features of the vignette, particularly how they depict Kamko. Initially most striking, perhaps, both to today's reader and to the contemporary reader of Broughton or Leake is the fact that the story of Ali's father's death is in some way predictable; that is, several of its features are almost standard in the genre. The features of the story, in fact, read like a fairy tale by the brothers Grimm: an evil stepmother, penniless orphans, feuding villagers, family vendettas. (Indeed, each of these standard features is present not just in the tales of Ali's early childhood but also of the childhood of Veli.) In the more elaborate accounts, we even read of the torching of Islam's home, of the *Frankenstein*-like immolation of his town by angry villagers. Thus, the story is exotic and alien, but also somehow predictable and familiar. This paradox of simultaneous proximity to and distance from the subject matter, as mentioned, is a common theme in Western biographical writings on Ali. The tales of both Veli's and Ali's early childhood provide one example of it.

A second standard feature or theme of the biographies of Ali and Kamko is a sort of gender reversal, whereby Kamko's abnormal and inhumane aspect is illustrated by her propensity for fierce, cruel, and man-like behavior, whereas Ali's deviance resides in part in behaviors thought to be effeminate or peculiar for his gender. For instance, Ali is typically described as having "fine" or "delicate" features. As Plomer puts it: "Ali at twenty was irresistible, handsome, with long fair hair and blue eyes, full of fire and charm, intelligent, graceful and talkative. He was not very tall, but finely made."[6] Similarly, Lord Byron, in his epic poem *Childe Harold's Pilgrimage*, writes of Ali's face as peculiarly gentle, belying the violence of which he was capable:

> In marble-paved pavilion, where a spring
> Of living water from the centre rose,
> Whose bubbling did a genial freshness fling,
> And soft voluptuous couches breathed repose,
> ALI reclined, a man of war and woes:

[6] Plomer 1970, 34.

Yet in his lineaments ye cannot trace,
While Gentleness her milder radiance throws
Along that aged venerable face,
The deeds that lurk beneath, and stain him with disgrace.[7]

His cruelties are belied by the female face of "Gentleness," by the mild lines of his face, and by the soft, voluptuous setting in which he is depicted. Ali is thus portrayed in both masculine and feminine terms.

We see another, and far less subtle, example of this gender reversal or blurring in the case of Kamko. With the death of her husband, Kamko is reborn, as it were, as a man: she comes out of the harem, takes up the band of followers left behind by Veli, and assumes his role as brigand leader. Davenport's biography is explicit about the effect Veli's death had on his widow:

> Khamko was not a mere theorist; she had courage enough to execute any plan which her interest or her feelings could suggest. During the life-time of her husband, she gave, indeed, no signs of being qualified to act the part of a heroine; but no sooner were his eyes closed in death than her latent spirit blazed forth. Far from being intimidated by the calamitous circumstances in which she was placed, she not only resolved to stem the torrent of ill fortune which threatened to overwhelm her, but also, hopeless as the design might seem, to restore her family to its pristine splendour. Abandoning at once the habits of her sex, she threw aside the distaff and the veil, and appeared in arms. With an Amazonian spirit, she put herself at the head of her late husband's remaining followers, and she is said not even to have spared personal blandishments and favours, to increase the number of her partisans.[8]

With the death of her husband Kamko takes off her veil and the modesty it implies and embarks on a life of promiscuity, weaponry, and war.

On this topic most remarkable perhaps is the 1978 biography of Ali by Tasos Vournas, *Ale Pasas Tepelenles: Tuyrannos e idiofues politikos (Ali Pasha of Tebelen: Tyrant or skilled politician?)*. Vournas describes Kamko in exclusively masculine terms: "To his mother Ali owes all of his physical and psychic qualifications. This obstinate Albanian woman, really a man-woman, who lived an intense and powerful life . . . [had] a strong and inflexible character, and the soul of a man in a female body, attractive to men, and spread her influence far beyond the realm of her household."[9]

Even accounts of Kamko's death contain by way of subtext the implication that she was not truly female, that she was in some fundamental

---

[7] Canto 2, verse 62, lines 550–559.
[8] Davenport 1878, 27–28.
[9] Vournas 1978, 13–14.

way more man than woman: she is said to have met her death at the hands of a combination of "hydrothorax" (an ill-defined condition of the chest) and uterine cancer.[10] Even in death the markers of her femininity were destroyed.

Why is this masculine, defeminized depiction of Kamko so central to all accounts of Ali's life? Kamko is a satisfying character in the context of Western biographies of Ali because she provides a vivid and horrifying example of the inverted, twisted nature of the oriental. She is, as we have seen, variously described as subhuman, superhuman, a monster, a fiend; *always*, however, she is distinctly masculine. She is the inverse of all that a woman is expected to be. She is not nurturing, but rather a bloodsucking monster; she does not tend to her home, but rather goes out into the world, into the realm of men, to plunder and kill and fight.

Although Kamko was, indeed, by all accounts (including Ali's[11]) a formidable personage, this fact alone does not satisfactorily account for her central place in biographies of Ali. She is of vital interest to Ali's Western biographers because she corroborates the general sense of the otherness of the Oriental, and she does so in no uncertain terms. Moreover, this corroboration is accomplished not just in the depiction of her as the inverse of her true gender, but also in the fact that she makes her son the opposite of what he should be. One of Kamko's most central functions in the biographies is that of domineering, emasculating bully vis-à-vis her son. Ali's dubious sexuality is explained, in part, by his "dysfunctional" relationship with his mother. As a result there is an anachronistically Freudian element in these stories, as if Ali's earliest biographers gropingly realized that they would find in his childhood an explanation for the peculiarities of his adulthood.

· · · · ·

The feminization of Ali at the hands of Kamko begins in earnest immediately following the death of Veli and Kamko's subsequent "rebirth" as a manlike warrior.

Shortly after her triumph over Tebelen, Kamko's two stepchildren died,[12] and she was left with the responsibility only for Ali and Shainitza.

---

[10] Davenport 1878, 50ff.

[11] The French consul Pouqueville, stationed for several years in Ioannina (and ultimately imprisoned there by Ali), reports that Ali once told him that he owed all that he had to his mother, and that she had "twice given him life"—once at his birth and once when he became vizier.

[12] Plomer writes: "Her two stepchildren now died suddenly within a short time of each other, and it was said, no doubt on excellent authority, that she had poisoned them" (Plomer 1970, 32).

With an eye to defending them and the family's interests, she launched a series of raids on the towns of her district. Kamko's initial success after the death of her husband, however, rapidly gave way to failure. The Kormovites, who at first had sided with her against Tebelen, turned against her. So too did the town of Gardiki, which was able, by way of feigning alliance with Kamko, to take her and her daughter prisoner.

The repercussions of this event were to be long-lasting indeed. While under the control of the Gardikiotes, Kamko, by most accounts, was repeatedly raped by male villagers and spent the better part of what remained of her life attempting to avenge herself on the Kormovites and Gardikiotes for this wrong.[13]

Ali was to be the instrument for Kamko's revenge. All chronicles agree: no sooner was Kamko released from her torment at the hands of the Gardiokiotes than she began urging Ali to rectify the wrong.[14] She viewed his initial failure as evidence of his effeminacy and impotence. Just as upon her husband's death (in Davenport's account) Kamko "threw aside" the distaff (casting off her femininity), now she told Ali to "take [it] up" (to take on the signifiers of femininity). This precise image—of Ali being told to spin, like a girl—was so evocative to his biographers that some version of it is included in virtually all accounts of Ali's early life. All the accounts are explicit in their sexual implications. Here I provide only a few examples.

The Hungarian novelist Mór Jókai published his *Janicsarok Vegnapjai* in 1853. In chapter 7 ("The Albanian Family"), Jókai provides a fictionalized biography of Ali's early relationship with Kamko. By Jókai's account, Ali, after his father's death, set about plundering the countryside to provide for his mother and sister. "And whenever he returned home without money," recounts Jókai, "his mother, Kamko, would rail upon and chide him, and let him have no peace until he had engaged in fresh and more lucrative robberies."[15] Ali, as Jókai has it, was so unsuccessful that he had to sell his sword for the paltry sum of ten sequins in order to obtain some money for his demanding mother.

> When Dame Khamko saw her son return home disarmed she was greatly incensed and exclaimed:
> "What hast thou done with thy sword?"
> "I have sold it," answered Ali, resolutely.
> At this the mother flew into a violent rage, and, catching up a bludgeon,

[13] For one of the earliest accounts of Kamko's suffering at the hands of the Gardikiotes, see Leake 1835, 1:29.

[14] By Pouqueville's account, Kamko was ransomed for a vast sum by a sympathetic Greek merchant in Argyrocastro who had heard of her plight (Davenport 1878, 29).

[15] This and the following passages are from R. Nisbet Bain's 1898 translation (Jókai 1898, 107ff.).

belabored Ali with it until she was tired. The big, muscular lad allowed himself to be beaten, and neither wept nor said a word, nor even tried to defend himself.

"And now dost see that spindle?" cried Dame Khamko. "Learn to spin the thread and turn the bobbins quickly; thou shalt not eat idle bread at home, I can tell thee. A man who can sell his sword is fit for nothing but to sit beside a distaff."

So Ali sat down to spin.[16]

It does not take a Freudian analyst to recognize the semiotic implications of Jókai's account. As punishment for giving up his sword—the signifier of warriorlike, manly behavior (not to mention its obvious possibilities as a phallic symbol)—Ali is told to take up the distaff—the signifier of femininity. The word *distaff* means not just the specific object, the staff used for holding flax or wool in spinning, but also women's work in general, or the female domain. Indeed, it can also refer to women in general, and, until the middle of this century, it was used attributively, as in the expression "the distaff side," namely, the female branch of a family. These meanings and their implication would most certainly not have been lost on the readers of the English translation of Jókai's novel.

Distaff, too, is the word of choice in Davenport's 1878 biography of Ali. In the opening pages of his work, Davenport describes one of Ali's early, unsuccessful raids on the Kormovites. Having met fierce resistance in Kormovo, Ali returned home to Kamko, who sat eagerly awaiting the news of her revenge. Ali instead told her that he had failed. "Stung to the heart by the disappointment of her hopes, and by the shame which he had brought upon himself, his mother met him with the bitterest of reproaches and invectives. Holding out her distaff to him, she furiously exclaimed, 'Go, coward! go and spin with the women of the harem; it is a trade which suits thee far better than that of arms.'"[17] What Jókai left implicit Davenport made explicit: Ali is more suited to the company and practices of women than of men.

This image of the emasculated Ali was still popular half a century later, when Plomer, too, made the spinning episode central to his account of Ali's childhood: "Khamko was furious and told him that he would be better employed with a distaff than a gun, and that the proper place for such a cissy [*sic*] was in the harem."[18] Plomer's depiction is the most direct of all, and it puts into contemporary parlance the gist of all of Ali's biographies: Ali was bullied by his mother, treated like a sissy, and emasculated because of his failure to avenge her rape.

[16] Jókai 1890, 107–8.
[17] Davenport 1878, 31.
[18] Plomer 1970, 33–34.

Fig. 5. The Youthful Ali Bey, Shewn by his Mother to the Partisans and Vassals of his Father's House

This basic tale, told over and over again by all of Ali's chroniclers, is significant in that it lays the groundwork for much of the later discussion on his sexual appetites and proclivities and for his penchant for cruelty. Most important, it dovetails with accounts of Ali's later supposed homosexual tendencies—homosexuality representing, in Ali's Western biographies, the logical outcome of gender-inverted behavior. Just as the young Ali used a distaff (like a woman), so too, write his biographers, did he in later life sleep with men (like a woman). Ronald Inden has written of the historiographic tendency of Indologists to conceive of the object of their study as being somehow feminine.[19] This strategy of feminization is nothing other than a means of robbing the studied object of power, a means, quite literally, of emasculating it.[20]

This strategy is clearly at work in all Western accounts of Ali. We have seen that his early boyhood is depicted as a series of humiliations and feminizations suffered at the hands of his man-woman mother, Kamko. This strategy of disempowerment continues with the gratuitous (and purely speculative) discussion of Ali's sexual "perversities."

Interesting, but perhaps not surprising, is the fact that the only biography lacking any such characterizations of Ali and his mother is also the only non-Western biography. Ahmet Moufit's 1903 *Tepedelenli Ali Pasas, 1744–1822*,[21] published in Turkish in Istanbul in 1903, makes no reference to either Kamko's masculinity or to her son's feminine qualities.[22]

. . . . .

All of Ali's biographers imply that his habit of maintaining a huge harem of women was a mere tip of the hat to the conventions of his day, and that in reality he found the company of young men infinitely preferable. Vaudoncourt, for instance, wrote that "he is almost exclusively given up to Socratic pleasures, and for this purpose keeps up a seraglio of youths, from among whom he selects his confidants, and even his principal officers, he had five or six hundred women in his harem."[23]

The fascination with Ali's sexual proclivities is part of the broader concern with his sensual appetites. His perversity and otherness resided in part, according to his biographers, in his complete lack of self-restraint. As an English physician who once attended Ali in Ioannina wrote of him, "In the gratification of his depraved appetites, Ali Pasha, of all modern

[19] Inden 1990, 122ff.
[20] Lewis 1996; Grewal 1996; Gikandi 1996; Morgan 1996; Phillips 1997; Mills 1991; Lowe 1991.
[21] Moufit A. H. 1324.
[22] Moufid was a descendant of Ali's sister, Shainitza.
[23] Cited in Plomer (1970, 79).

sensualists the most sensual, exceeded whatever the most *impure imagination can conceive*, whether it may have drawn its sullied stores from scenes of high-varnished debauchery, or from the obscurely tinted perspective of the low haunts of infamy and vice."[24]

In his biography of Ali, M. Gabriel Remerand writes: "Ce qui frappait en effet chez Ali Pacha, c'etait la violence de ses passions";[25] he also comments on Ali's inability to control himself when angry: "Il était cependant incapable de dominer sa colère qui se manifestait par une contraction violente de ses traits et qui éclatait en de térribles explosions de fureur."[26]

The French infantry captain Bellaire, in his account of French military activities in the Ionian Islands, also takes the time to hint at Ali's sexual appetites and salaciousness. Describing a meeting between the French representative Scheffer and Ali (which, by the way, Bellaire did not personally witness), Bellaire writes that Ali several times during the meeting went over to a carved screen, which comprised one wall of the conference room, and peeked through it at the women of his harem, so incapable was he of preventing his sexual appetites from intruding into his business affairs.[27]

Moral and Religious Depravity

A second major theme of Western biographies of Ali is the lax and hypocritical religious observances of the Muslims in general and of Ali specifically. This, too, is an intimate component of the West's strategy of biographically Othering and disempowering Ali. This portrayal of Ali is a double-edged sword: First, Ali is suspect by dint of his being a Muslim (Islam being, of course, nothing more than a depraved form of Christianity); second, he is guilty for not showing appropriate respect for his religion.

The general picture that emerges is of someone largely indifferent to matters of religion. We read repeatedly, for instance, of the fact that he made no programmatic attempt to persecute the Orthodox populations of his land on the basis of their religious belief. On the contrary, it seems clear that Ali was given to treating the Orthodox in a privileged fashion, as they were central to the trade of his region and thus to his personal prosperity and that of his capital. Leake, for instance, tells the story of a traveling dervish who complained of the favored status of the Greeks in Ioannina and urged Ali to restrict the Greeks at least in their dress.[28] Sim-

---

[24] Ibid., 80.
[25] Remerand 1928, 92.
[26] Ibid.
[27] Bellaire 1805, 24.
[28] Leake 1835, 4:494ff.

ilarly, numerous accounts in the travel literature on Ali note the relatively healthy status of the churches and church education within his territories. Churches, we learn, were converted into mosques only as punishment for specific acts of rebellion, as in the case of the Souliote villages, whose inhabitants were in an ongoing state of insurrection against Ali. Ali had a policy of persecution only insofar as it corresponded to his program for personal financial gain.

Leake tells us that the favorite in Ali's harem was a Christian Albanian from near Tebelen: "She is still a Christian, and allowed to have her chapel, and service performed by a papas in the palace. Indeed, [Ali] never troubles himself to make religious converts of either sex; on the contrary, it is more common to see boys who are brought up in the serai in his service, reading and writing with the Greek papas than with the Turkish hodja. Nor has Ali ever deprived any of the higher class of Greeks of their daughters."[29]

Ironically, Ali's leniency is often presented not as a policy of tolerance for Christianity but as an indication of his own depravity qua Muslim. Moreover, when Ali does seem to act in a fashion that would perhaps indicate that he did possess some religious sensibility or reverence, his behavior is described not as pious or religious but as "superstitious." M. Gabriel Remerand, for example, writes of Ali that "superstitieux a l'extrême, il ne tentait d'ailleurs en temps ordinaire aucune enterprise sans consulter devins et derviches; il leur faisait interpréter ses songes et accordait a leurs explications une créance qui déterminait souvent le sens de ses actions."[30]

Leake is particularly snide in his commentary on the religion of the Albanian Muslims in general and of Ali in specific. He writes of "how little the Musulman Albanians care for the ceremonies or doctrines of their religion."[31] He makes much of the fact that Ali drank wine openly. He also deprecatingly comments that the fast of Ramadan represented no real hardship, particularly in the winter months, when it got dark so early and dawn broke so late that there were only a few hours during which the prohibitions against food and drink were in effect.[32]

Broughton's description of the Ramadan he spent in Ali's company goes even further, delineating the fasting season as one not of privation and spiritual concentration but of merriment:

> [The beginning of Ramadan] was hailed, at the rising of the new moon on the evening of the 8th [of October], by every demonstration of joy: pistols

---

[29] Ibid. 4:225.
[30] Remerand 1928, 100.
[31] Leake 1835, 1:36.
[32] Ibid., 37.

and guns were discharged in every quarter of the city. The Turks continued
firing long enough to exhaust their cartridge-pouches; and as they used balls,
according to custom, the Greek inhabitants closed their window-shutters
and remained at home; a precaution very necessary, for two bullets passed
within a very audible distance of our host's gallery. The minarets of all the
moscks were illuminated, and everything seemed to show that the ap-
proaching season was not considered as one of penance, but devoted to merriment. In truth, although during this month the strictest abstinence, even
from tobacco and coffee, is observed in the daytime, yet with the setting of
the sun the feasting commences, and a small repast is served, then it is
the time for paying and receiving visits, and for the amusements of Turkey,
puppet-shows, jugglers, dancers, and story-tellers. At one o'clock in the
morning, after prayers, the dinner commences, and the carousal lasts till day-
break, when the Turks retire to rest, and do not rise till mid-day.[33]

By Broughton's account, Ramadan is in Ali's lands entirely bereft of religious or spiritual content, and its ersatz privations merely serve as a foil
for revelry and all-night "carousal." Likewise, the fast of Ramadan is
often portrayed as a feeble, and far less reverential, equivalent of Lent.

It is unclear just what Ali's religious beliefs really were. Reading between the lines, it seems evident that he was somewhat casual in his approach to Islam. By numerous accounts, he did indeed drink wine, although in moderation, and he observed fasting in only the most nominal
ways. Broughton, who was present with Ali in Tebelen for the month of
Ramadan in 1809, which that year corresponded with October on the
Gregorian calendar, tells us that Ali did keep a fast for the month; but he
is also quick to point out the relative laxity of the Albanians as compared
with the Turks when it came to the observances of Islam.[34] The fact that
at the time of this observation Ali was in his hometown of Tebelen rather
than in the more cosmopolitan capital of Ioannina also mitigates somewhat against the assumption that the keeping of Ramadan represented
true seriousness of religious belief; more than one traveler commented
that Ali tended to be more conservative in his religious practices when visiting the Albanian territories of his youth.[35]

Insofar as he considered himself a Muslim, he seems to have been most
attracted to the Bektashi order, and there are repeated references to his
patronage of mendicant sufis. There are several accounts of his endowing
a Bektashi *tekkeh* (lodge) in Tríkkala, and he had lodgings built in several

---

[33] Broughton 1855, 1:66.

[34] Ibid., 94.

[35] Leake 1835, 1:36. This is a reference to the fact that when among his native Toskhides
and Liapidhes, Ali tried to set a good example and hide from the people the fact that he
drank wine.

towns in his dominions for visiting dervishes and *shaykh*s. Ahmed Moufit writes that his direct ancestors included a Mevlevi dervish by the name of Nazif.[36]

Biographies commissioned by Ali or written by Turks tend to make the most of his religious belief, as in the versicular work of Hadji Seret, who formalistically conceives of Ali's war against the Souliotes as a religious one, referring to the Orthodox rebels as the "Din Düşman" (enemies of the faith).[37] (There seems, however, to be no indication that the war between Ali and the Souliotes marked anything more than a personal vendetta on the part of Ali, to whom the territories of Souli held no importance but whose ongoing refusal to submit to his rule galled him. He had no particular interest in the Souliotes as Christians, and in fact it can be argued that he ought, culturally, to have favored them as being, like himself, of Albanian rather than Greek, Vlach, or Turkish descent.)

Henry Holland reports that Ali was interested in "the philosopher's stone and the elixir vitae,"[38] and Ibrahim Manzur Effendi writes of Ali's devotion, in the later years of his life, to a mendicant Persian mystic (Cheik Ali), who spent a good deal of time at Ali's court, died in Ioannina, and to whom Ali erected an extravagant marble mausoleum.[39] Broughton reports that at the time of his visit to Ioannina, Ali was entertaining several mendicant dervishes in his court. All accounts are unanimous in their portrayal of Ali as the foolish dupe of superstitious nonsense peddled by opportunistic charlatans. Even the courtier Ibrahim Manzur Effendi is disparaging in his portrayal of Ali's devotion to these mystics, and describes Ali's sycophancy in the presence of the aforementioned Cheik Ali.[40]

·   ·   ·   ·   ·

Ali cannot win. On one hand, he is criticized for not being religious enough and is only grudgingly granted any religious sensibilities while his beliefs are seen as superstitious silliness. On the other hand, when Ali is portrayed as religious, his beliefs are debunked as opportunistic or politically expedient. Leake writes of the Bektashi order:

> It is their doctrine to be liberal towards all professions and religions, and to consider all men as equal in the eyes of God. . . . The Vezir, although no prac-

[36] Skiotis 1971, 225 n. 3.
[37] Hadji Seret, National Library of Greece.
[38] Holland 1815.
[39] Ibrahim Manzur Effendi 1827.
[40] Again, I must note that Ibrahim Manzur Effendi, although one of Ali's courtiers, was European. Only when he came into the employ of Ali did he exchange his native name—Samson Cerfbeer de Medelsheim—for a Muslim one. This, however, is not certain. The true identity of Manzur Effendi is debated. He seems to have been the Frenchman Bessieres but may have been de Medelsheim.

tical encourager of liberty and equality, finds the religious doctrines of the Bektashli exactly suited to him . . . it was an observation of the bishop of Trikkala, that Aly takes from everybody and gives only to the dervises [*sic*], whom he undoubtedly finds politically useful. In fact, there is no place in Greece where in consequence of this encouragement these wandering or mendicant Musulman monks are so numerous and insolent as at Ioannina.[41]

Philhellenism and Orientalism

In order to understand the motivation behind this consistent denigration of Islam in general and Ali's religious belief in particular, it is important to note that Western travelogues and biographies of Ali are not just critical of the religious status of the Muslims they describe but also portray the Greek Orthodox as similarly impure, superstitious, and depraved.

The "Turks" (a designation that includes Ali, his Albanian origins notwithstanding) are compared with the West and found lacking; the Greeks of today are compared with the Greeks of yesteryear and are found lacking. The comparison in the Oriental instance is one of geography, of the Orient vis-à-vis the West, whereas the comparison in the Greek instance is one of chronology.

Implicit, then, is the algebraic equation of the Greeks of yesteryear with the Europeans of today. The Greek Orthodox and the Muslims are, to put it bluntly, tarred with the same brush. As Broughton somewhat startlingly writes, "The Greeks, taken collectively, cannot, in fact, be so properly called an individual people, as a religious sect dissenting from the established church of the Ottoman Empire."[42] Indeed, the descriptions we have of the religious practices of the Greek Orthodox citizenry of Ali's lands bear no small resemblance to those of the Muslims. Leake, for instance, writes of the Greeks' "superstitious practices," describing their use of amulets and charms, their belief in vampires, and their habit of sewing bones to the forelegs of sheep so as to ward off evil spirits.[43] Their faith is typically described as "corrupted" and its practitioners as lacking in education.[44]

The root impulse behind much of the Orientalist discourse generated by the European visitors to Ali's lands is indicated by this equation of the Greeks with the Muslims by virtue of their shared, religiously depraved outlook. The travelers who came to Ioannina and the environs did so not

[41] Leake 1835, 4:285.
[42] Broughton 1855, 2:11.
[43] Leake 1835, 4:215ff.
[44] For a powerful argument against dividing "superstition" and "orthodoxy" into different religious categories, see Stewart 1991.

just to see Ali and the Ottoman East, but to search out vestiges of glorious Hellas, considered the fount of European civilization.

Ali's lands were appealing not merely because they were the closest Ottoman territories. They also encompassed some of the Greek classical sites most familiar to the European literary and philosophical imagination. Such well-known classical geographic features as the Oracle of Dodoni and Mount Olympus were encircled by Ali's borders, and the numerous visitors to Ioannina were interested in it not just as Ali's capital but, more important, as the most prosperous city in the core territories of classical Greece.

Ali, then, was seen against the classical history of Epiros rather than of the Ottoman Empire. Davenport, for instance, did not liken Ali to such immediately comparable figures as Mehmet Ali of Egypt but located him in a historical line of Epirotes: "The martial and conquering but magnanimous Pyrrhus, the patriotic and invincible Scanderbeg, and the subtle, treacherous, and sanguinary Ali of Tepeleni."[45]

The implications of Ali's geographic situation and the effect of philhellenism and the Western attitude of the day toward Greece fused in peculiar ways. The paradoxical depiction of religion evidenced by Western travel accounts pertaining to Ali is a prime example. The denigration of the Muslim faith and of Ali's practice of it is a central theme of all Western travel accounts and biographies of Ali. The remarkable assumption on which this portrayal rests is that the Christian West knows better than Ali what is the correct way to be a Muslim. Such too was the Christian West's attitude toward Orthodox strands of Christianity. Both Orthodox Christianity and Islam were criticized as "superstitious" and backward. One British observer of Ali's day wrote of the Ottoman state that "the superstition on which it is founded is stupidly gross and universally present," and decried members of the Islamic religious hierarchy for their belief in "ghosts, genii, and the like."[46] The Greeks, however, are judged little better. Having rhapsodized over their ancient forebears, the same observer states: "Such a nation could not have fallen under the yoke of a Turkish conqueror, had she not been prepared for that disgrace by a long period of debasement and superstition."[47]

The manner in which both the religion of the Greeks and that of Ali and his Albanians are similarly denigrated is a direct result of the structurally identical position they hold, as religions, vis-à-vis the West. Again we would do well to remember the "intimate estrangement" that is a central feature of the Orientalist vision.

Christianity has long regarded Islam as constituting a sort of heretical,

[45] Davenport 1878, 1.
[46] Eton 1798, 121–25.
[47] Ibid., 337.

severely flawed version of itself.[48] Islam's inclusion (interpreted by Christianity as co-opting) of figures central to both Christianity and Judaism (Abraham, Moses, Jesus, and so on) in its list of prophets feeds directly into this attitude. Islam is not wholly other but rather discomfitingly similar in many respects to the primary religious faiths of Europe. This is precisely the relationship between Western forms of Christianity and the Orthodox Christian forms that prevail in the East.

The legacy of the Great Schism has been a long-standing claim on the part of the Western church (in both its Catholic and Protestant denominations) that Greek and Russian Orthodoxy represent a heretical, flawed version of true Christianity. The Greeks were guilty of a form of heresy. Further, with the rise in the late eighteenth and early nineteenth centuries of European philhellenism, the Orthodox Greeks of Ali's lands came to be compared not just with the Christians of Europe but also with the Greeks of old. And again, this represented a category with which the West felt itself to be intimately familiar. Ancient Greece, after all, was thought to be the cradle of Western civilization, and the scholar-travelers who visited Ali's Epiros were well versed in the literature and traditions of the ancient Greeks. The Greeks, then, are, like the Muslims, in a position of double jeopardy: they measure up neither to the imagined standard of classical Hellas nor to the "correct" form of Christianity as practiced in the West.

Thus the simultaneous proximity and distance that Ali represented from a geographic standpoint was perfectly echoed in the relationship between Western European Christianity and both Islam and Orthodoxy. Just as Ali was technically European yet wholly other by dint of his connection to the Ottoman imperial system, so too was he both similar and dissimilar to the West in his (albeit nominal) adherence to Islam, a religion that was at once considered akin to and freakishly different from Christianity.

The circumstances of "intimate estrangement" between the West and the Orient are greatly heightened in the case of Ali, who ruled, after all, within the confines of Europe. There is a second, even more significant difference between the case of Ali and those considered by Said. The literatures on which Said and his successors base their theory invariably have as their backdrop the mechanisms of colonialism and imperialism. Said writes that for the British the Orient was always consummately represented by India, always understood through the experience of colonial possession.[49]

Ali's lands, however, were never under the domination of European

[48] Levonian, 1940; Daniel 1958; Bennett 1992.
[49] Said 1979, 169.

colonial/imperial systems. Whereas many territories of the Ottoman Empire (the Fertile Crescent, for instance, or Egypt) came under French and British control, the territories of mainland Greece did not. Moreover, from the point of view of foreign affairs, Britain's (and to a lesser extent France's and Italy's) experience with Ali was one not of political domination of the Oriental but of insecurity, confusion, and dependence. The sense of domination and control, then, had to derive from some other source for the British.

The source in which Britain and, to a lesser extent, France found a sense of control and superiority over Ali and his lands was philhellenism and the Hellenic Ideal. Olga Augustinos argues that travel literature on Greece is decisively colored by Europe's long-standing claim to the ancient Greek past. "European travel literature on Greece, although it typifies in many respects the approach of Renaissance and post-Renaissance travelers to non-European peoples, has a unique dimension. The links with its classical past, real or imagined, made it seem closer to the West, while its subjugation to Ottoman rule placed it in the penumbra between East and West."[50]

By Ali's time, the Hellenic Ideal had propelled numerous Europeans eastward to Greece. With the texts of Homer and Pausanias as their guides, these travelers hoped to find the places and people about whom they had read so much in the course of their classical education. So literalistic were these travelers in their interpretations of their classical works that several believed they had found the relics of the *Odyssey* and the *Iliad*. The death mask of Agamemnon, Helen's jewelry, Nestor's cup—these and other items were eagerly sought out, and some believed they had found them. Such "discoveries" were met with great excitement. As David Constantine puts it, "It is like the Invention of the True Cross; certainly of that order of excitement."[51]

The result of such fascination with the relics of classical Hellas was that the lands of Greece came to be regarded as a kind of vast, self-service museum, where travelers could see (and, in many instances, take home) the artefacts of the classical past. As Lord Broughton wrote of this European acquisitiveness, "No one likes to pass through such a country without collecting a little."[52] These were not artefacts of just any classical past; they were regarded as an integral part of Europe's own history, for part of the Hellenic Ideal was the belief that ancient Greece was the cradle of all Western civilization. As Percy Bysshe Shelley wrote in his introduction to his lyrical drama *Hellas*, "We are all Greeks." This, then, was the logic whereby Europe "colonized" Greece—by making it if not a physical satellite, then at least an intellectual and ideological one.

---

[50] Augustinos 1994, ix.
[51] Constantine 1984, 92.
[52] Broughton 1855, 1:156.

The travelers to Ali's court, politicians and tourists alike, were all strongly guided by this ideal of Hellenism. Leake's 1824 *Journal of a Tour in Asia Minor*, for instance, was subtitled *With comparative remarks on the ancient and modern geography of that country.* John Cam Hobhouse (Lord Broughton), Henry Holland, William Gell, Edward Dodwell, William Eton, Thomas Smart Hughes—all include numerous and lengthy references to the classics in their travel accounts. All of these travelers were steeped in the notion that they were not just visiting Ali, but were on pilgrimage to lands to which they held some sort of personal claim. Whether they reacted with horror to what they perceived as the degenerate state of the modern Greeks or with joy at the thought of seeing the preserved, surviving features of classical Hellas, these travelers invariably had as their point of reference the Greece they knew through academic study of the classics.

Captain Leake, the British representative in Ali's court, frequently cites Livy, Hesiod, and other ancient sources as he tromps around the countryside. General Bellaire cites Virgil's *Aeneid* as if it were a guidebook: "Bientôt nous perdimes de vue les hautes tours des Phaeciens. Ayant rangé les côtes de l'Épire, nous relachames dans le port de Chaonie, et nous prîmes le chemin de Buthrote."[53] Even those who traveled to Epiros for reasons of modern diplomacy were at least nominally educated in the classics, and their interest in travel in the area was in large part defined by the quest to find the ancient sites.

The classics were also used as a hermeneutic lens through which the practices of the East were made explicable. When, for instance, Leake describes the morning sessions in which members of Ioannina's general populace came to pay obeisance to Ali, he cites for comparison Euripides' account of similar acts of fealty shown to the leaders of yore. Likewise, Leake subscribes to the view, highly popular in academic European circles of his day, that Greek Orthodoxy represented the direct descendant of classical Greek religious practices:

> Many of the churches occupy probably the sites of ancient temples, which, on the establishment of Christianity, were converted to the service of the new religion, with little or no change of structure, although a succession of repairs may now have left in them no vestiges of Hellenic antiquity that can easily be recognized. Nor is it improbable that many of the customs and ceremonies in honour of the protecting saints are the same as those which once appertained to the worship of Dione, Aphrodite, Dionysus, or Apollo.[54]

This, then, is the backdrop against which not just Greece but also its ruler are seen. Ali is not just understood to be a "typical" Oriental, but is

[53] Bellaire 1805, 134.
[54] Leake 1835, 4:84.

seen as the oppressor and abuser of the legacy of ancient Hellas. As for the disappointing incongruity between the imagined Greeks of old and the present-day specimens, many travelers attributed it to the contaminating influence of Ali. Leake, for instance, observes that the Greeks are "all deceitful," claiming that they have no choice but to be so because of Ali's tyrannies. Other incongruous characteristics are likewise attributed to Ali and his oppressive predecessors. "[T]imidity," writes Leake, "is the necessary consequence of the Turkish yoke following long ages of the debasing tyranny and superstition of the Byzantine Empire. But through this unamiable covering the ancient national character continually breaks forth."[55]

Counterparts for Ali were also found in the classical past, and Ali was compared to Greek oppressors and warriors of old. In *Voyage dans la Grèce*, Pouqueville writes of his excitement at going to meet the pasha. "My curiosity was keenly piqued: finally I was going to see a very famous man, a new Theseus, an old warrior covered with scars, a satrap grown white in the craft of war, the modern Pyrrhus of Epirus; I had been told all this."[56]

.   .   .   .   .

The European travelers who visited Ali's lands felt they had a personal claim to the peoples and territories over which he ruled. This sense of intellectual and historical possession compensated for the evident weakness that France and Britain, in particular, felt in relation to Ali's formidable strength, influence, and control over mainland Greece, the Adriatic, and the Aegean. Simultaneous with this, it contributed to the heightened othering of Ali in the texts that these travelers published upon their return home.

The standard orientalist mechanisms by which the object of study is made Other—gender inversion, dehumanization, demonization, and so on—were all the more potent in the case of Ali. His connection to the supposed descendants of classical Hellas—assumed to be noble, honest, democratic, strong of body, and pure of heart—made him, by contrast, appear all the more depraved, deceitful, wily, evil, and despotic. And if the mechanisms of othering became more potent in Ali's case, they were all the more necessary. The lack of any imperial/colonial control over Ali's lands, coupled with his primacy in the region, demanded an alternative basis for a European sense of dominance over him. The romantic ideal of ancient Greece provided Europe with a surrogate imperialism, whereby

[55] Ibid., 1:14.
[56] Pouqueville 1826–27, 1:115.

Ali's lands could be ideologically and philosophically claimed, controlled, and colonized.

The Hellenic Ideal made it possible for Europeans to feel that they "knew" the lands of Greece historically and geographically, that they understood its cultural habits, and that they had a better sense of its true origins than its own inhabitants did. Moreover, this ideal gave the French and English travelers to Ali's court a mechanism that compensated for the political and strategic tenuousness of their own positions by providing a hermeneutic lens through which the people they saw there seemed feeble, degenerate, and ignorant when compared with the glory of ancient Hellas. Finally, since these people—albeit degenerate and much reduced—were, after all, considered the forebears of all Western civilization, their disappointingly nonclassical characteristics somehow had to be excused and explained. Ali provided a ready and easy target for the blame. Linked to the Ottoman regime and the Muslim faith, he was described as the source of all contamination and degeneration of the ideals of ancient Greece. The European travelers who visited his lands were therefore greatly invested in seeing him in the most alien terms possible. Ali *had* to be other, for only in seeing him as such could Europeans fully feel their imagined affinity with Greece.

TEN

ALI'S MANIPULATION OF THE ORIENTALIST IMAGE

DIPLOMATIC MATERIALS dating from the height of Ali's career demonstrate that he was in a position of relative strength vis-à-vis both the French and the British; yet the question of this strategic, and political relationship is ignored in favor of anecdotal accounts describing his childhood, his idiosyncrasies, and his treacheries. And just as the Orientalizing features of the literature on Ali overlook or elide his military and diplomatic successes, so too do they attempt to do away with other manifestations of his growth and self-conscious evolution as a ruler. As Ali attempted, through military and diplomatic strategy, to gain the approbation and admiration of Europe, he deployed symbology in his ongoing shift away from the ideologies of the Ottoman Empire. His dress, his behavior, and the decor of his homes were carefully choreographed to portray him in very specific terms to his European audience.

Just as his efforts in international diplomacy were ignored, so too Ali's more symbolic gestures of interest in the political and social worlds of Western Europe were largely overlooked by his biographers and the anterior travel accounts from which they worked. His attempts to use the political vocabulary and cultural trappings of Europe were consistently dismissed as the tasteless and childish pretensions of a silly and idiosyncratic ruler. Never were they taken seriously as a self-conscious statement of Ali's own understanding of himself as ruler or even as a symbolic image of how he would like to have been seen in the eyes of the West. This represents a major oversight, which is one of the Orientalist tendencies discussed in preceding chapters and has the same aim: to compensate for and elide the structurally weak relationship of Europe vis-à-vis Ali.

There is, however, another layer in the representational relationship governing Western accounts of Ali. The Orientalist view did not merely provide Europe with the means to control and manipulate Ali; it also provided Ali with a way of controlling and manipulating Europe. He was aware of the Western, Orientalist vision of him and used it to his advantage. He understood that the West sought in him verification of its vision of the Orient, and recognized that the Oriental was expected to behave in certain typecast, formulaic ways, and in many cases he acted accordingly. Ali reveled in playing the part of the idiosyncratic, cruel and illogical despot, and staged carefully planned Orientalist vignettes to thrill his visitors and validate their established view of the Orient.

In so doing he managed to divert the attention of Europe from matters he wanted to keep to himself. So long as the focus was on his personal pe-culiarities, the "perversities" of his character, and the idiosyncrasies of his manner, it was less likely that he would be perceived as a viable military competitor and targeted for systematic suppression. He used amusing and colorful behaviors as a shield for the fact that he was secretly negotiating with several powers at the same time. Insofar as his European diplomatic visitors were aware of his multiple—and theoretically mutually exclu-sive—alliances, they attributed it to a general untrustworthiness, illogi-cality, and confusion. They regarded these as evidence not of a threat to European security but of the opposite: Ali was incapable of formulating a clear foreign policy and therefore need not be considered seriously. Such an interpretation was useful to Ali, even if he had to forego the hope of being regarded as the political equal of the rulers of France and England. In short, the Orientalist view of a weak and irrational despot was useful not just to Europe, as a way discursively to establish power over Ali, but also to Ali himself.

There is then in Ali's life a peculiar, ongoing tension between his desire to be held in high, competitive esteem by his Western European neighbors and his realization that it was perhaps in his best interests to be seen as weak, silly, and fundamentally nonthreatening. Ali's manipulation of Ori-entalist descriptions of the Eastern despot demonstrates a remarkable level of self-awareness and represents a very shrewd if inchoate dimension of his foreign policy.

．　．　．　．　．

Ali's territories are typically described as constituting a non-nationalist, autonomous principality.[1] Although his subject populations—the vast majority of whom were Greek—have been noted for their nationalist im-pulses and cultural links to Enlightenment Europe, there is little evidence that Ali conceived of his desire for independence in such terms. The en-tire period of his rule is devoid of any explicit appeals to nationalist group identity, save the most opportunistic and half-hearted one. He was pri-marily interested in holding power *over* his subjects, not in fighting to gain power and freedom *for* a specific group of people. When in the last years of his life he appealed to the Greeks in nationalist terms, claiming to be a member of the Filiki Etairia (friendly society), it is clear that he did so not out of any sense of affinity with them but because he saw that his own success might be entirely contingent on the success of the planned Greek insurrection against the Ottoman Empire.[2] Ali's own sense of group iden-

[1] Hobsbawm 1962, 140.

[2] In the event, the opposite was true: the success of the first outbreak of the Greek War of Independence in 1821 can in large part be attributed to Ali's "insurrection" against the

tity came from the ancient legacy of Albanian banditry and the concomitant pseudo-nobility; any independent state that he envisioned almost certainly would have been dominated by this Albanian military, aristocratic elite.

In historiographic terms, the result of this evident lack of nationalist interest is the assumption that Ali was unaffected by, or, more typically, oblivious of the ideologies undergirding the new political forms taking shape in Europe.[3] Hans Georg Schenk's view of Ali typifies this perspective. "The only thing which the Pasha really learned from the West in general, and France in particular, was absolutism or political centralization."[4] Ali's hopes, according to this view, remained ever internal, concerned with consolidating power within his own borders but largely unconcerned with the world around him. Typical of such depictions is the denigration and underplaying of Ali's status and his identification as nothing more than a broad-based crook. Schenk, for instance, continues: "Under his rule other klephts did not stand much chance, unless they were under the orders of the chief robber [Ali]. And then, having lost their independence, they could be called klephts no longer, nor as yet civil servants."[5]

Ali's sensibilities as ruler do not demonstrate any particular grasp of or interest in the mechanisms of nationalism, yet it is a gross misstatement to write that Ali learned nothing from the West save "absolutism" and "centralization." The observation, in fact, is wrong on several scores. Ali's policy of centralizing power predominated during the first period of his rule, prior to his direct exposure to Europe, when he was consolidating control over various Ottoman provincial territories and was concerned not with European but with Ottoman opposition. Ali did not "learn" absolutism and centralization from the West; in his absolutist and centralizing rule he was merely demonstrating the natural outcome of traditional Albanian tribal politics.

Ali did, however, learn several other tactics from the powers of Europe. The fact that Ali did not turn himself into a constitutional monarch, become an ardent fighter for Albanian nationalism, or explicitly reject the ideology of empire can hardly be taken to mean that he was oblivious of and unaffected by such "new" European concepts as state, democracy, atheism, and constitution. Ali was extremely interested in these features of European culture, and to some extent he shaped himself accordingly.

Porte, which tied up significant Ottoman troops, energy, and attention during the crucial first phases of the Greek movement for independence.

[3] This was quite aside from the question of a *Nations Before Nationalism* sort of argument (Armstrong 1982).

[4] Schenk 1947, 164.

[5] Ibid.

There is a great need to reconsider the years of historiography that have allowed Ali and others like him to stand only as "petty despots," "semi-autonomous satraps," and "backward" Ottoman governors whose insularity leaves them impervious to a broader sociointellectual climate.[6]

This refusal of most historiography to see in Ali any degree of ideological sophistication or any sort of consistent political philosophy was a product first of the European travelers who visited his lands, then of the histories and biographies based on their travel accounts. It is linked to an Orientalist vision that is deeply invested in viewing such regional governors as totalitarian and antidemocratic, in part because such characteristics are the opposite of those with which Europe most liked to describe itself. We have seen how this method of description through inversion is one of the most marked characteristics of Orientalist discourse, and seen it at work in the context of Ali's diplomatic dealings with the West.

The symbolic dimensions of Ali's self-styling as a ruler, too, are diminished through the mechanisms of Orientalism. Although concepts such as symbolism and ideology are far more difficult to document than are diplomatic relations, they are worth more than the fleeting and dismissive attention that Ali's contemporary Western interlocutors granted them.

. . . . .

For several centuries prior to Ali's rise to power Albania had by no means been sheltered from the events in Europe. Of all the various and widespread territories of the Ottoman Empire, Albania enjoyed a particularly close relationship to Western Europe. The first and most obvious reason is the territories' geographic proximity. Perched on the westernmost borders of the empire, the lands of Albania, Epirus and the Morea were closer to France, Malta, and the Italian city-states than they were to their central government in Istanbul. The long tradition of Albanian mercenary activity combined with this geographic closeness to produce a regional population that was relatively cosmopolitan, in many instances bilingual, and well attuned to the shifting alliances of the European powers. Leake, among other contemporary travelers in Ali's lands, noted that at the turn of the eighteenth century virtually all Albanian men spoke Albanian and Greek, as well as at least one European language (French, English, or Italian).[7] Similarly, he reports that almost all Albanian members of Ali's court had done service abroad, and that some continued to receive pensions from the king of Naples, who had a resident in Ioannina.[8] At the turn of

---

[6] Shaw 1988. Historians of Albania, too, portray Ali in this way. See, for example, *Southern Albania: Under the Acroceraunian Mountains* (Baerlein 1968).

[7] Leake 1835, 1:86ff.

[8] Ibid., 100ff.

the century various Khimariote Albanian captains had their own military corps in Naples and would return home periodically to recruit new troops. Economic activity, too, had long been a link between the Balkans and Western Europe. Finally, unlike other Balkan Ottoman territories bordering on Western Europe (Bosnia, for instance), there was a long-standing intellectual relationship between Ioannina and European institutions of learning.

As a result, Ioannina was a highly cosmopolitan milieu and maintained direct access through trade, education, and military activities to the ideologies, tastes, and habits of Europe. Ali, the former petty bandit from Albania, gradually became more interested in the material and intellectual features of contemporary European society. As the emphasis of his trade, foreign affairs, and political aspirations shifted from Istanbul and the Ottoman regime toward Europe, so did his cultural and intellectual interests.

Of these interests, the figure who exerted the greatest influence on Ali's later career and life was Napoleon Bonaparte. Along with this fascination came a general infatuation with the notion of France and all things French. The impact of Bonaparte on Ali's psyche cannot be overestimated. It is well known that the Greeks, along with other Ottoman subjects, were powerfully influenced by the French Revolution and the Napoleonic Wars. French revolutionary ideology was no less well known to Ali than it was to his subjects. Pouqueville, the French resident consul in Ioannina, reports: "La révolution Française était, dans ces derniers temps, le sujet de toutes ses conversations."[9] Pouqueville makes repeated comments on Ali's obsessive interest in the French, and he recounts tales of the pasha's incessant interrogation of his French prisoners, whom he pumped for any information he could glean about France and with whom he engaged in discussions of political and religious ideology.

Although Pouqueville's bias toward the French is evident, other writers, too, corroborate Ali's interest in French politics and philosophy.[10] Ali's sense that such French borrowings lent him cachet is documented by British travelers who tell of his bragging of a close relationship with Bonaparte in the hope of impressing and intimidating them. He was clearly interested in giving his visitors the impression that he was the type of ruler who would hobnob with the most prestigious political figures of Europe.

One particularly amusing anecdote is provided by Lord Broughton, who portrays Ali's fascination with the French as puerile and pretentious. Broughton writes that he and his party were visiting Ali when "he showed us some pistols and a sabre and then took down a gun that was hanging

---

[9] Pouqueville 1805, 25.
[10] Eton 1798, 372–373; Broughton 1855, 107–8; Baerlein 1968, 24; Shaw 1988, 269.

over his head in a bag, and told us it was a present from the king of the French. It was a short rifle, with the stock inlaid with silver, and studded with diamonds and brilliants, and looked like a handsome present; but the secretary informed us that, when the gun came from Napoleon, it had only a common stock, and that all the ornaments had been added by his highness, to make it look more like a royal gift."[11]

Whether Broughton's account is accurate (did Ali embellish the gun? did he actually receive it from Bonaparte?) is not as important as the impression Ali wished to give his English visitors. Ali desired that the English see him as a ruler worthy of receiving the royal gifts of Napoleon, equal to him in stature and certainly independent as a ruler. The message of equivalence between Ali and the French would have been all the more impressive to the English, as they were the long-time enemies of the French Republic. Similar in import are several of Holland's conversations with Ali regarding his relationship with the French.[12]

To this end Ali decorated his homes with items redolent of French imperialism. Leake describes his visit to Ali's new quarters in his castle stronghold: "A magnificent room, which he has just finished in his new serai in the kastro, is probably not surpassed by those of the Sultan himself. It is covered with a Gobelin carpet, which has the cypher of the King of France on it, and purchased by the Pasha's agent at Corfu."[13] Note, though, that this carpet is not viewed as Ali's attempt to liken himself to Napoleon—which it most obviously is—but is interpreted in light of the sultan in Istanbul; the assumption is that the Ottoman regime, rather than the nations of Europe, is Ali's index for self-importance. Leake, however, seems oblivious (or feigns obliviousness) of the true meaning of Ali's gesture.

Leake's account downplays this attempt at sharing in French symbology by framing it within the Oriental context in other ways as well. For instance, he juxtaposes Ali's attempts at "Europeanness" with what he perceives as the manifest evidence of Ali's true, backward, and uncivilized nature. Two hundred pages deeper into his account, Leake returns to another description of Ali's ostentatious new carpet. This time, however, he situates his description within a broader discussion of Ali's greediness, a discussion that serves to undermine the symbological importance of Ali's choice of decor.

> The Pasha's avaricious disposition carries him to such a length, that he never allows any worn-out piece of furniture, or arms or utensils to be thrown

[11] Broughton 1855, 1:99.

[12] Holland 1815. It was to Holland, among others, that Ali spoke of Napoleon's promise to grant him the kingship of Albania.

[13] Leake 1835, 1:223.

away, but lays them in places well-known to him, and would discover the
loss of the smallest article. In the dirtiest passages and antichambers *[sic]*
leading to some of the grandest apartments of his palace, and which have
cost some thousands to fit up, the worn out stock of a pistol, or a rusty sword,
or a scabbard, or some ragged articles of dress, may be seen hanging up,
which his numerous domestics never venture to remove, well knowing that
it would be remarked by him. This mixture of magnificence and meanness is
very striking in every part of the palace. His great apartment, covered with
a Gobelin carpet, surrounded with the most costly sofas, musical clocks and
mirrors, is defended by cross iron bars, rougher than would be considered
tolerable in the streets of London. They are intended to keep his servants
from passing through the windows when the chamber is locked.[14]

This passage manages simultaneously to verify several Orientalist
stereotypes and to ignore the symbolic implications of its central feature,
a description of Ali's fine furniture and ornamentations. Ali's fundamentally coarse nature is revealed by the presence of windows that are covered with bars so rough as to be intolerable to an Englishman; the bars
also demonstrate Ali's untrustworthiness. Worn-out junk is heaped about
the palace, and Ali keeps avaricious inventory of every last rag in his residence. Ali's lavish furniture is at odds in this setting, and, by Leake's account, he is basically a suspicious, coarse, and boorish peasant whom no
amount of finery will redeem.

Hobhouse, too, was treated to a tour of Ali's architectural and decora-
tive Europeanizations. In an account of his visit to Ioannina, Hobhouse
describes the garden gazebo at Ali's summer residence. It sits in the midst
of a beautiful jungly garden, with deer and antelope frolicking in a neighboring field. It

> is in the form of a pavilion, and has one large saloon (I think an octagon)
> with small latticed apartments on every side. The floor of the saloon is of
> marble, and in the middle of it there is a fountain containing a pretty model,
> also in marble, of a fortress, mounted with small brass cannon, which, at a
> signal, spouts forth jets of water into the fountain, accompanied by an organ
> in a recess, playing some Italian tunes. The small rooms are furnished with
> sofas of figured silk, and the lattices of the windows, as well as the cornices,
> are gilt and highly polished. The shade of an orange-grove protects the pavil-
> ion from the sun, and it is to this retreat that the Vizier withdraws during the
> heats of the summer, with the most favoured ladies of his harem, and indulges
> in the enjoyment of whatever accomplishments these fair ones can display
> for his gratification. Our attendant pointed out to us, in a recess, the sofa on

[14] Leake 1835, 1:405–6.

which Ali was accustomed to sit, whilst, on the marble floor of the saloon, his females danced before him to the music of the Albanian lute.[15]

Again, the British visitor chooses to minimize the symbolic implications of Ali's choice of decor by emphasizing the broader setting in which it appears. Broughton not only describes the Italianate fountain, but also paints for his reader the imagined scenes for which the fountain is the setting. Here Ali's appetites are "indulged" and "gratified" and Ali is entertained by dancing women. The effect is a complete Orientalization of the setting. Even the European-style fountain of which Ali was so proud (and with which he obviously hoped to impress his visitors) is subsumed in the quintessentially orientalist vision of a lecherous despot surrounded by young and fawning women.

Similarly, in his description of the new carpet, Broughton, like Ali himself, selects for description items rife with symbolism, but symbolism that implies the opposite. The ragged clothes, the coarsely barred windows, the worn-out odds and ends kept about the palace—all imply Ali's backwardness, avarice, and lack of culture.

Ali's use of the French style as his standard for domestic decoration was not merely an aesthetic choice. It was directly linked to his admiration of Napoleon and his aim of attaining comparable fame. His foreign visitors, however, although recognizing the dramatic difference between Ali's furnishings and those favored by his cultural milieu, show an unwillingness to accept the possibility that Ali was using European decor and architecture as a symbol of his political aspirations. Of Ali's garden kiosk, for example, Broughton notes: "The pavilion and its gardens bespeak a taste quite different from that of the country"; but he goes on only to observe: "Most probably the Vizier was indebted to his French prisoners for the beauties of this elegant retirement. We were told it is the work of a Frank."[16]

. . . . .

That Ali wanted not simply to be associated with the French but to be viewed as their equal, as a worthy opponent, is evident from his diplomatic negotiations with them. He viewed himself as their peer in diplomacy, strength, and cunning. Ali boasted to visitors that Napoleon had promised him the kingship of Albania as a reward for colluding with the French against the Ottoman Porte.[17] He was quick to add, however, that

[15] Broughton 1855, 1:59. Leake, incidentally, also includes a description of the same fountain, dismissing it as a "silly bauble" (Leake 1835, 4:152).

[16] Broughton 1855, 1:59.

[17] Similarly, Ali was reported to have been promised kingship by the Russians. The ac-

he was not interested in becoming a French vassal.[18] He wanted total independence and declined the French offer. Similarly, he was cool to Russian promises of independent kingship.

The French promise of kingship is also referred to in the 4,500-verse *stoihoi politikoi* of Hadji Seret,[19] one of Ali's courtiers. Hadji Seret, too, writes that Ali scorned the offer, being too wise to hand over his independence to the French. In borrowing the symbols and tastes of France Ali's aim was not to demonstrate his friendship with France but to obtain what France stood for: independence, modernity, power, and supremacy.

In the same way that Ali decorated his homes as to demonstrate his independence and modernity to passing visitors, he adjusted his behavior so as to appear more European to his guests. Aware of the significance he held in the greater picture of regional politics, he was clearly self-conscious about how he presented himself to the outside world. European travelers make repeated and explicit references to his obvious attempts to present himself in a particular light. For example, Leake writes that "Aly, since he has become of political importance in Europe, shows some wish that foreigners should have a favorable opinion of him." Not one to miss the opportunity to make something of Ali's renowned cruelties, however, Leake continues: "Nevertheless, he has little scruple in alluding to those actions of his life which are the least likely to obtain such favour, though he generally endeavors to give such a colouring to them as shall make them appear less criminal."[20] The import both of his European decor and of his "Western" behavior and his attempts to make a good impression were downplayed. It seems to elude Leake's attention entirely that just as Ali's "good" manners were deliberately planned, so too might have been his bragging of past atrocities, cruelties, and criminal acts.

This skepticism toward Ali's attempts to appear polite is echoed by his European biographers. Remerand, for example, writes: "Les etrangers étaient réçus généralement par Ali avec la meilleure grace. Il savait se montrer affable et accueillant et laissait le plus souvent la meilleure impression a ceux qui l'approchaient pour la première fois."[21] The implication was that once one got to know him better, Ali was revealed as the true beast

---

counts of Broughton, Vaudoncourt, and Hughes refer to Ali's supposed collusions with Prince Potemkin of Russia. Ali is said to have had initial contact with Potemkin in the 1787 war between Austria, Russia, and Turkey, during which Ali distinguished himself. At this time he entered into secret correspondence with Potemkin; thus if the Turks lost the war to Russia, he would have a new ally under the new regime. See in particular *Travels in Greece and Albania* (Hughes 1830) and *Memoirs on the Ionian Islands, including the life and character of Ali Pacha* (Vaudoncourt 1816), as well as *Life of Ali Pasha* (Davenport 1878).

[18] Holland 1815.
[19] Hadji Seret, National Library of Greece.
[20] Leake 1835, 4:220.
[21] Remerand 1928, 96.

that he was. Similarly, Plomer strikes up the theme of Ali's barely concealed true character, copying wholesale Leake and Pouqueville's description of his manners. Of Pouqueville's first meeting with him (in the autumn of 1805) he writes, "Pouqueville now noticed . . . that when he was not indulging in his famous guttural laugh he knew how to say things not without a certain charm."[22] Ali is not charming, but rather knows how to give the impression of being charming. Again, the implication is that Ali's manner is simply one of thinly veiled backwardness and boorishness.

Ali's *politesse* (feigned or otherwise), however, was clearly intended not just to give a generically "good" impression, but to give the specific impression of Ali's being a ruler among his peers. This is clearly evinced by the way in which his long-term visitors were treated. Such visitors were viewed paternalistically, treated with an overprotectiveness that was, in its completeness, a form of control. Broughton writes that he is referred to at all times throughout his travels in Ali's regions as "the vizier's guest."[23] Ali took on a benevolent, controlling, and, above all, executive role in his dealings with foreign visitors, and he evidently regarded foreign travelers as visitors in *his* lands, not in those of the sultan or the Ottoman Empire at large. He never presented himself as a representative of the Ottoman Porte.

More illustrative still of Ali's comportment and attitudes as an independent ruler is Broughton's description of the way in which Ali discussed with the British their recent military successes in the area: "During this interview Ali congratulated us upon the news which had arrived a fortnight before, of the surrender of Zante, Cephalonia, Ithaka, and Cerigo, to the British squadron: he said he was happy to have the English for his neighbors; that he was sure they would not serve him as the Russians and the French had done, in protecting his runaway robbers; and that he had always been a friend to our nation, even during our war with Turkey, and had been instrumental in bringing about the peace."[24]

Ali was certainly acting in a fashion quite different from the official stance of the Ottoman Empire regarding Britain, at that time extremely chilly, to say the least. He was also interested in portraying himself as a leader of the caliber and rank of the leaders of France and England, congratulating the British, as it were, nation to nation. His absolute lack of reference to the official stance of the Porte, combined with his veiled demand that the British turn over to him the Greek robbers who took refuge in the islands, makes clear his self-perception as a wholly independent ruler. The fact that Ali was still involved in secret negotiations with the

[22] Plomer 1970, 129.
[23] Broughton 1855, 1:68.
[24] Ibid., 98–99.

French (unknown to Leake) only makes clearer Ali's sense of parity with the British and his conviction that he was a clever and accomplished "player" in the world of international diplomacy.

Ali's behavior, his choice of decor, and his European architectural borrowings were not merely imitative. They also bore the mark of his careful self-definition as a ruler and were designed to give his visitors the semiotic impression that he was of a stature comparable with that of European leaders. These symbolic efforts, however, were downplayed and overlooked in accounts by European travelers. These travelers, invested in an Orientalist vision of Ali, were unable to look beyond Ali's immediate background and context. The qualities of fixity, timelessness, and backwardness were canonical features of the Oriental type as known to the European literary imagination, and therefore Ali's symbolic gestures were dismissed as ignorant whimsies and silly, hollow imitations of Europe.

At the same time Ali was also deeply invested in the Orientalist views by which these foreign visitors were guided. Just as it was advantageous for the Europeans (whose position vis-à-vis Ali was not, from a strategic point of view, always secure) to view Ali as backward, irrational, and nonthreatening, so too was it at times advantageous to Ali to be seen in such terms. Several episodes in the history of Ali's contacts with the West demonstrate behaviors that seem contrived to convey this very impression. In his visits with the French and British travelers to his court, Ali was participating in an ongoing performance every aspect of which was designed to give a particular impression to those who came. Sometimes this performance took the form of an adoption of the material symbols of European kingship. At other times it involved the use of an independent, diplomatic tone, designed, like these material symbols, to convey the impression of Ali's being an equal of the rulers of Europe. At still other times, however, this performance depended on a deliberate heightening of precisely the non-Western characteristics that Ali's European visitors expected to see.

The two characteristics his Western visitors most often attributed to Ali were cruelty and irrationality. This should come as no surprise, these traits being almost ubiquitous in eighteenth- and nineteenth-century accounts of the Oriental. Virtually all biographies and the anterior travelogues on which they are based give detailed accounts of specific episodes in Ali's life: his drowning of a group of Greek women in Lake Ioannina; his revenge upon the Gardikiotes, who in Ali's childhood had raped his mother; his bloodthirsty attacks on the Orthodox Albanian people of Souli. All these are provided as illustrations of his fickle and irrationally cruel nature. Indeed, such accounts eclipse in length and emphasis virtually all other aspects of his life, despite the fact that the accounts are relatively insignificant to the story of his rise to power, his negotiations with Europe, and his gradual break with the Ottoman Porte.

These tales represent what I have referred to as the highly anecdotal quality of European texts on Ali. The anecdote functions as a means of diminishing Ali's importance, heightening his Otherness, and deflecting attention (for both the reader and the European writer) from the genuine power and control he enjoyed at the pinnacle of his career. These stories were evidently in wide circulation during his lifetime, and it seems likely that Ali himself on several occasions told them to his visitors.[25]

The Story of Lady Frosine

The first of these anecdotal tales, the *pniximon*, or drowning tale, involves Ali's arbitrary murder of a large group of young Greek Ioanninite women. It is included in virtually every European travel account, biography, and history even tangentially related to Ali.

The story is as follows: Ali's eldest son, Muktar, the pasha of Lepanto, was given to violent physical passions.[26] He consequently pursued a wide array of women, thus arousing the jealousy of his wife, Pasho, who monitored his affairs and sent out hired spies after him. In the course of his philanderings, Muktar is said to have fallen in love with a beautiful young Greek woman by the name of Frosine, who, although married, enjoyed a certain amount of freedom, as her husband, a merchant, spent a good deal of time away from Ioannina.

So it was that Muktar and Frosine became involved in a highly publicized and time-consuming extramarital liaison. Frosine, it is said, was not devoted to Muktar (as he was to her) but was flattered by the attentions of so prominent a citizen. Thinking to turn her connection with the pasha's son to her material advantage, Frosine pursuaded Muktar to give her a valuable and distinctive ring that he wore regularly. Muktar, blinded by his obsession with Frosine, did not see this request as the simple act of gold digging that it so obviously was, and obliged her request, touched that she would want to own one of his personal effects. Frosine promptly turned the ring over to a jeweler, telling him to hock it on her behalf.

The jeweler, immediately recognizing the great value of the ring, went

---

[25] Holland, Leake, Pouqueville, and Broughton (to name but a few) on several occasions had private audiences with Ali and recount that Ali bragged to them of the "exploits" mentioned here.

[26] Of these passions, Plomer writes: "[Muktar] was so little given to delay in the gratifying of them that he had been known to rape women publicly in the streets in broad daylight" (Plomer 1970, 102).

to the only place where he would find a buyer wealthy enough to afford such an item. Thus the jeweler ended up at the palace (from whence, of course, the jewel had originally come) and brought the ring before Pasho, with whom he had done some business. Pasho quickly recognized the ring and made the jeweler tell her how it had come into his possession. She flew into a jealous rage when she learned of the ring's true provenance and vowed revenge against Frosine.

Conveniently, at this time Ali was called by the Porte to aid in the suppression of the pasha of Adrianople, who was in revolt against the empire. Not wishing to go, Ali feigned illness and sent Muktar instead.[27] No sooner had Muktar left than Pasho, accompanied by her sister Zobeide (to whom Ali's second son, Veli, was married), sought an audience with the pasha. Raving, it is said, with jealousy, Pasho and her sister begged that Ali punish Frosine for the perceived wrongs committed against Pasho.

Promising his assistance, Ali had Frosine taken into custody and requested that Pasho furnish him with the names of any other women who might have caused her harm by attracting Muktar's attentions. Without delay, Pasho presented Ali with a list of several other names,[28] and these women too were rounded up and thrown into the dungeon with Frosine. All were sentenced to death. A few nights later the women were taken from the dungeon to the shores of Ioannina's lake where they were forced into waiting boats, tied up in sacks, and thrown into the water as adulteresses.[29]

This is almost certainly a true story, and over time it has become important not just to the corpus of literature on Ali but also to the Greek national consciousness. The body of Frosine is said to have been recovered from the lake and buried at the monastery of Hagion Anargyron, in Ioannina. The Orthodox Church declared Frosine a Christian martyr; the Greeks even adopted her as a symbol of rebellion in their fight for independence from the Ottoman regime. Greek popular song celebrates her to this day.

> T'akousate ti gineke sta Yiannena, ste limne,
> pou pnixane tis dekafta me ten kura Frosune;
> . . . De sto'lega, Frosune mou, krupse to dahtulidi

[27] Ali was, with reason, paranoid about the Porte, knowing that it wanted to do away with him, and honored such requests only when absolutely necessary.

[28] The precise number varies from account to account. Fifteen, sixteen, and seventeen are the most commonly cited figures.

[29] Another version of this tale appears in the contemporary accounts of Broughton, Hobhouse, Holland, Hughes, Leake, Bessieres, Malte-Brun, Pouqueville, and Vaudoncourt. Virtually all subsequent biographers include it, in many instances in a very detailed (and embellished) form.

yiati an to mathe o Alepasas the na se fae to fidi;
. . . Fusa voria, fusa, thrakia, gia n'agriepse e limne,
na vgale tes archontisses kai ten kura Frosune.
. . . Frosun', se klaiei to spiti sou, se klaine ta paidia sou,
Se klain ola ta Yiannena, klaine ten omorfia sou . . .[30]

(Did you hear what happened at Ioannina, at the lake? / Where they drowned
the seventeen, along with Lady Frosine? /. . . Didn't I tell you, my Frosine,
to hide the ring? / Because if he finds it, Ali Pasha, the snake will want to eat
you /. . .[31] Blow, North Wind; Blow, Easterlies, that the lake might become
wild / that they can put [into it] the young ladies and lady Frosine /. . . Frosine, your house weeps for you, your children weep for you / All of Ioannina
weeps for you, weeps for your beauty . . .)

With ballads such as this, Frosine has become a central feature of the
Greek folk landscape. Through the repetition of this tale in numerous
travel accounts, her story was also, for a time, well known to a European
audience. Both Greek ballad tradition and European travel writing used
the story as a lens through which Ali's cruel and merciless nature was magnified. To this day, the story of Kyra Frosine is an unavoidable feature of
any visit to Ioannina. James Merrill wrote in his 1973 poem *Yannina*:
"And in the dark gray water sleeps / One who said no to Ali. Kiosks all
over town / Sell that postcard, 'Kyra Frossini's Drown . . .'"[32]

In the Greek instance, the understanding of Frosine as a martyr or independence fighter necessarily heightened the Orientalist vision of Ali,
who in Greek tradition functions not just as Frosine's murderer but also
as the antagonist of both the Orthodox Church and the Greek independence movement. In the instance of European travel accounts, the story
of Frosine functioned as corroborating evidence of the correctness of the
orientalist vision. While it verified this view, it also perpetuated it. As mentioned, the endless repetition of specific anecdotes pertaining to Ali served
as a device through which the Orientalist representations were simultaneously fed and verified. The tale of Lady Frosine clearly functioned in
this fashion.

Two audiences—the Greek Orthodox and the European—were fused
together through philhellenism. The Greek hatred of Ali that such stories
generated was shared by the Europeans who became so interested in the
Greek cause during the first years of the Greek War of Independence. The
long-standing Orientalist biases against the Oriental type were fed and

[30] Politis 1914, 16–17.

[31] "Na se fae to fidi" (may the snake eat you) was a favorite expression of Ali's, referring
to the snake, himself, and his treatment of his enemies. In Hadji Seret the phrase is "Na sas
troge to fidi" (National Library of Greece).

[32] Merrill 1973.

augmented by this portrayal of Ali as anti-Greek, and the European philhellene sentiment was distilled into an out-and-out hatred of Ali.

Ali and the Gardikiotes

Stories of Ali's childhood play a central role in the larger accounts of his
life penned by his European visitors. By far the most common tale is that
of Ali and the Gardikiotes, which shares with the story of Kyra Frosine
the themes of Ali's vengefulness and cruelty.

The story is as follows: Ali's mother, Kamko, was forced, upon the
death of her husband, to fend single-handedly for her son Ali and his sister, Shainitza. Having put herself at the head of a band of her late husband's followers, Kamko took on the role of Albanian brigand and set
about leading her followers in battle against her perceived enemies.
Among these were the neighboring villages of Kormovo and Gardiki. The
Gardikiotes, feigning alliance with Kamko and her gang, were in reality
colluding with the Khormovites to squelch this reckless woman. Hearing
of their collusion, Kamko promptly declared war against the two towns.
After much fighting, Kamko and Shainitza were taken prisoner by the
Gardikiotes and thrown in the dungeon in Gardiki. They were, by most
accounts, extremely ill treated at the hands of their captors. The strong
implication of the less explicit versions is that the two women were beaten
and raped; less modest accounts state explicitly that Kamko and Shainitza
were repeatedly violated by the Gardikiote warriors who guarded them.
Ali, more fortunate than his womenfolk, managed to escape his enemies
but was unsuccessful in his attempts to obtain the release of Kamko and
Shainitza.

After a lengthy captivity (it is unclear precisely how long they were
held), the two women were freed through the interventions of one Malikovo, a Greek merchant in Argyrocastro who had heard of their plight
and felt sorry for them.[33] It is said that he paid the vast sum of four thousand pounds sterling for their release.[34] No sooner had Kamko obtained
her release than she began harassing Ali to exact revenge upon the people
who had done her these great wrongs. Her thirst for vengeance, according to the tale, was only augmented by Ali's first unsuccessful attacks upon
the Kormovites, against whom he could do nothing. We have seen that
Kamko upbraided her son as an emasculated weakling for these early
defeats.

[33] It is likely, too, that this merchant, as a Greek, knew well that it was best to stay in the
good graces of the leading Albanian Muslim families of the area. In the event, Ali is said to
have rewarded Malikovo in 1807 by poisoning him in Eleftherohori.

[34] Davenport 1878, 27.

Years passed, during which Ali repeatedly failed to exact the revenge demanded by his mother. Shainitza and Kamko, however, could not forget, and both, it is said, demanded Ali's vow that he would avenge them. Kamko's dying words ostensibly included the demand that Ali seek out her enemies and take revenge against them. Shainitza, too, is reported to have spent days at a time brooding over the injustices of the Gardikiotes and Kormovites.

At the time of Ali's accession to the *paşalık* of Ioannina, numerous quasi-independent Greek and Albanian towns of the region (the so-called *eleftherochoria*) reversed their policy of resistance to the Ottoman regime and declared their fealty to Ali. His influence and reputation in the area were such that it was evidently perceived as a lesser evil to be his ally than to be independent and subject to his aggressions. Among these villages was Kormovo, whose residents were well aware of Ali's long-standing hatred toward them. Ali, it is said, accepted the Kormovite surrender and promised to forgive them their wrongs if they would expel from town the few families to whom he objected. Then, feigning great friendship, he approached the town with several hundred armed *scipetars* (Albanian warriors). Telling the Kormovites that he did not wish to burden them by quartering his numerous soldiers in their town, he suggested that they retreat to the nearby monastery of Tribukhi, where he proposed that the Kormovite leaders meet with him to sign articles of alliance and friendship. The hapless Kormovites, eager for a long-awaited end to their feud with Ali, set off for the designated rendezvous. There Ali and his men set upon and killed them all.[35]

It was not until 1812, however, about fifty years after the instigating deed had been done, that the demands of Ali's sister and his deceased mother were fully met. The Gardikiotes, having learned well from the misfortune of the Kormovites, managed for several years to see through Ali's overtures and feigned friendships. Finally, however, they too were to meet their end at his hand, when, after years of "alliance" with Ali against the peoples of Souli, the Gardikiotes let down their guard, thinking that he had at last forgiven them (or, more precisely, their forefathers, as most of the original offenders had died by then) the ancient wrong.

So it was that six hundred Gardikiote males accepted Ali's offer in the spring of 1812 to meet him, unarmed, at the Valiare Khan, a roadside khan, or public resting place, between Gardiki and Ioannina. There they were met by Ali, who fed them a feast in the walled courtyard of the khan.

---

[35] Accounts vary as to the timing of Ali's revenge against the Kormovites. Davenport and Pouqueville, for instance, who are frequently at odds with one another, are in agreement, stating that these events occurred after Ali's accession to the *paşalık* of Ioannina. Hughes disagrees, writing that they took place before. Leake in his *Travels in Northern Greece* states that they occurred in 1795 (Leake 1835, 1:29). This last estimate, however, seems late.

No sooner had they set to eating, however, than the gates were closed and Ali's Albanians opened fire on them from without the walls. All six hundred men were killed.

Immediately upon the conclusion of this slaughter, Ali had the doors to the khan permanently sealed and commissioned a Greek inscription to be placed above the door. The verse's narrative voice is at times that of the Gardikiotes, at others that of Ali:

> He that wishes to destroy the house of Aly, wishes surely to lose his life . . . when Aly was a little boy, deprived of his father, with no brother, and only a mother, we ran with arms in our hands to cut him off. He escaped, skillful as he is, upon which we went to Kargiani and burnt his houses. It is now fifty years since. It is for that deed that he slew us at the khan; that he has sent our chief men to the island of the lake of Ioannina, and there put them to death; that he has dispersed our families among all the kazas under his authority, has razed our unfortunate town to the ground, and ordered that it may remain a desert forever. For he is a very just man, and in like manner slew the Kormovites, and ordered that not one should remain alive. . . . When I consider this terrible slaughter, I am much grieved, and I desire that so great an evil shall never occur again. For which reason I give notice to all my neighbors that they must not molest my house, but be obedient, in order that they may be happy. This sad event took place the 15th of March, 1812, in the afternoon.[36]

So it is that half a century after the fact, Ali managed to punish the Gardikiotes for their abuses of Shainitza and Kamko.[37]

. . . . .

As did the story of Lady Frosine, this account of Ali's slaughter of the peoples of Kormovo and Gardiki fulfilled an important role in the Orientalist construct of him. It demonstrated several canonical Orientalist traits at once: cruelty, an overweening loyalty to Kamko, total untrustworthiness, lack of mercy, and, above all, inability ever to forgive a wrong.

Moreover, it provided an explanation for the deep suspicion with which Ali regarded everybody else. His own deviousness was understood as being the source of his deep distrust of everyone—a fact made much of in the travel accounts of the period. Leake wrote: "Aly is his own Kehaya and Hasnadar, trusts not even his own sons, and transacts everything himself, except where writing is required, when he dictates to a Turkish or

---

[36] Leake 1835, 4:178.

[37] This story, too, is virtually universal in the accounts of the chroniclers who visited Ali's lands. It is absent, of course, from those who traveled before 1812 (Leake, for instance). All visitors, however, note Ali's extreme dislike of the Gardikiotes and Kormovites.

Greek secretary."[38] Finally, like the tale of Lady Frosine, the history of Ali's dealings with Kormovo and Gardiki provided a colorful and entertaining story. The European diarists-travelers to Ali's lands were no less concerned with crafting an entertaining and marketable account than are most novelists today.

These stories, however, did not only function as a central feature of the West's representation of Ali. They were also important to Ali's construct of himself. Even as Ali undertook to adorn himself with the markers of "Europeanness" and modernity, so too did he capitalize on the stereotypical, Orientalist depiction of him so popular in the West. Ali, it is true, altered his behavior for the benefit of his visitors. We have seen, for example, Leake's observation that Ali behaved in such a way as to give a "favorable impression" to him. The clear implication is that Ali did so by attempting to disguise his "true" nature—presumably backward, cruel, and irrational. Leake, after all, finishes his observation by writing: "Nevertheless, he has little scruple in alluding to those actions of his life which are the least likely to obtain such favour, though he generally endeavours to give such a colouring to them as shall make them appear less criminal."[39] By Leake's account, Ali is ill able to play the role of civilized and dignified host (try as he might), for he is not clever enough to keep quiet when it comes to his criminal "endeavours." His braggadocio gets the better of him and belies his attempts to portray himself in a light favorable to Europeans.

A more logical explanation, however, for Ali's bragging is not that he was simply unable to control himself but that in telling such stories he hoped to have a specific effect on his audience. The way in which Ali related tales of his more cruel and oriental exploits was not uncontrolled or spontaneous but careful and deliberate. In the instance of the slaughter of the Gardikiotes, for example, Ali did not just brag; he also commissioned a verse commemorating the event. This verse was prominently placed so it would be widely seen—almost all of his European visitors, as well as local travelers, passed by the site of the Valiare Khan. Similarly, it is clear from contemporary European accounts that Ali himself was one of their primary sources for the story of Kyra Frosine's drowning.

What does it mean that Ali himself made a point of sharing these and other exploits with his European visitors? According to his European interlocutors, he was simply unable to suppress his desire to boast, and thus revealed things he would have been better off, from a political point of view, to keep to himself. According to this view, Ali's bragging about atrocities is evidence that his attempts at Western (that is, "civilized") be-

---

[38] Leake 1835, 1:37
[39] Ibid., 4:220.

Fig. 6. The Vizier Ali Pasha, Giving the Fatal Signal for the Slaughter of the Gardikiotes Shut up in the Khan of Valiare

havior were superficial and ill conceived, that his European pretensions were mere mimicry and carried no deeper symbolic or ideological import. Foolishly thinking he would impress his visitors, Ali told tales that in fact disgusted them.

This interpretation is based on several assumptions. First, Ali, although shrewd enough to negotiate successfully with the French and British over the course of several years and symbolically aware enough to make a show of his French decor, is so stupid as to unthinkingly blurt out stories bound to shock his audience. Second, Ali, as an Oriental, must be irrational and illogical. It is these traits, then, that are assumed to underlie his braggadocio.

Finally, there is the disingenuous and contrived assumption that the European audience finds his stories only abhorrent and atrocious. In reality, such tales as those of Lady Frosine and Ali and the Gardikiotes held tremendous value as sources of titillation and entertainment. Again, they were included in the vast preponderance of accounts written on Ali. Had they been merely tasteless and abhorrent, they would tactfully have been omitted, along with all the neglected material pertaining to the pasha's life which was thought too boring, recondite, or irrelevant. They were written down because they held cachet as thrilling and lurid entertainment. Tales of Ali's atrocities were a significant source of entertainment and played an important role in validating the West's assumptions of the Oriental as cruel, vengeful, and irrational.

Writers of eighteenth- and nineteenth-century Oriental travel accounts understood that such lurid tales of Ali's cruel and senseless antics were an important and salable feature. The travelogue was well established as a popular genre in Western Europe, and its popularity depended in no small part on the inclusion of colorful tales of whimsical Orientals and their inscrutable and grotesque exploits.

Just as the travelers who visited Ali's court understood the necessity of these canonical, fixed tropes, so too did Ali himself. His exposure to the West had taught him the importance of such concepts as constitutionality and nation, Gobelin carpets and Italianate fountains. It also taught him the expected behavior of the Oriental, and he deliberately satisfied the Western appetite for Orientalia by bragging of his conquests, cruelties, and rapaciousness. Thus Ali adjusted his behavior not just to give the impression of being Western, but also—and paradoxically—to give the impression of being the quintessential Oriental of the European representational imagination.

European travel accounts are full of bemused delight at Ali's perceived attempts to appear wiser, more educated, and more Western than he in fact was. Much is made, for instance, of the question as to whether he was literate, all visitors taking up the debate and weighing in with evidence corroborating one side or the other. Leake and Holland, for instance, claim to have personally witnessed Ali Pasha in the act of writing and reading but state that his penmanship was awkward and childlike. Others argue that what they saw was mere bluster, and that Ali was virtually illiterate but made a great show of holding pen and paper in front of visitors so as to give the impression of literacy. Ibrahim Manzur Effendi, a courtier who had free access to the pasha, writes that he is certain that Ali could neither read nor write, but that he pretended to do both.[40] No attention, however, is paid to the fact that even as Ali contrived to appear more Western and "advanced," so also did he often intentionally heighten his Oriental and "backward" nature.

Ali did so not only by disseminating tales but also by behaving in a bizarre, irrational, and illogical fashion when in the presence of his European visitors. Such behavior was, according to the assumptions of the Western Orientalist view, corroborating evidence of that view. What the Orientalist weltanschauung could not accommodate, however, was the possibility that Ali was *intentionally* meeting his visitors' expectations, tailoring his behavior so as to give precisely the desired impression. To allow for such a possibility would be to imply that Ali was not, in fact, thoroughly irrational, backward, and oblivious of Europe's representational fantasies of the East.

It is entirely reasonable, however, to assume that if Ali could act more Western for his audience's benefit, he could also intentionally act more Oriental. Just as he understood, through his contacts with the West, the importance of such symbols as a French imperial carpet or a jewel-encrusted diplomatic gift, so too did his dealings with Europe teach him of the Orientalist vision of which he was so central a part. And just as the travelers who wrote of him consistently missed the symbolic implications of his Westernisms, so too did they overlook the intentionality that underlay his Orientalisms.

In many instances, the extreme eccentricity evidenced by Ali's behavior makes it impossible to think that it was anything but artifice. Ibrahim Manzur Effendi relates that one of Ali's more peculiar amusements was to speak, according to his whim, Turkish, Greek, or Albanian, with absolutely no consideration of the linguistic capabilities of the person or persons whom he was addressing. The result was one of extreme confusion and discomfort for Ali's audience and extreme amusement for Ali. "One of Ali's strange amusements was to speak either Turkish, Greek, or Albanian, as it pleased him for the moment, without any reference to the person whom he addressed, whether he understood the Vizier or not. Ali sometimes employed a Greek interpreter who knew neither the language

[40] Ibrahim Manzur Effendi 1827, 331.

of the Vizier nor of his guest." Broughton goes on to tell the amusing story of one such victim: "A Maltese jeweler who was treated in this way put up his wares and walked out of the room; and Ali, persisting in his Turkish, called to him to come tomorrow."[41] Broughton is greatly taken with the humor of this event (which he claims to have witnessed firsthand), and is so blinded by his assumption that Orientals are bizarre and irrational that he does not even pause to consider how truly bizarre is the event he describes.

Ali, as Broughton knew, understood the necessity of interpreters; he did, after all, have several in his employ and used them when negotiating with his European visitors. Ali himself spoke two languages fluently (Albanian and Greek) and knew at least a bit of a third (Turkish). Yet it was one of his "strange amusements" to speak in what he knew was an unintelligible language to several of his lesser visitors, and he did so in front of Broughton. The only intentionality that Broughton is willing to attribute to this event, however, is Ali's desire for self-amusement. Much more reasonable, though, is the proposition that the vignette was staged not for the pasha's benefit but for Broughton's. Moreover, it apparently had the desired effect: it corroborated Broughton's view of Ali as peculiar, irrational, and whimsical, for it made its way into Broughton's account precisely as evidence of these traits. If confusing one's visitors by speaking an unintelligible language was thought to be amusing, how much more so to do it with a surprised and gawking audience standing by to watch! Ali clearly reveled in the fact that he was expected to behave in bizarre, unintelligible, and Oriental ways, and his amusement derived not just from doing so but also from having an audience.

Similarly, one of his favorite activities with his European visitors was to give demonstrations of his weaponry, much of which had been given to him by the French and the British. Leake tells the story of one such demonstration. "In the evening he has some mortar practice at Bunila, with an old five or six inch mortar, which has been considerably damaged by its employment in the siege of Souli. They fire loaded shells, one of which explodes close to a party of Greeks standing upon a height, but fortunately without hurting any of them. The Pasha laughs heartily at the joke. We then visit the foundry, the roof of which seems likely to fall."[42]

Once again, it seems likely that Ali's amusement derived not so much from his lackadaisical attitude toward his lethal weapons as from his awareness of the audience's presence.

· · · · ·

[41] Broughton 1855, 1:114 n.
[42] Leake 1835, 1:223.

It is certain that in Ali's day Western travel writers were aware of being engaged in a collective enterprise of cultural representation of the Orient. They were also aware that this representational process was at times committed not so much to portraying a "true" or accurate picture of the Orient as to creating a tale that would entertain the West and meet its expectations of that Orient. The French infantry captain Bellaire, in his *Précis des opérations générales de la division française du Levant,* which details the French defense of the Ionian Islands, includes commentary not just on military matters but on the character and habits of Ali Pasha as well. This, as we have seen, is typical of the accounts of European travelers to Ali's lands. Typical also in Bellaire's case is the fact that he as author is aware of the orientalist tendencies of many accounts such as his, and fears that their authors have been guided less by the desire to give an accurate portrayal of events than by the hope of titillating the reader with entertaining and exaggerated tales of Ali's antics: "[Ces] ouvrages [sont] faits avec goût et érudition; mais quelques-uns d'entr'eux se sont plus occupés d'écrire dans le genre poetique que de peindre les choses telles qu'elles étoient. Mon but, en publiant mes observations sur ces differens pays, a été de rectifier certaines erreurs commises par ces voyageurs, et surtout de traiter les parties oubliées ou negligées dans leurs descriptions."[43]

The "poetic genre" of which Bellaire speaks is nothing other than a version of what we, in this day and age, would call Orientalism. It is guided by a love of strange and entertaining tales, and focuses on the anecdotal at the expense of the accurate.

Just as Bellaire and his fellow diarists were to some extent aware of the Orientalist authorial assumptions of their writings, so too was Ali familiar with the Oriental type so popular in the West. We have seen the cosmopolitan nature of Ioannina, its large merchant community, its expatriate families, and its educational institutions. So too the high number of foreign visitors to the region, a number of whom, like Lord Byron, set up house in Ali's capital. In addition to these many sources of Western influence, Ali had a large number of Europeans in his employ. Most of these foreign employees were French, and a number of them were, through the interventions of their patron, married off to local girls in the hope that local ties would guarantee the longevity of their service. These "Franks" worked as engineers, carpenters, and other skilled laborers. Many visitors wrote of the Milanese builder, employed to build a foundry, and Ali's Italian smith and Dalmatian watchmaker.[44]

Ali's inner circle, too, was populated with foreigners. Marco Quirini,

[43] Bellaire 1805, vi.
[44] Leake 1835, 1:43.

his secretary for foreign affairs, for instance, was a Roman who converted to Islam and changed his name to Mehmet Effendi.[45] Quirini, a Roman Catholic priest, had been promised the bishopric of Bombay, but did not take it; instead, meeting with the French in Malta en route to Egypt, he took a position as Bonaparte's secretary-interpreter (he is said to have been fluent in Arabic). After three months he grew tired of the job and set sail for Europe but was taken prisoner by a "Dulciniote cruizer" and brought to Ioannina.[46] Ali, thrilled to have such a well connected personage in his lands, first made Quirini his prisoner and then employed him. Another foreigner, a Frenchman, was known to be one of the pasha's closest confidants and advisers.[47] Broughton was accompanied on his travels in Epiros by the court secretary Colovo, an Italian expatriate.[48] Also in the employ of the court was a French doctor, who had formerly served as a physician to the French army in Egypt. Finally, many of the Albanian soldiers who worked for the pasha had been mercenaries in the armies of Italy and France. These soldiers had spent years, even decades, abroad, were bilingual, and considered themselves expert in European culture.

Ali had direct access to European ideologies and intellectual interests through his immediate contacts in Ioannina, a number of whom were highly educated and sophisticated. It is certain that Ali had some knowledge not just of the European political climate but also of the cultural and intellectual one. I am not suggesting that Ali thus became somehow vicariously educated or sophisticated in his intellectual and philosophical outlook. It is, however, clear that he was able to grasp in a rudimentary way some of the essential features of the European intellectual climate of his day and that he employed them against the very people from whom he had learned them. Many visitors, for instance, remarked on Ali's interest in atheism and on his own apparent disregard for religion. He used the concept as a device to tease his French prisoners. Leake tells us anecdotally that "at the time that Christianity was out of favour in France, he was in the habit of ridiculing religion and the immortality of the soul with his French prisoners; and he lately remarked to me, speaking of Mahomet, *kai ego eimai profites sta Yiannena*: and I too am a prophet at Ioannina."[49]

. . . . .

---

[45] Quirini ultimately returned to Europe and recanted his conversion.
[46] Leake 1835, 1:54.
[47] Broughton 1855, 1:94.
[48] Ibid., 70.
[49] Leake 1835, 4:285.

Part of the European intellectual climate of the day was the fascination with the Orient and the stock figure of the Oriental. Just as Ali came under the influence of such concepts as atheism, constitutionality, and nation, so too was he affected by the West's Orientalist vision of him and his lands. And just as he manipulated these other concepts, so too, in his dealings with Europe, did he exploit its Orientalist fantasy. Apparently irrational acts were designed to play to this fantasy and were intentionally performed in the presence of a European audience.

ELEVEN

CONCLUSION

THE CASE OF ALI and his interactions with Europe indicates that
by the late eighteenth century the assumptions of Orientalism were
familiar not just to the Western writers who employed them but
also to the Orientals whom they were used to describe. This bears significant implications not just for the specific history of Ali and the European
powers but also for post-Saidian theories pertaining to study of the non-
Western other.

Since the 1978 publication of Said's *Orientalism*, historians of all
stripes, particularly of the Islamic Middle East and India, have produced
countless works on the mechanisms of power in the historical construction of cultural, national, and ethnic identity. Indeed, so dramatic has been
the influence of Said's book that since its appearance the term *Orientalism* has come to take on an entirely different meaning. *Orientalism* used
to denote simply those fields of study concerned with the Orient, with the
non-European East. Philologists, historians, anthropologists, and lin-
guists—any one concerned in any way with the study of the Orient (particularly with the Islamic Middle East and the Indian subcontinent)—
were regarded, and regarded themselves, as Orientalists. Now, however,
at least in all but the most intransigently old-school academic milieus, the
term *Orientalist* carries connotations of naïveté, colonialist superiority,
and cultural absolutism. Indeed, the term as associated with this latter def-
inition has come into such common use in historical circles as to have suffered the fate of other buzzwords or truisms; it has taken on a meaning
so general, and is now so omnipresent, that its use seems almost hackneyed, or at least not particularly insightful or useful as a tool of historical analysis. And this quite aside from the fact that even in its original
Saidian incarnation, the theory is not without its significant flaws and
oversimplifications.

As we have seen, the story of Western Europe and its fascination with
Ali quite obviously bears the hallmarks of Saidian Orientalism. The vocabulary with which Ali is described and the attitude displayed by his
Western chroniclers are textbook examples of Said's model. This is, however, only one interpretive dimension of the complex relationship between
Ali and the Western powers with whom he did business. The West was
obsessively drawn to Ali and in him saw all the expected features of the
classic Oriental despot. The orientalist model, however, does not accommodate the fact that Ali reciprocated Europe's interest and compulsively

amassed as much information as possible about the British and the French, attempting in many instances to adopt features of their culture. At the most basic level it is clear that Ali himself was affected by, and adjusted himself to, his *own* specific encounter with what was to him the other. This adjustment was based on his understanding and manipulation of the European fascination with him qua Oriental. He knew that he was expected to act in certain ways, and he behaved accordingly. His dress, his ostensibly irrational manner, his erratic behavior, his much advertised cruelties—all were intentionally heightened and designed by Ali to confirm the West's view of him as the quintessential Oriental Despot. His willingness to act a part provided for him by the eighteenth-century European Orientalist imagination represents a clever and cynical manipulation of his European visitors.

Ali's visitors, however, could not afford to entertain the possibility that this was the case. One of the central functions of Orientalist depictions of Ali was to compensate for European diplomatic weakness in the eastern Adriatic. In order to fulfill this function it was essential that Ali, if at times militarily and strategically superior to the Europeans, be consistently inferior in intellect, reason, and morality.

I have argued that the European travel literature on which much of this book is based reveals as much about this simultaneous sense of inferiority and superiority vis-à-vis Ali as it does about Ali himself. It provides, albeit inchoately, a commentary on Europe's contemporary situation. Self-reflection and self-criticism are, in the educative tradition of Locke, at the heart of much of this literature, just as Marcus and Fischer have argued that today they are at the heart of much anthropological ethnography. As Marcus and Fischer observe, however, this viewpoint, in its more modern, anthropological incarnation has recently been undercut with the publication of a number of works analyzing the distortions and assumptions that characterize the history of Western scholarship aiming to portray non-Western peoples. Such works have provided ample corroboration of the basic problematics identified most famously by Said. Works such as *Orientalism* have highly problematized the task of the Western writer who would document the other. Such writing now appears naive, irrelevant, and, at worst, impossible.

As Marcus and Fischer also observe, however, Said and many writers like him for the most part provide no alternative approach; that is, they are combative, rather than constructive, and make no (nor, to be fair, mean to make) significant inroads into the question of just how it is that other "voices" and cultural viewpoints are to be represented. Said, according to Marcus and Fischer, represents a fundamentally "polemical" point of view and, most troublingly, "practices the same sort of rhetorical totalitarianism against his chosen enemies as he condems."[1] Despite the 1994 addition of an afterword to *Orientalism,* in which he tries to rebut such accusations and expresses his dismay at having been thus "misunderstood," the criticism of Marcus and Fischer, among others, remains salient.

This, then, is one of the two primary legacies of Said: an ever burgeoning literature that ostensibly exposes the claims of the West to a hegemonic power over the East, and that demonstrates that this claim to power is inevitably part of the very discourse with which the West describes the other. In the wake of this new body of literature, the historical and anthropological enterprise of describing the "other" seems virtually bankrupt.

The second legacy of *Orientalism* is one adumbrated by Said himself. In the work's introductory pages he writes: "One ought never to assume that the structure of Orientalism is nothing more than a structure of lies and myths which, were the truth about them to be told, would simply blow away."[2] Said's warning notwithstanding, precisely this attempt has been one of the primary results of his work. Recent years have seen a veritable inundation of works attempting somehow to "set the record straight" or "make right the wrong" that has been wrought by the West and the history of its study of the other. More subtle and sophisticated variants of this approach include the so-called subaltern school, which has produced a prodigious amount of literature over the last decades with the aim of "giving voice" to the dispossessed groups of history. Best intentions notwithstanding, the upshot is in most instances no less patronizing and hegemonic than is the literature to which it is a response.

The story of Ali and Europe makes clear the highly complex, multivalent nature of the process of cultural representation. Ali was not merely an object of representation but also a participating subject in the representational process surrounding him. To borrow the vocabulary of literary theory, his participation in that process took the form of a dialogic response to a representational "conversation." Ali's willing participation in the Orientalist vision can perhaps best understood as his rejoinder to that vision. Bakhtin explains:

> Discourse lives, as it were, on the boundary between its own context and another, alien context.
>
> In any actual dialogue the rejoinder also leads such a double life: it is structured and conceptualized in the context of the dialogue as a whole, which consists of its own utterances ("own" from the point of view of the speaker)

---

[1] Marcus and Fischer 1986, 2.
[2] Said 1994, 6.

and of alien utterances (those of the partner). One cannot excise the rejoinder from this combined context made up of one's own words and the words of another without losing its sense and tone. It is an organic part of a heteroglot unity.[3]

It is possible, as we have seen, to isolate specific moments marking Ali's representational participation.[4] Ali's participation in the process of cultural representation was integral to that process and altered its literary product.

A model such as this helps free cross-cultural representation from the post-Saidian bind. So long as the process of cultural representation is conceived of in unidirectional, monolithic terms, description of the other is of necessity an act of control, domination, and cultural totalitarianism. Consequently, the academic study of the other is problematized and burdened with ever more convoluted attempts to demonstrate cultural "sensitivity" and "respect" and to otherwise distance the scholar from its negative aspects as identified by Said and his successors.

Such attempts, however, only corroborate the basic assumption against which they supposedly rail: the voice that describes inevitably controls that which is described. The fallacious assumption underlying this problematic is that power, particularly discursive power, is the exlusive property of only one clearly articulated voice, and that it is held over the others whom that voice describes, manipulates, and controls. As we have seen in the case of Ali, however, power of different sorts is embedded at all levels of the discursive process. The Orientalist vision, although very much in evidence in the case of Ali, was by no means the exclusive property of the West. It was used not only by travelers, diplomats, scholars, and biographers to describe Ali, but also by Ali himself to guide the West's vision of him. The encounter between Ali and the West is not one of Orientalist unidirectionality and control; rather it constitutes a dialogue in which Ali was one of several participants.

We have seen that the two primary legacies of Said's *Orientalism* have been the problematization of writing about the other and the development of a series of historiographic approaches aiming to free that other from a hegemonic and oppressive West. A third, and perhaps no less important concomitant, has been the complete and total devaluation of historical travel literature as a viable source for writing history. It is assumed that

---

[3] Bakhtin 1981, 284.

[4] According to Bakhtin's model, these specific moments are only the smallest fraction of the sum total of his participation in the process of cultural representation because a dialogic "rejoinder" need not be verbal. It can consist of any interaction between the "speaker" and the alien "partner." Finally, of course, the markers "partner" and "speaker" change with point the of view. For obvious reasons, the evidentiary bias in the current discussion is textual.

such literature represents nothing other than the consummate illustration of Said's point. Such literature, although clearly in many ways voyeuristic and distorted, is extremely valuable as a source not just for the cultures it describes but also for the cultures by which it is produced. Travel literature not only provides a repository of quaint, amusing, and colorful Orientalia, but also constitutes an extremely rich source for writing history. This is especially the case if it is read alongside other materials that can shed light on the specifics of its cultural, social, and political context.

Just as cultural representation is a multidirectional process, so too is travel, which is the economic, educative, and diplomatic activity standing as a backdrop for much of this study.[5] The Greek and Hellenized Vlach merchants of western Greece, Albanian mercenary soldiers, university students of the Balkan elites: all traveled to France, Germany, Italy, and Russia. There they were exposed to the material and intellectual cultures of Europe, which they in turn brought home to their families and contacts in Ioannina, Preveza, Arta, and Tríkkala. The simultaneous sense of familiarity and alienness that European visitors felt in Ali's lands derived from such cultural syncretisms, as well as from the Hellenic Ideal and its strong proprietary interest in the relationship between Greece and the West. One of the primary aims of the Grand Tour and its offshoots, however, was to experience precisely that which was *not* familiar, to witness strange and exotic things that could be found only by leaving home.[6] The sense of foreignness, peculiarity, and incomprehensibility was of necessity heightened. This heightening was not, of course, a conscious or deliberate act, but something that naturally occurred because of the complex array of political, cultural, and historical concerns that informed Europe's relationship to Greece.

The West's literary, musical, and artistic vision of Ali was indeed in many ways an Orientalist one, but this Orientalism was informed by feelings of insecurity and inferiority as much as by a sense of superiority and control. It was an amalgam of cultural and political factors. Philhellenism (which provided Europe with a surrogate form of colonialism in the south Balkans), the belief in travel as a pedagogical device, a generic fascination with Islam and the Orientals who practiced it, and shifting attitudes toward the evident decline of the Ottoman Empire were all recruited in the fight for dominance in the Adriatic. Thus Ali Pasha was cast in belittled and degraded terms not just because these were most familiar to standard Orientalist discourse, but also because such a portrayal helped combat Europe's sense of insecurity and weakness regarding him.

Ali was a convenient point of intersection for all of these preoccupa-

---

[5] For more on the centrality of travel to the formation of cultural representations, see Wolff (1994) and, in the specific context of the Balkans, Stoianovich (1994).

[6] Locke 1989, 262–65.

tions. From the philhellene point of view he was the oppressor of the Greeks; from the standpoint of the Eastern Question he appeared as one of the primary culprits for Ottoman weakness. If geopolitically at times more powerful than the French and British, that power could be overlooked or diminished through the themes and strategies of the Orientalist literary tradition.

The Orientalist vision recruited by Ali's Western chroniclers was, in turn, reified in the history of subsequent scholarship on him. This took the form primarily of neglect; as an anecdotally amusing figure Ali was given much attention, as a key player in Ottoman and modern Greek history he was virtually ignored. What little scholarly attention was paid to him was (with a few notable exceptions) still concerned with his anecdotal exploits rather than with his political, economic, and international impact.

Finally, Greek and Turkish nationalist concerns have colored depictions of Ali Pasha, for he is an enemy of sorts to both Greek and Turkish tradition. That Ali did grave harm to the Ottoman state and particularly to numerous Greek, Vlach, and Albanian communities under his control is clear. The fact that descriptions of Ali are Orientalist does not mean that they are wholly inaccurate, and it is evident that his cruelties and avarice, his wild rages and dictatorial government, although stock characteristics of the Oriental despot, were also quite real. But added to the specific dislike of Ali is a good portion of, in the Greek instance, an uglier and more generic anti-Muslim sentiment. The lack of interest in Ali in Turkish academic circles can in turn be traced in part to a widespread if low-grade antipathy for Greece. It scarcely need be said how unwise it is for scholars to take their lead from such impulses, and how easy it is for them unknowingly to do so.

Ali Pasha of Ioannina is a looming figure in the contexts of both the Ottoman and Greek past and the broader history of the relationship between Western Europe and the Orient. Part of this history is his Orientalist representational legacy, but it also includes the economic and cultural transformations Ali effected, his impact on the Greek War of Independence, and his diplomatic relations with Western Europe. The Muslim Bonaparte, as Byron's eptithet suggests, should be remembered as the point of intersection for the complex set of social, cultural, and diplomatic concerns that characterized Greece in the early nineteenth century.

BIBLIOGRAPHY

ARCHIVAL MATERIALS

Archives Nationales de France, Paris

MINISTÈRE DES AFFAIRES ÉTRANGÈRES.
Correspondance Consulaire
  Athènes 3 (1792–1824)
  Corfou 2–4 (1793–1816)
  Janina 1 (1800–1807)
  Patras 1 (1717–1810)
  Zante 6–7 (1792–1807)
Correspondance Politique
  Autriche 367–380 (1796–1807)
  Îsles Ioniennes 1–7 (1796–1808)
  Turquie 190–217 (1794–1808)

Başbakanlık Arşivi (BA), Istanbul

Hatt-ı Hümayun Tasnifi, 21034L; 21056; 21026
Ayniyat Defterleri, 610, 3–4, 22
Mühimme Defterleri, 163, 65
Dahiliye, 11047, 14418
Timar, 4971, 2710, 2699
Zaptiye, 1102

The British Museum, London

British Museum Additional Manuscripts
  20, 183, f. 13 and 67
  20, 182, f. 87
  34919, f. 20
    The Papers of Lord Broughton—John Cam Hobhouse
    The Papers of General Sir Richard Church
    The Papers of Lord Collingwood
    The Papers of William Martin Leake
    The Papers of Lord Nelson

Haus-, Hof-, und Staatsarchiv, Vienna

Turkei VI, 8

The National Library of Greece, Athens

Hadji Seret, Vios Ali Pasas

Public Record Office, London

PRO/FO 42/3 (Foresti to Grenville)

PRO/FO 78/96 (Meyer to Castlereagh; Meyer to Maitland)
PRO/FO 78/44, nos. 1, 5, 9, 10 (Morier)
PRO/FO 78/47, nos. 4, 9 (Morier)
PRO/FO 78/53, nos. 5, 6, 7, 13, 14 (Morier)
PRO/FO 78/57, no. 3 (Leake to Canning)
PRO/FO 352 (The Papers of Stratford Canning)
PRO/FO 136 (Ionian Islands)
State papers 105, vols. 126, 129, 133

Vivliothiki Korai, Chios

No. 493 (the autobiography of Korais)

OTHER PRIMARY SOURCES

Adair, Robert. 1845. "Memoirs of the British Ambassador to Istanbul" In *Negotiations for the Peace of the Dardanelles*. 2 vols. London.

Albin, P. 1911. *Les grands traités politiques*. Paris.

Anderson, M. S. 1970. *The Great Powers and the Near East, 1774–1923*. London.

Aravantinos, P. 1880. *Sylloge demodon asmaton tes Epeirou*. Athens.

Bartholdy, J. C. S. 1807. *Voyage en Grèce fait dans les années 1803 et 1804*. 2 vols. Paris.

Beaujour, Felix. 1800. *Tableau du commerce de la Grèce, formé d'après une année moyenne, depuis 1787 jusqu'en 1797*. Paris.

———. 1800. *A View of the Commerce of Greece, formed after an annual average from 1787 to 1797*. London.

———. 1974. *Pinakas tou Emporiou tes Ellados sten Tourkokratia, 1787–1797*. Athens.

Bellaire, J. P. 1805. *Précis des opérations générales de la division française du Levant chargée, pendant les années V, VI, et VII de la défense des îles et posséssions ex-venitiennes de la mer Ionienne, formant aujourd'hui la République des Sept-Îles*. Paris.

Bessieres, J. 1822. *Mémoire sur la vie et la puissance d'Ali Pacha*. Paris.

Best, J. J. 1842. *Excursions in Albania*. London.

Birge, J. K. 1965. *The Bektashi Order of the Dervishes*. London.

Botzaris, Notis. 1962. *Visions Balkaniques dans la préparation de la Révolution Grecque (1798–1821)*. Geneva.

Bowen, G. F. 1850. *The Ionian Islands under British Protection*. London.

Broughton, Lord (John Cam Hobhouse). 1855. *Travels in Albania and other Provinces of Turkey in 1809 and 1810*. 2 vols. London.

Brue, Benjamin. 1870. *Journal de la campagne que le grand visir Ali Pacha a faite en 1715 pour la conquête de la Morée*. Paris.

Byron, Lord (George Gordon). 1901. *Letters and Journals*. Edited by R. E. Prothero. 6 vols. London.

Clogg, Richard, ed. 1976. *The Movement for Greek Independence, 1770–1821: A Collection of Documents*. London.

Cockerell, R. A. 1903. *Travels in Southern Europe and the Levant (1810–1817)*. London.

Collingwood, G. L. N. 1829. *Collingwood's Life and Correspondence*. London.

Czartoryski, (Prince) Adam. 1888. *Memoirs of Prince Adam Czartoryski and His Correspondence with Alexander I*. 2 vols. London.

Davenport, W. 1823. *Historical Portraiture of leading events in the Life of Ali Pacha, Vizier of Epirus, Surnamed the Lion, in a Series of Designs, Drawn by W. Davenport*. London.

Dearborn, H. A. S. 1819. *A Memoir on the Commerce and Navigation of the Black Sea, and the Trade and Maritime Geography of Turkey and Egypt*. 2 vols. Boston.

de Bosset, C. P. 1819. *Proceedings in Parga and the Ionian Islands*. London.

———. 1822. *Parga and the Ionian Islands*. London.

Diplomatika Engrafa. 1863. Athens.

Dodwell, E. 1819. *A Classical and Topographical Tour through Greece*. 2 vols. London.

Dupre, Louis. 1825. *Voyage à Athènes*. Paris.

Eton, W. 1798. *A Survey of the Turkish Empire*. London.

Eynard, J. G. 1831. *Lettres et documents officiels relatifs aux derniers événements de la Grèce*. Paris.

Fauriel, C. 1824–25. *Chants populaires de la Grèce moderne*. 2 vols. Paris.

Filitti, J. 1915. *Lettres et extraits concernant les relations des principautés roumaines avec la France (1720–1810)*. Bucharest.

Firmin Didot, Ambroise. 1826. *Notes d'un voyage fait dans le Levant en 1816 et 1817*. Paris.

Flaubert, Gustave. 1979. *The Letters of Gustave Flaubert, 1830- 1857*. Translated and edited by Francis Steegmuller. Cambridge.

Gaultier de Claubry, Xavier. 1864. *Aperçu d'un mémoire sur l'occupation des îles Ioniennes par les Français en 1797, 1798, 1799, d'après la correspondance du général Chabot*. Paris.

Gell, William. 1823. *Narrative of a Journey in the Morea*. London.

Grasset de Saint-Saveur, Andre. 1800. *Voyage historique, littéraire et pittoresque dans les îles et possessions ci-devant venitiennes du Levant*. 3 vols. Paris.

Hobhouse, John Cam (Lord Broughton). 1813. *A Journey through Albania and other provinces of Turkey in Europe and Asia to Constantinople during the years 1809 and 1810*. 2 vols. London.

Holland, Henry. 1815. *Travels in the Ionian Isles, Albania, Thessaly, Macedonia &c. during the years 1812 and 1813*. London.

Hrysanthopoulos, Fotios. 1899. *Apomnemonevmata peri tes Ellenikes Epanastaseos*. Edited by S. Andropoulos. Athens.

Hughes, Thomas S. 1830. *Travels in Greece and Albania*. 2 vols. London.

Ibrahim Manzur Effendi. 1827. *Mémoires de la Grèce et l'Albanie pendant le gouvernement d'Ali Pacha*. Paris.

Kolokotrones, Theodoros. 1856. *Ellenika upomnemata, etoi epistolai kai diafora engrafa aforonta ten Elleniken epanastasen apo 1821 mehri 1827*. Athens.

———. 1892. *Kolokotrones, the Klepht and the Warrior*. Translated by Elizabeth Mayhew Edmonds. London.

————. 1969. *The Greek War of Independence*. Edited and translated by Elizabeth Mayhew Edmonds. Chicago.

Lair, Jules, and Emile Legrand. 1872. *Lettres de Constantin Stamaty à Panagiotis Kodrikas sur la Révolution Française*. Paris.

Lamarre-Piquot. 1918. *Souvenirs de l'Aide-Major Lamarre-Piquot (1807–1814)*. Paris.

Lassels, R. 1670. *Voyage of Italy*. London.

Leake, William Martin. 1814. *Researches in Greece*. London.

————. 1824. *Journal of a Tour in Asia Minor: With Comparative Remarks on the Ancient and Modern Geography of that Country*. London.

————. 1830. *Travels in the Morea*. 3 vols. London.

————. 1835. *Travels in Northern Greece*. 4 vols. London.

Lear, Edward. 1851. *Journal of a Landscape Painter in Albania and Illyria*. London.

Loir, Sieur du. 1654. *Les voyages du Sieur du Loir*. Paris.

Loukopoulos, D., ed. 1931. *O Roumeliotes Kapetanios tou 1821 Andritsos Safakas kai to arheion tou*. Athens.

Makriyannes, I. 1966. *Makriyannis: The Memoirs of General Makriyannis, 1797–1864*. Edited and translated by H. A. Lidderdale. London.

Napoléon I. 1809. *Correspondance*. Paris.

————. 1823–25. *Mémoires pour servir a l'histoire de France, sous Napoléon. Écrits a Saint-Hélène, sous la dictée, par les généraux qui ont partagé sa captivité*. Paris.

————. 1859–64. *Correspondance de Napoléon Ier*. Vols. 2–16. Paris

Oddy, J. Jepson. 1805. *European Commerce, Shewing New Secure Channels of Trade with the Continent of Europe*. London.

Papadopoulos, T. H., ed. 1952. *Studies and Documents Relating to the History of the Greek Church and People under Turkish Domination*. Brussels.

Perraivos, Christophores 1857. *Istoria tou Soulliou kai Tis Pargas*. Athens.

Politis, N. G., ed. 1914. *Eklogai apo ta tragoudia tou Ellenikou Laou*. Athens.

Pouqueville, F. C. H. L. 1805. *Voyage en Morée, a Constantinople et en Albanie*. 3 vols. Paris.

————. 1816. *Viaggio in Morea et Constantinopoli et in Albania negli ani 1798, 1799, 1800, e 1801*. 4 Vols. Milan.

————. 1820. *Travels in Albania*. London.

————. 1820–21. *Voyage dans la Grèce*. 5 vols. Paris.

————. 1826–27. *Voyage de la Grèce*. 6 vols. Paris.

Protopsaltis, E., ed. 1955–59. *Apomnemonevmata agoniston tou '21*. 20 vols. Athens.

Regnault, Amable. 1855. *Voyage en Orient*. Paris.

Scrofani, Xavier. 1801. *Voyage en Grèce de Xavier Scrofani, Sicilien, fait en 1794 et 1795*. Translated by J. F. C. Blanvillain. Paris.

Sonnini, C. S. 1801. *Voyage en Grèce et en Turquie*. Paris.

Stephanopoli, Dimo, and Nicolo Stephanopoli. 1800. *Voyage de Dimo et Nicolo Stephanopoli en Grèce, pendant les années V et VI*. 2 vols. Paris.

Vane, Charles, ed. 1848–53. *Memoirs and Correspondence of Viscount Castlereagh*. London.

Vaudoncourt, Guillaume. 1816. *Memoirs on the Ionian Islands including the life and character of Ali Pacha*. London.
Walsh, R. 1828. *Voyage en Turquie et à Constantinople*. Paris.
Xanthos, Emmanouel. 1845. *Apomnemonevmata peri tes Filikes Etaireias*. Athens.

SECONDARY SOURCES

Aksut, A. K. 1925. *Tepedelenli Ali Paşa*. Istanbul.
Alcaini, C. 1823. *Biographie des Wesirs Ali Pascha von Janina*. Vienna.
Allen, W. E. D. 1919. *The Turks in Europe*. London.
Anderson, M. S. 1966. *The Eastern Question, 1774–1923*. London.
Andreades, A. 1912. "Ali Pacha de Tebelin: Economiste et financier," *Revue des études grecques* 25, no. 111:427–60.
Antonius, George. 1938. *The Arab Awakening*. London.
Aravantinos, P. 1856–57. *Hronografia tes Epeirou*. Athens.
———. 1909. *Epeirotikon Glossarion*. Athens.
Aravantinos, Spiros. 1895. *Istoria Ale Pasa tou Tepelenle*. 2 vols. Athens.
Armstrong, John. 1982. *Nations Before Nationalism*. Chapel Hill, N.C.
Asdrachas, Spyros J. 1972. "Quelques aspects du banditisme social en Grèce au XVIIIe siècle." *Études Balkaniques* 4:97–112.
Augustinos, Olga. 1994. *French Odysseys: Greece in French Travel Literature from the Renaissance to the Romantic Era*. Baltimore.
Baerlein, Henry. 1968. *Southern Albania: Under the Acroceraunian Mountains*. Chicago.
Baeyens, Jacques. 1973. *Les Français à Corfu*. Paris.
Baggally, John W. 1936. *The Klephtic Ballads in Relation to Greek History*. Oxford.
———. 1938. *Ali Pasha and Great Britain*. Oxford.
Bakhtin, M. M. 1981. *The Dialogic Imagination*. Translated by Caryl Emerson and Michael Holquist. Edited by Michael Holquist. Austin.
Balic, Smail. 1995. "Is There Any Religious Motivation for the Bosnian Conflict?" In *Muslims and Christians in Europe*, edited by Ge Speelman, Jan van Lin, and Dick Mulder. Kampen, Holland.
Beauchamp, Alphonse. 1822. *The Life of Ali Pacha of Janina, Vizier of Epirus*. London.
———. 1822. *Vie d'Ali Pacha, vizir de Janina*. Paris.
Behdad, Ali. 1994. *Belated Travelers: Orientalism in the Age of Colonial Dissolution*. Durham, N.C.
Beldiceanu, Nicoara. 1980. *Le Timar dans l'état Ottoman*. Wiesbaden.
Bennett, Clinton. 1992. *Victorian Images of Islam*. London.
Bernard, R. 1935. *Essai sur l'historie de l'Albanie moderne*. Paris.
Boppe, Auguste. 1902. *Le Regiment Albanais (1807–1814)*. Paris.
———. 1914. *L'Albanie et Napoléon (1797–1814)*. Paris.
Boue, Ami. 1854. *Turquie d'Europe*. 2 vols. Vienna.
Boulanger, Nicolas Antoine. 1764. *The origin and progress of despotism in the Oriental, and other Empires of Africa, Europe, and America*. Translated by John Wilkes. Amsterdam.

Braude, Benjamin, and Bernard Lewis, eds. 1982. *Christians and Jews in the Ottoman Empire*. 2 vols. New York.

Bringa, Tone. 1995. *Being Muslim the Bosnian Way*. Princeton.

Brown, L. Carl, ed. 1996. *Imperial Legacy: The Ottoman Imprint on the Balkans and the Middle East*. New York.

Bulgari, N. T. 1859. *Les Sept îles Ioniennes et les traités qui les concernent*. Leipzig.

Burke, John, and Stathis Gauntlett, eds. 1992. *Neohellenism*. Melbourne.

Camariano, Nestor. 1966. "Nouvelles informations sur la création et l'activité de la typographie grecque de Jassy (1812–1821)," *Balkan Studies* 7, no. 1:61–76.

Camariano-Cioran, Ariadna. 1964. "La guerre Russo-Turque de 1768–1774 et les Grecs" *Revue des études sud-est européennes* 2:513–47.

———. 1984. *L'Épire et les pays roumains*. Jannina.

Camba, Pietro. 1825. *A Narrative of Lord Byron's Journey to Greece*. London.

Campbell, John, and Philip Sherrard. 1968. *Modern Greece*. London.

Cantemir, Dimitrie. 1734–35. *The History of the Growth and Decay of the Ottoman Empire*. Translated by N. Tindal. London.

Capps, Edward. 1963. *Greece, Albania, and Northern Epirus*. Chicago.

Carter, Eric, James Donald Squires, and Judith Squires, eds. 1993. *Space and Place: Theories of Identity and Location*. London.

Cesare, Giovanni Martino. 1979. *La Massimiliana: La Ioannina*. Munich.

Chaconas, S. G. 1942. *Adamantios Korais: A Study in Greek Nationalism*. New York.

Charlton, David. 1986. *Gretry and the Growth of Opéra-Comique*. New York.

Christowe, Stoyan. 1941. *The Lion of Yanina*. New York.

Ciampolini, L. 1827. *Le guerre dei Sulliotti contro Ali Bascia di Janina*. Florence.

———. 1846. *Storia del Risorgimento della Grecia*. Florence.

Clogg, Richard. 1982. "The Greek Millet in the Ottoman Empire." In *Christians and Jews in the Ottoman Empire*, edited by Benjamin Braude and Bernard Lewis, vol. 1, 185–207. New York.

———. 1996. *Anatolica*. Aldershot, Hampshire.

———. ed. 1973. *The Movement for Greek Independence*. London.

Cocker, Mark. 1992. *Loneliness and Time: The Story of British Travel Writing*. New York.

Constantine, David. 1984. *Early Greek Travellers and the Hellenic Ideal*. Cambridge.

Dakares, S. I. 1959. *Odegos Nesou Ioanninon*. Athens.

———. 1971. *To Nesi ton Ioanninon*. Athens.

Dakin, Douglas. 1955. *British and American Philhellenes during the War of Greek Independence, 1821–1833*. Thessaloníki.

———. 1972. *The Unification of Greece, 1770–1923*. London.

———. 1973. *The Greek Struggle for Independence, 1821–1833*. Berkeley.

Dalven, Rae. 1990. *The Jews of Ioannina*. Philadelphia.

Danforth, Loring. 1995. *The Macedonian Conflict: Ethnic Nationalism in a Transnational World*. Princeton.

Daniel, Norman. 1958. *Islam and the West: The Making of an Image*. Edinburgh.

Dascalakis, Apostolos. 1937. *Rhigas Velestinlis: La Révolution Française et les preludes de l'independence hellénique*. Paris.

———. 1966. "The Greek Marseillaise of Rhigas Velestinlis," *Balkan Studies* 7, no. 2:273–96.

Davenport, Richard Alfred. 1837. *The Life of Ali Pasha, of Tepeleni, Vizier of Epirus, surnamed Aslan, or the Lion*. London.

———. 1878. *The Life of Ali Pasha, Late Vizier of Jannina: Surnamed Aslan, or the Lion*. London.

Davison, Roderic. "'Russian Skill and Turkish Imbecility': The Treaty of Kuchuk Kainardji Reconsidered." In *Essays in Ottoman and Turkish History, 1774–1923*, edited by Roderic Davison, 29–50. Austin.

Demos, Raphael. 1958. "The Neo-Hellenic Enlightenment (1750- 1821)" *Journal of the History of Ideas* 19:523–41.

Denitch, Bogdan. 1992. *After the Flood*. Hanover, N.H.

———. 1994. *Ethnic Nationalism*. Minneapolis.

Dimandouros, Nikiforos, et al., eds. 1976. *Hellenism and the First Greek War of Liberation (1821–1830): Continuity and Change*. Thessaloníki.

Dimakis, Jean. 1968. *La Guerre de l'Independence Grecque vue par la presse française*. Thessaloníki.

Dimaras, H. 1953. *O Korais kai e Epohe tou*. Athens.

———. 1969. *La Gréce au temps des Lumières*. Geneva.

Dimopoulos, A. G. *L'opinion publique française et la Révolution Grecque*. Nancy.

Dodd, Philip. 1982. *The Art of Travel: Essays on Travel Writing*. Totowa, N.J.

Douin, G. 1917. *La Mediterranée de 1803 à 1805: Pirates et Corsaires aux îles Ioniennes*. Paris.

Driault, E. 1904. *La politique orientale de Napoléon, Sebastiani, et Guardane*. Paris.

Dumont, A. 1874. *Le Balkan et l'Adriatique*. Paris.

Duval, Amaury. 1820. *Exposé des faits qui ont precédé et suivi la cession de Parga*. Paris.

Eisner, Robert. 1991. *Travelers to an Antique Land*. Ann Arbor.

Evangelides, T. 1896. *Istoria Ale Pasa tou Tepelenle, satrapou tes Epeirou*. Athens.

———. 1936. *E paideia epi Tourkokratias*. 2 vols. Athens.

Fabian, Johannes. 1983. *Time and the Other*. New York.

Farwell, Beatrice. 1981. *French Popular Lithographic Imagery, 1815–1870*. Chicago.

Finlay, George. 1861. *A History of the Greek Revolution*. 2 vols. Edinburgh.

———. 1970. *A History of Greece from Its Conquest by the Romans to the Present Time*. Vols. 5 and 6. Oxford.

Foscolo, U. 1850. *Narrazione delle fortune e della cessione di Parga*. Florence.

Foss, Arthur. 1978. *Epirus*. London.

Foucault, Michel. 1980. *Power/Knowledge*. Edited by Colin Gordon. New York.

Frangos, George D. 1973. "The Philiki Etairia: A Premature National Coalition." In *The Struggle for Greek Independence*, edited by Richard Clogg, 87–103. London.

Gailhard, John. 1678. *The Compleat Gentleman; or, Directions for the education of youth as to their breeding at home and travelling abroad*. London.

Gatos, Georgios K. 1965. *Istoria ton Ioanninon*. Athens.

Gikandi, Simon. 1996. *Maps of Englishness: Writing Identity in the Culture of Colonialism*. New York.

Gluck, Christoph. 1923. *La rencontre imprévue*. Paris.

Godo, Sabri. 1970. *Ali Pashe Tepelena*. Tirana.

Gordon, Thomas. 1844. *History of the Greek Revolution*. 2 vols. London.

Gourgouris, Stathis. 1996. *Dream Nation: Enlightenment, Colonization, and the Institution of Modern Greece*. Stanford.

Grassini, C. 1829. *Storia di Ali Tebelen, Bascia di Janina*. Milan.

Greenfeld, Liah. 1992. *Nationalism: Five Roads to Modernity*. Cambridge, Mass.

Gretry, André Ernest Modeste. 1771. *Zémire et Azor*. Paris.

———. 1862. *Zémire et Azor: Opéra-Comique en 4 actes*. Paris.

Grewal, Inderpal. 1996. *Home and the Harem: Nation, Gender, Empire, and the Cultures of Travel*. Durham, N.C.

Guha, Ranajit, ed. 1985. *Subaltern Studies IV*. New Delhi.

Guha, Ranajit, and Gayatri Chakravorty Spivak, eds. 1988. *Selected Subaltern Studies*. Oxford.

Hechter, Michael, and Margaret Levi. 1979. "The Comparative Analysis of Ethnoregional Movements," *Ethnic and Racial Studies* 2/3:262–74.

Henderson, G. P. 1971. *The Revival of Greek Thought, 1620–1830*. Edinburgh.

Hickock, Michael Robert. 1997. *Ottoman Military Administration in Eighteenth Century Bosnia*. Leiden.

Hobsbawn, Eric. 1959. *Social Bandits and Primitive Rebels*. Glencoe, Ill.

———. 1962. *The Age of Revolution, 1789–1848*. New York.

———. 1969. *Bandits*. London.

———. 1995. *Nations and Nationalism since 1780*. Cambridge.

Hobsbawm, Eric, and Terence Ranger. 1983. *The Invention of Tradition*. Cambridge.

Hugo, Victor. 1829. *Oeuvres complètes de Victor Hugo*. Paris.

Idromenos, M. S. 1889. *O uper tes ethnikes apokatastaseos agon ton Eptanision, 1815–1864*. Corfu.

Ilou, Philippe. 1969. "Pour une étude quantitative de public des lectures grecs à l'Époque des Lumières de la Révolution (1749–1832)" *Association internationale d'études du sud-est Europe* 4:475–80.

Inalcık, Halil, and Donald Quataert, eds. 1994. *An Economic and Social History of the Ottoman Empire, 1300–1914*. New York.

Inden, Ronald. 1990. *Imagining India*. Oxford.

Irschick, Eugene F. 1994. *Dialogue and History*. Berkeley.

Isambert, M. 1900. *L'Independence Grecque et l'Europe*. Paris.

Jackson, Peter, and Jan Penrose, eds. 1994. *Constructions of Race, Place, and Nation*. Minneapolis.

Jelavich, Barbara. 1996. *History of the Balkans: Eighteenth and Nineteenth Centuries*. Cambridge.

Jervis, Henry Jervis-White. 1852. *History of the Island of Corfu and of the Republic of the Ionian Islands*. London.

Jókai, Mór. *Photo the Suliote: A Tale of Modern Greece.* London.

———. *1898. The Lion of Janina; or, the Last Days of the Janissaries.* Translated by R. Nisbet Bain. New York.

Jonquiere, Vicomte de la. 1914. *Histoire de l'Empire Ottoman.* 2 vols. Paris.

Kafadar, Cemal. 1995. *Between Two Worlds: The Construction of the Ottoman State.* Berkeley.

Kakridis, John T. 1963. "The Ancient Greeks and the Greeks of the War of Independence," *Balkan Studies* 4:251–64.

Kaplan, Caren. 1996. *Questions of Travel: Postmodern Discourses of Displacement.* Durham, N.C.

Karpat, Kemal. 1973. *An Inquiry into the Social Foundations of Nationalism in the Ottoman State.* Princeton.

———. 1982. "Millets and Nationality: The Roots of the Incongruity of Nation and State in the Post-Ottoman Era." In *Christians and Jews in the Ottoman Empire,* edited by Benjamin Braude and Bernard Lewis, vol. 1, 141–69. New York.

Keyder, Çağlar. 1987. *State and Class in Turkey.* London.

Kitromilides, Paschalis M. 1985. "The Last Battle of the Ancients and Moderns: Ancient Greece and Modern Europe in the Neohellenic Revival," *Modern Greek Studies Yearbook* 1:79–91.

Knight, E. F. 1880. *Albania.* London.

Kokkinos, D. 1970–72. *Istoria tes Neoteras Ellados.* Athens.

Krapsiti, Vasili. 1988. *E Istoria ton Ioanninon.* Athens.

Kurat, Akdeş Nimat. 1970. *Türkiye ve Rusya, XVIII yüzyıl sonundan Kurtuluş Savaşına kadar Türk-Rus ilişkileri (1798– 1919).* Ankara.

Kurgiannes, M. 1984. *To Pasaliki Ioanninon sten Epohe tou Ale Pasa Tepelenle (1788–1822).* Athens.

Laios, G. 1961. *O Ellenikos Tupos tes Viennes.* Athens.

Lair, Jules. 1904. *La captivité de François Pouqueville à Constantinople.* Caen.

Lambrides, I. 1887. *O Tepelenles Ale Pasas.* Athens.

Lambros, S. 1916. "Peri paideias en Ioanninois epi Tourkokratias," *Neos Ellenomnemon* 13.

Lane, Frederick C. 1958. "Economic Consequences of Organized Violence," *Journal of Economic History* 18:401–17.

Lazarou, Ahilleos. 1965. *Glykoharama Neoellenikes Paideias.* Peiraeus.

Leake, William Martin. 1826. *An Historical Outline of the Greek Revolution.* London.

Legrand, Emile. 1886. *Complainte d'Ali de Tebelen, Pacha de Janina.* Paris.

Levonian, Lootfy. 1940. *Studies in the Relationship between Islam and Christianity, Psychological and Historical.* London.

Lewis, Bernard. 1953. "The Impact of the French Revolution on Turkey." *Journal of World History* 1:105–25.

———. 1968. *The Emergence of Modern Turkey.* Oxford.

———. 1968. "Some English Travellers in the East" *Middle Eastern Studies* 4:296–315.

Lewis, Reina. 1996. *Gendering Orientalism: Race, Femininity, and Representation.* London.

Locke, John. 1989. *Some Thoughts Concerning Education.* Edited by John W. Yolton and Jean S. Yolton. Oxford.

Loria, Diego. 1845. *Ali Tebelen: Pascia di Janina.* Naples.

Lortzing, Albert. 1904. *Ali Pascha von Janina.* Leipzig.

Lowe, Lisa. 1991. *Critical Terrains: French and British Orientalisms.* Ithaca.

Lunzi, Conte. 1863. *Della Repubblica Settinsulare.* Bologna.

Macfie, A. L. 1996. *The Eastern Question, 1774–1923.* Harlow, Essex.

Malakis, E. 1925. *French Travellers in Greece (1770–1820): An Early Phase in French Philhellenism.* Philadelphia.

Malte-Brun, Conrad. 1822. *Tableau historique et politique de la vie d'Ali-Pacha.* Paris.

Mantran, Robert. 1984. *L'Empire Ottoman du XVIe au XVIIIe siècle.* London.

Marchand, Suzanne L. 1996. *Down from Olympus: Archaeology and Philhellenism in Germany, 1750–1970.* Princeton.

Marcus, George, and Michael Fischer. 1986. *Anthropology and Cultural Critique.* Chicago.

Mardrus, J. C., and Powys Mathers. 1989. *The Book of the Thousand Nights and One Night.* 4 vols. New York.

McGrew, William W. 1976. "The Land Issue in the Greek War of Independence." In *Hellenism and the First Greek War of Liberation (1821–1830)*, edited by Nikiforos Diamandouros et al., 111–29. Thessaloníki.

McKnight, James Lawrence. 1965. "Admiral Ushakov and the Ionian Republic: The Genesis of Russia's First Balkan Satellite". Ph.D. diss., University of Wisconsin.

Merrill, James. 1973. *Yannina.* New York.

Mihalopoulos, F. 1930. *Ta Ioannina kai e Neoellenike Anagennese (1648–1820).* Athens.

Miller, William. 1836. *The Ottoman Empire and Its Successors, 1801- 1927.* Cambridge.

———. 1913. *The Ottoman Empire.* Cambridge.

———. 1922. *The Turkish Restoration in Greece.* London.

Mills, Sara. 1991. *Discourses of Difference: An Analysis of Women's Travel Writing and Colonialism.* New York.

Morgan, Susan. 1996. *Place Matters: Gendered Geography in Victorian Women's Travel Books about Southeast Asia.* New Brunswick.

Morier, D. R. 1951. *A Tale of Old Yanina.* Edited by J. W. Baggally. London.

Moufit, Ahmet. 1993. *Ale Pasas o Tepelenles (1744–1822).* Translated by A. Iordanoglu. Ioannina.

———. A. H. 1324[1903]. *Tepedelenli Ali Paşa, 1744–1822.* Istanbul.

Napier, Sir Charles James. 1833. *The Colonies: Treating of Their Value Generally.* London.

Napier, W. 1857. *Life of General Sir Charles Napier.* 4 vols. London.

Oikonomou, Manthos. 1959. "O Prothupourgos tou Ale Pasa," *Epeiroteke Estia* 8.

Orhonlu, Cengiz. 1967. *Osmanlı İmparatorluğunda Derbend Teşkilatı.* Istanbul.

Osborn, J. M. 1963. "Travel Literature and the Rise of Neo-Hellenism in England." *Bulletin of the New York Public Library* 65, no. 5:279–300.

Otetea, A. 1966. "Les grandes puissances et le mouvement Hetairiste dans les principautés roumaines," *Balkan Studies* 7, no. 2:379–94.

Palmer, Alan Warwick. 1992. *The Decline and Fall of the Ottoman Empire*. London.

Pantazopoulos, N. J. 1967. *Church and Law in the Balkan Peninsula during the Ottoman Rule*. Thessaloníki.

Papadopoulos, S. 1970. *To Ergo tes Filikes Etaireias sten Epeiro*. Ioannina.

Pappas, Paul C. 1985. *The United States and the Greek War for Independence, 1821–1828*. New York.

"Parga." 1819. *The Edinburgh Review* 32, no. 64:263–93.

"Parga." 1820. *Quarterly Review* 23:111–36.

Patseles, N. 1936. *E Oikonomike Politike kai o Ploutos tou Ale Pasa ton Ioanninon*. Athens.

Paulini. 1849. *Le tre constituzione, 1800, 1803, 1817, delle sette isole Ionie*. Corfu.

Pauthier, G. 1863. *Les îles Ioniennes pendant l'occupation française et le protectorat anglais*. Paris.

Payne, John Howard. 1823. *Ali Pacha; or, The Signet Ring: A Melodrama in Two Acts*. New York.

Petropulos, John A. 1976. "Forms of Collaboration with the Enemy during the First Greek War of Liberation." In *Hellenism and the First Greek War of Liberation (1821–1830)*, edited by Nikiforos Diamandouros et al, 131–43. Thessaloníki.

Phillips, Richard. 1997. *Mapping Men and Empire: A Geography of Adventure*. New York.

Plomer, William. 1936. *Ali the Lion*. London.

———. 1970. *The Diamond of Jannina: Ali Pasha, 1741–1822*. New York.

Porter, Dennis. 1991. *Haunted Journeys: Desire and Transgression in European Travel Writing*. Princeton.

Pouqeville, F. C. H. L. 1825. *Histoire de la regénération de la Grèce*. 4 vols. Paris.

———. 1835. *Grèce*. Paris.

Pratt, Mary-Louise. 1992. *Imperial Eyes: Travel Writing and Transculturation*. New York.

Pratt, Michael. 1978. *Britain's Greek Empire*. London.

Rados, C. 1921. *Napoléon Ier et la Grèce*. Athens.

Reid, James. 1993. "Social and Psychological Factors in the Collapse of the Ottoman Empire, ca. 1780–1918," *Journal of Modern Hellenism*, no. 10:117–56.

Remerand, M. Gabriel. 1928. *Ali de Tebelen: Pacha de Janina (1744–1822)*. Paris.

Richards, Theophilus. 1823. *The Life of Ali Pacha of Jannina, later Vizier of Epirus, surnamed Aslan or the Lion*. London.

Rodocanachi, E. 1899. *Bonaparte et les îles Ioniennes, 1797–1816*. Paris.

Romano, Ruggiero. 1951. *Le commerce du royaume de Naples avec la France et les pays de l'Adriatique au XVIIIe siècle*. Paris.

Said, Edward. 1979. *Orientalism*. New York.

———. 1994. *Orientalism*. New York.

Saint Clair, W. 1972. *That Greece Might Still Be Free: The Philhellenes in the War of Independence*. London.

Salamanga, D. S. 1959. *Suntehnias kai epangelmata epi Tourkokratia ton Ioanninon*. Ioannina.

———. 1965. *Peripatoi sta Giannina: Istoriko-Laografika Semeiomata*. Ioannina.

Sarafuddin, Mohammed. 1994. *Islam and Romantic Orientalism: Literary Encounters with the Orient*. London.

Sathas, Konstantinos. 1870. *Istorikai Diatrivai*. Athens.

———. 1889. *Tourkokratoumene Ellas, 1435–1821*. Athens.

Schenk, Hans Georg. 1947. *The Aftermath of the Napoleonic Wars*. London.

Segounis, F. 1932. "Anekdotos allelografia ton Zosimadon," *Epeirotike Hronografia 7*.

Seton-Watson, R. W. 1918. *The Rise of Nationality in the Balkans*. New York.

Shaw, Stanford. 1988. *History of the Ottoman Empire and Modern Turkey*. Vol. 1. Cambridge.

Silvestro, Betty Mack. 1959. "Western European Travellers to Mainland Greece, 1700–1800." Ph.D. diss. University of Wisconsin.

Simopoulos, Kyriakos. 1975. *Xenoi taxidiotes sten Ellada*. Athens.

———. 1979. *Pos Eidan oi Xenoi ten Ellada tou 21*. Athens.

Skiotis, Dennis N. 1971. "From Bandit to Pasha: First Steps in the Rise to Power of Ali of Tepelen, 1750–1784" *International Journal of Middle East Studies* 2:219–44.

———. 1976. "The Greek Revolution: Ali Pasha's Last Gamble." In *Hellenism and the First Greek War of Liberation (1821–1830)*, edited by Nikiforos Diamandouros et al., 97–109. Thessaloníki.

Sorel, Albert. 1902. *La question d'Orient au XVIIIe siècle*. Paris.

Soria, D. 1847–48. *Ali Tebelen, pascià di Janina*. Turin.

Spencer, Terence. 1954. *Fair Greece, Sad Relic: Literary Philhellenism from Shakespeare to Byron*. London.

———. 1959. *Byron and the Greek Tradition*. Nottingham.

Spender, Harold, ed. 1924. *Byron and Greece*. New York.

Spivak, Gayatri, Donna Landry, and Gerald Maclean, eds. 1996. *The Spivak Reader*. New York.

Springborg, Patricia. 1992. *Western Republicanism and the Oriental Prince*. Austin.

Spurr, David. 1993. *The Rhetoric of Empire: Colonial Discourse in Journalism, Travel Writing, and Imperial Administration*. Durham, N.C.

Staab, Robert Lee. 1980. "The Timar System in the Eyalet of Rumeli and the Nahiye of Dimetoka in the Late Fifteenth and Sixteenth Centuries." Ph.D. diss. Salt Lake City.

Stavrianos, L. S. 1957. "Antecedents to the Balkan Revolutions of the Nineteenth Century," *Journal of Modern History* 19:335–48.

———. 1963. *The Balkans since 1453*. New York.

Stewart, Charles. 1991. *Demons and the Devil: Moral Imagination in Modern Greek Culture*. Princeton.

Stoianovich, Traian. 1960. "The Conquering Balkan Orthodox Merchant," *Journal of Economic History* 20 no. 2:234–313.

———. 1962. "Factors in the Decline of Ottoman Society in the Balkans," *Slavic Review* 21:623–32.

———. 1994. *Balkan Worlds: The First and Last Europe*. Armonk, N.Y.

Stoneman, Richard. 1984. *A Literary Companion to Travel in Greece*. Harmondsworth, England.

Strangford, Viscountess. 1864. *The Eastern Shores of the Adriatic*. London.

Sugar, Peter. 1977. *Southeastern Europe under Ottoman Rule, 1354–1804*. Seattle.

Sugar, Peter F., and Ivo J. Lederer, eds. 1969. *Nationalism in Eastern Europe*. Seattle.

Teignemouth, R. N. 1923. "A Splendid Scoundrel," *English Review* 2 (July–December): 373–79.

Thesprotos, Kosmas and Athanasios Psalidas. 1964. *Geografia Alvanias kai Epeirou*. Ioannina.

Tomadakes, Nikolaos. 1953–83. *Neoellenika dokimia kai meletai*. Athens.

Tregaskis, Hugh. 1979. *Beyond the Grand Tour: The Levant Lunatics*. London.

Tsigakou, Fani-Maria. 1981. *The Rediscovery of Greece: Travellers and Painters of the Romantic Era*. London.

Tzauras, V. 1921. *To Mantevma tes Magissas kai o Thanatos tou Ale Pasa*. Corfu.

Van der Veer, Peter. 1994. *Religious Nationalism*. Berkeley.

Vane, Charles, ed. 1848–53. *Memoirs and Correspondence of Viscount Castlereagh, second marquess of Londonderry*. 12 vol 5. London.

Vasdravelles, I. K. 1948. *Armatoloi kai Kleftes eis ten Makedonian*. Thessaloníki.

———. 1970. *Piracy on the Macedonian Coast During the Rule of the Turks*. Translated by T. F. Carney. Thessaloníki.

Vavaretos, G. 1930. *O Ale Pasas apo ten allen plevran*. Athens.

Von Hahn, J. J. G. 1854. *Albanesische Studien*. Jena.

Vournas, Tasos. 1978. *Ale Pasas Tepelenles: Turannos e idiofues politikos?* Athens.

Vranoussis, Leandros. 1986. "Post-Byzantine Hellenism and Europe: Manuscripts, Books, and Printing Presses," *Modern Greek Studies Yearbook* 2:1–71

Webster, C. K. 1925. *The Foreign Policy of Castlereagh, 1815- 1822*. London.

White, David Gordon. 1991. *Myths of the Dog-Man*. Chicago.

White, Hayden. 1973. *Metahistory*. Baltimore.

Wolff, Larry. 1994. *Inventing Eastern Europe: The Map of Civilization on the Mind of the Enlightenment*. Stanford.

Wood, A. C. 1935. *A History of the Levant Company*. London.

Woodhouse, C. M. 1952. *The Greek War of Independence: Its Historical Setting*. London.

———. 1969. *The Philhellenes*. London.

———. 1992. "The Transition from Hellenism to Neohellenism." In *Neohellenism*, edited by John Burke and Stathis Gauntlett, 31- 48. Melbourne.

Yanagisako, Sylvia, and Carol Delaney, eds. 1995. *Naturalizing Power: Essays in Feminist Cultural Analysis*. New York.

Zacharopoulos, N. 1983. *E Paideia sten Tourkokratia.* Thessaloníki.

Zakythinos, D. A. 1947. *La Grèce et les Balkans.* Athens.

———. 1976. *The Making of Modern Greece.* Oxford.

Zerlentos, P. G. 1921. *Ale Pasa: Sytheke eptanession kai Ale Pasa etei 1803.* Athens.

Zotos, D. A. 1938. *E Dikaiosune eis to Kratos tou Ale Pasa.* Athens.

INDEX